## Advance Praise for
# *OVERCOMING: Lessons in Triumphing Over Adversity and the Power of Our Common Humanity*

"In *Overcoming*, Dr. Gus White has fashioned a timely and terrific treatment of the human condition and instructive roadmap for negotiating one of the most perilous periods in American history.... A prescription of hope for an ailing nation beset by racial and ethnic disharmony and a pandemic that has struck us at our most vulnerable core. An inspiring journey certain to lift spirits and help us all to overcome."

—**Arne Duncan**, former Secretary of Education under President Barack Obama

"*Overcoming* is a book about optimism and courage.... The writing is plain and direct. It is also evocative. This book will move you and reinforce your will to overcome and even benefit from life's most severe challenges."

—**Louis Sullivan**, former Health and Human Services Secretary

"*Overcoming* is a beautiful and deeply moving book that reminds us of our common humanity and of the reservoir of resilience that resides in all of us. I love the fact that the reader learns about so many strategies to survive and even grow from the many stresses, traumas, and tragedies that we will face at some point in our life, and that we learn these strategies through the eyes and actions of everyday heroes. To me, *Overcoming* is a true gift that inspires the reader to rise up to their best self and join the human family so that we together can confront, overcome, and grow from the challenges that life presents us."

—**Dr. Steven Southwick,** bestselling author of
*Resilience: The Science of Mastering Life's Greatest Challenges*

"In this latest book, Dr. White reminds us of our shared values through portraits of twenty exemplary individuals who have overcome extreme physical, mental, economic, and social hardships, and against all odds have succeeded, without abandoning hope and their faith in human solidarity. This book is an ode to humanity, and could not be more timely. It reminds us that what unites us as human beings is more enduring than what divides us."

—**Vartan Gregorian**, president of the Carnegie Corporation

"Resilience is a popular term today and it has become ever more important as world crises deepen with no end in sight.... Reading about these heroic struggles, our backs straighten, our confidence in the future is reborn, and our self-pity melts away.... We can all feel buoyed by these profiles in determination."

—**Ruth Simmons**, president of Prairie View A&M University

"Dr. Augustus White presents us with inspiring and invaluable stories of resilience at a time when resilience has never mattered more. Triumphing over adversity, he forcefully reminds us, is a team sport. His book offers powerful illustrations of an essential truth: 'No one makes it alone.'"

—**Drew Gilpin Faust**, former president of Harvard University

"This new book from Dr. Gus White is most timely. Natural and man-made traumas assault us as individuals and communities.... This exceptional book tells the stories of how individuals face the challenges of debilitating illness and other life crises, and how these challenges reveal the primary elements of our essential human resilience and ability to overcome the hard challenges we all inevitably face in our lives."

—**Dr. Gregory Fricchione**, Associate Chief of Psychiatry
at Massachusetts General Hospital

"Dr. Augustus White has taken the stories of twenty individuals and woven them into a compelling book focusing on resilience and the common strain that comes from humankind when we think beyond ourselves and contribute to the goodness that can be found in our daily lives. For me, these stories gave me both a sense of hope and a belief in the future of humankind."

—**Gordon Gee**, former president of Ohio State University

# OVERCOMING

## LESSONS IN TRIUMPHING OVER ADVERSITY AND THE POWER OF OUR COMMON HUMANITY

## DR. AUGUSTUS WHITE III

### WITH JON LAND
### AND DAVID CHANOFF

Post Hill
PRESS

**Post Hill Press**
New York • Nashville
posthillpress.com

Published in the United States of America
1  2  3  4  5  6  7  8  9  10

*Dedicated to my wife, Anita.*
*My daughters: Alissa, Atina, and Annica.*
*My grandchildren: Leah, Logan, Alfred, Astrid, and Aaden.*
*My mother and father: Vivian Dandridge White*
*and Augustus Aaron White.*
*With much love.*

# CONTENTS

*I don't think of all the misery but of the beauty that still remains.*

—Anne Frank

# FOREWORD

# Adversity

By Mike "Coach K" Krzyzewski

What I believe separates good teams and individuals from great ones is the manner in which they handle adversity. Do you let it beat you, or do you use it to make yourself better?

Adversity can teach you more about yourself than any success, and overcoming an obstacle can sometimes feel even better than achieving an easy victory. Additionally, you can discover things about your endurance, your ability to turn a negative into a positive, and your personal strength of heart.

One of the greatest comments I ever heard about adversity came from the current Duke University president, Richard Brodhead. He said to me, "You outlive your darkest day." In other words, failure can never be your destination. In adverse circumstances, you must remind yourself that this day is not your last. You will get through it, but can you use it to get better? Improvement comes as the result of adversity; it comes from learning about limits and how to break those limits. Whenever I face adversity, I look at the problem and then beyond the problem. I look for the solution and then I look for the positive impact it will have on me, my team, or my family.

In the summer of 2003, after doing a speaking engagement in Colorado Springs, I heard on television the frightening news that my former Duke point guard Jason Williams had been in a horrific motorcycle accident. I immediately made calls to find out about Jason and learned that he was in serious condition and had been taken to a trauma center in Chicago. The initial prognosis was that he had a chance of losing his leg and never being able to walk again. I immediately changed my original schedule and flew to Chicago to be with him.

On the flight, I thought about Jason's current condition and all that he had already accomplished in his young life: he was a Duke graduate, a National Champion, a two-time National Player of the Year, and he had his jersey retired and hanging from the rafters in Cameron Indoor Stadium.

One thing that had always blown me away about Jason is that he was never afraid to make mistakes. In the 2001 National Championship game, Jason had hit only one three-pointer in ten attempts, but going into the last few minutes of the game, I called a play for him to shoot another three. He was not afraid to take that next shot. And he hit the three that proved to be the biggest shot in the last few minutes of the game. As a result, we all became National Champions. Jason was fearless because he grew up with great parents, knowing that he had their unconditional love and support and that a mistake was never the end-all. I tried to offer him the same type of support during his college career. His fearlessness made him one of the best players I have ever coached.

I will always remember walking into Jason's hospital room, seeing him in that condition, and hugging his crying mother and father. As I bent over and kissed him on his forehead, Jason said to me, "Coach, thanks for being here."

I then proceeded to talk to Jason in positive terms about the fact that he would not only walk again but also would be in the NBA again. I gave him a holy saint's medal of mine that I had carried with me for years. Every time he looked at the medal, I wanted him to look beyond the adversity he was currently facing and to remember that those who love him will be behind him throughout his recovery and the rest of his life. I wanted to give him a destination beyond the devastation. I said to him, "Jason, this medal is very special to me, but I want to lend it to you. You have to promise to give it back to me the day that you play in your next NBA game. And you can be sure that I will be there."

The doctors would talk about the solution to Jason's medical problems, but I wanted to be sure that, mentally and emotionally, he was looking beyond the problem and that his destination was not adversity, but success.

I have always known that Jason has the heart of a champion, and with him it is best to let him follow his instincts. Winners expect to win. And Jason expects that he will come out a champion yet again. His limits have been tested in a very serious way. But he is approaching this scary situation and his arduous recovery with the same fearlessness with which he played every game of basketball. He has used his recovery time to develop himself as a student of the game, attending as many games as possible, asking questions of other players and coaches, and even doing television commentary during some games. Because I know Jason has a winner's heart, it doesn't surprise me to watch as he has gone from not knowing whether or not he will walk again to having the opportunity to begin playing basketball.

The adversity did not beat him. Rather, he has used it as an opportunity to grow as a person and to learn a great deal about what a strong man he is, mentally, emotionally, and physically. Jason looked at his adversity and beyond, and his champion heart has him running and jumping again, less than three years later. What a winner!

—From *Beyond Basketball: Coach K's Keywords for Success*
by Mike Krzyzewski with Jaimie K. Spatola, Hachette Book Group, 2006. Reprinted with permission.

# The Courage That Matters—My Take

*"No one can predict whether we'll ever return to something like the life we used to know."*

That's from Uri Friedman writing for the *Atlantic* magazine in May of 2020, postulating on what the future of a coronavirus-dominated world will look like. Scary prospects indeed, if not downright terrifying.

We started *Overcoming* way back in the fall of 2019, what seems like another age now. At that point, neither we nor anyone else had the slightest inkling that the world would be facing a life-changing pandemic that has upended every aspect of our lives. Nothing we do now is the same. So much we took for granted has been stripped away or altered, at times beyond recognition. Normalcy has become a relative, ever-evolving term as we find ourselves in the midst of a paradigm shift that seems certain to redefine life as we know it.

So how are we to cope?

Although COVID-19 didn't exist when we began this book, the answer lies in the message contained in these pages. You are about to meet a group of extraordinary individuals distinguished not by their fame or fortune but by their ability to face down often incredible levels of adversity. They are black, white, and Latino; male and female, young and old.

They are you.

They are me.

They are our fellow humans.

They represent all of us and, in doing so, encapsulate our capacity for resilience in the face of often insurmountable obstacles. They have suffered devastating injuries, endured tragedy, overcome setbacks determined to destroy them, and experienced all manner of commonly perceived disabilities. They have beaten stereotypes, flouted societal limitations, witnessed unimaginable horrors, and survived devastating heartache. They have persevered through loss, abuse, pain, and mourning to become heroes in their own right.

They are a Lost Boy of Sudan finding a new life and second chance in America. They are a woman fighting for the rights of those sexually abused by priests, as she was. They are a once-paralyzed high school wrestler who returned to compete at an Olympic level. They are a blind psychotherapist, an award-winning actor with Down syndrome, a lung cancer survivor, a CrossFit athlete who didn't let the loss of an arm waylay her dreams. They are parents who found the strength to endure the loss of a child, a haunted survivor of the Boston Marathon bombing, a Navy SEAL suffering from post-traumatic stress disorder, one doctor who lost his dream only to forge a new one, and another doctor determined to help thousands of people live to realize their dreams in a distant, forgotten corner of the world.

They are you.

They are me.

None of them suffered from COVID-19, but their stories offer lessons and inspiration on how to negotiate the new roads before us, providing us with maps to help us find our way even if the route has changed. "It always seems impossible until it's done," Nelson Mandela once famously said. No counsel could be better suited for what we are facing now and will continue to face.

"We all want things to go back to normal quickly," wrote the *MIT Technology Review* of the crisis visited upon us in early 2020. "But what most of us have probably not yet realized—yet will soon—is that things won't go back to normal after a few weeks, or even a few months. Some things never will."

We need to find the resilience needed to cope with that. And, as with all things, it is easier to succeed by following the footsteps of those who've already managed to achieve what we seek. In that respect, the lessons contained in these stories can show us the way even as they keep our current plights in the perspectives where they belong—against a backdrop of success drawn from failure, hope out of tragedy, pleasure from pain.

And we will learn the strength and happiness that comes from extending a hand down to help another, even as you are stretching a hand up for help yourself. The hardship we are facing is unprecedented, and we must find similarly unprecedented levels of compassion if we are to not just survive, but thrive.

"Pandemics will always be characterized by their randomness, pitilessness, and power to sicken and kill," Jeffrey Kluger wrote for *Time* in February of 2020. "The human response, when it's at its best, is defined by collective courage and compassion, a 'not-on-our-watch' refusal to let a disease have its way with our fellow humans. And to limit the impact of—and ultimately to defeat—the current coronavirus pandemic, that's exactly what we'll need."

That's the power of our common humanity, and, more than anything else, we need that now. The belief that we are stronger together has never been truer. COVID-19 does not discriminate among race, age, culture, ethnicity, creed, religion, or any other factor that may tend to divide us. And so we must tighten the ties that bind us, because those ties are both the cure and the vaccine—if not for the virus itself, at least for its side effects, which are certain to linger the longest in disrupting the lives we are now forced to redefine.

We are all so much more similar than different. As an orthopedic surgeon, I can tell you that when you make the incision, when you look inside, everybody is the same. Open up the skin and underneath it's all one. The reality of the body tells you this. It's a reality doctors see constantly. Our humanness is greater than our cultural differences, our differences in status or rank, our racial differences. In the final analysis, we're just human, and now we need the power of our common humanity to help us spot a future through the clouds, to bring light to the darkness that threatens to consume us.

"The only courage that matters," wrote author and journalist Mignon McLaughlin, "is the kind that gets you from one moment to the next."

We're going to emphasize two themes in this book: one is our common humanity, the other is our resilience. The first will help us to understand and interact more humanely with one another. The second will help us to work better with ourselves. *Overcoming* will guide you from one hour to the next, one day to the next, one month to the next. The twenty-one people you are about to meet will show you how.

Because they are us. And we are them.

# Greetings from Dr. Gus White

My fellow humans…

The pioneering black physical anthropologist, physician, and civil rights leader Montague Cobb used to begin all his speeches with that salutation. In his day, medical and scientific audiences rarely heard addresses from black scientists. Cobb's "my fellow humans" was a greeting, but it was also an announcement. He was acknowledging the listeners in front of him as his fellow humans; by the same token, he was reminding them that he was *their* fellow human.

I've adopted Cobb's "my fellow humans" salutation for my own speeches, as an homage to both his greatness and the vital nature of the message the phrase imparts. Because we are better, and stronger, together than we are apart. The nature of people coming together for a common good seems ever so far-fetched in these tribal times, where we allow what separates us to define us far more than what bonds us together.

I, for one, refuse to accept that. If I've learned nothing else in my many years as a surgeon, it's that everyone's the same when you open them up, and one man bleeds the same as another. These last four years—the last one in particular—have been a trying experience for

Americans on both sides of the political spectrum. Indeed, we have too often lost track of the very trait that makes the good great and the great even better:

Our common humanity.

In the black South, when I was a child growing up in Memphis, Tennessee, the first thing an adult person would ask was, "What are you going to be when you grow up?" Or in my case, since my father had been a physician, "Your father was a fine man, a great doctor. You going to be a doctor like him?"

My physician father died when I was eight, but some of his influence must have rubbed off, because in our playground games of cowboys and Indians, I seemed to naturally want to take care of those who might have been hurt or wounded in the action.

My last book, *Seeing Patients*, covers my experience as a physician. It tells a personal story, but it also explores some of the root causes that steer all of us, physicians and nonphysicians, into discriminatory behaviors operating beneath the surface of conscious thought and moving us without our realizing it. When I was growing up in Memphis, it was widely believed that there were significant discrepancies in aptitude and intelligence between blacks and whites. Most black doctors saw only black patients. White doctors tended to treat black patients with the condescension and patronization common in that society. In those playground games, by the way, I treated whites and blacks alike, cowboys as well as Indians.

After my dad died, my mother and I were forced to move from our two-bedroom house into the home of my Aunt Addie and her husband, Uncle Doc, a pharmacist. We doubled up on couches and cots, and my college-educated mother got a job as a secretary at a high school, where she eventually became a teacher after remarrying, to a man I welcomed into our home as my stepfather. All the schools in the South were segregated back then, and the high school I attended was considered the best in terms of sports. My stepfather coached boxing and also served as an assistant coach on the football team. He

2

was very generous with his time to me. He taught me how to box and how to catch a football. I learned so much from him, including how important it is when an adult takes an interest in you.

My uncle, Doc Jones, also took a real interest in me. Fatherless boys long for role models, and he was a tough guy, never afraid to stand up for himself. He carried a gun and got into scrapes often over the years, including a shoot-out. He'd stayed home and worked so his younger siblings could go to school, becoming a pharmacist later in life. We'd go to cowboy movies at the local cinema on Saturday afternoons, and he'd even take me with him when he delivered prescriptions to his many customers. I'd ride with him in the front seat, feeling like I was king of the world.

"We're real partners, aren't we?" I'd ask him from the passenger seat, mining the language from all those cowboy movies.

And it sure seemed that way at the time. I don't think I knew what the word "mentor" meant back then, but those men were my first two, at least when it came to male role models. Because my initial mentor was none other than my mother.

She believed, above all else, how important it was to treat everyone with respect—those above, below, and 360 degrees around you. Her attitude was, "You can do it!" It didn't matter what "it" was—I could succeed and prosper no matter what. This encompassed a vital emotional component of mentoring. Indeed, my own mentees are fond of telling me that I expressed a confidence in them, a positivity that made them feel good about themselves because my mother made me feel good about myself. I often talk about the importance of smiling generously at others and being equally generous with sincere compliments. There is no greater gift one fellow human can give another than to make clear how much you believe in them.

My mother also placed tremendous emphasis and value on education, as had my father, and that set me on a road that would take me north to the Mount Hermon School for Boys (now Northfield Mount Hermon), a prestigious boarding school that accepted blacks and started me on my way to breaking down numerous color barriers deemed unthinkable at the time. I earned tuition money by waiting tables and sweeping floors—not because I was black, but because all students were required to do their assigned chores around the school grounds. It was one of the ways the school balanced the scales between races and socioeconomic levels, all students within the school's hallowed gates considered equals. I sang in the choir, excelled academically, and was the only member of my class to earn varsity letters in three different sports: wrestling, lacrosse, and football.

At Mount Hermon, the man who picked up where my stepfather and Uncle Doc left off was the wrestling coach, Vincent Campbell. He was a quieter mentor, not the most communicative or engaging. He wasn't great at verbalizing his feelings, but I prospered under his tutelage and served as captain of the wrestling team my senior year, the first African-American student elected to that role. Coach Campbell looked at me and didn't see a black kid; he just saw a kid. And years later that kid would be inducted into the Northfield Mount Hermon Hall of Fame.

Then came Brown University.

"When Augustus A. White III arrived at Brown in 1953," *Brown Alumni Magazine* wrote in a fall 2011 issue, "he joined a student body as whitewashed and WASPy as a beach house in Kennebunkport, Maine. The Hillel House wouldn't open for another decade. The first woman, the first African American, and the first Jew on the Corporation's Board of Fellows would have to wait until 1969. White was one of only five African Americans in his class."

"We, Brown's African American students, didn't feel affronted by this plain discrimination," I told the magazine for that same article. "Quite the opposite. We felt happy to be at a place so liberal that it accepted Negroes at all."

I worked grueling hours in order to play football—defensive end and wide receiver—in a career highlighted by a game against Dartmouth my senior season that saw the Big Green driving for a winning touchdown in the waning minutes of the fourth quarter. They'd gotten down to our six or seven yard line and seemed certain to be going in for the winning score. I'd been badly beaten on an earlier running play, and they came out in the same formation. As the ball was snapped, the offensive lineman tried to hook me to get me out of the way again. But this time I was ready. I threw him aside, made the tackle, and the clock ran out. There was also the game against Cornell where I caught a twice-deflected pass for a touchdown, and another touchdown I caught on Homecoming that gave us the lead in a game where we drubbed Harvard 21–12, for which I was recognized in the following day's *Providence Journal* and was also awarded the game ball.

That senior season held one of the most indelible memories: the day when Brown's, and the country's, first great African-American player, Fritz Pollard, was inducted into the College Football Hall of Fame at Brown Stadium. My teammate Archie Williams and I were standing on the sidelines when the man who led Brown to an appearance in the first ever Rose Bowl game in 1916 came strolling past us.

The greatest highlight of my own football career came in my final home game against Colgate on November 28, 1956, when my mother came north to watch me play for the first time ever at any level in the last game I would ever be in. We won the game 33–7, and I don't remember much about my own performance other than bursting with pride that the woman who'd raised me was finally there to share in such an important part of my life. I even composed a prayer for the game in her honor:

*Oh God,*
*When the final gun is shot and my final game is over*
*May I please know that on every play I had done my very best.*
*This way may I leave football and life.*
*Amen*

At the end of the season, I was named winner of the Class of 1910 Trophy, awarded to the senior with the highest academic average on the team. I don't know what life would've been like if I hadn't played football, if I'd focused on another sport instead. A lot of that has to do with the culture in which I grew up, how important football was to the culture of the South in a middle-class black community. Football was lauded. People respected and looked up to people who played the game. And that was so important to my identity as a young boy when I thought I was tough playing sandlot, even though I was a pip-squeak at the time. When I think of all the things I took from football, the first one that comes to mind is resilience. Football helped teach me how to pull myself back up after getting knocked down, the way I had been when my father died.

My mentor at Brown was a wonderful man named Tony Davis, a professor in the Psychology Department. He noticed me because I was a football player and wrestler, and he took an interest in me.

Walking out of class one day, he said, "Mr. White, may I speak with you? You're a good student and you might want to consider writing a thesis. Please make an appointment to come see me."

Well, I did, and down the road we ended up publishing a paper together. That was so important to me because no one had ever told me I was a good student before. Just having someone of Professor Davis's stature tell me that provided reinforcement and encouragement at a critical point in my life, and it made me a better student who expected and demanded more of myself. Life has that way of bringing people to you who have a huge impact when you need them the most, true mentors who help you not only realize your own potential, but exceed it.

"The influence White has had on Brown's racial and ethnic diversity reflects the steady, deliberate effort of an unlikely pioneer," that article in *Brown Alumni Magazine* continues. "A groundbreaking orthopedic surgeon, he was the first African American medical student at Stanford, the first black orthopedic surgeon at Yale, the first black professor of medicine at Yale, and the first black department chief at a Harvard teaching hospital. One of the world's most preeminent experts on the biomechanics of the spine, White has coauthored textbooks that remain seminal references for surgeons and clinicians. When his book for a popular audience, *Your Aching Back: A Doctor's Guide to Relief,* appeared in 1990, the *New England Journal of Medicine* decreed that it 'should be read by every person afflicted with low back pain, and perhaps everybody.'"

Years later, Tony Davis became my patient. He died recently, and his obituary mentioned me as one of his mentees, which meant a lot to me, even after all these years. I also read in his obituary that he was a fighter pilot in the Korean War. I wish I'd known that when he was alive and was disappointed that I hadn't, because he'd been so important to me. I guess he knew me better than I'd known him, and I felt like I'd missed something as a result. Mentees should make it a point to know their mentors, not just the reverse.

When I went to medical school at Stanford back in the late 1950s, there were strict quotas for black students. This was before the civil rights movement, a time when most medical schools in the country simply did not believe that a person of color might have the intelligence and diligence to become a doctor. Often, you had to work twice as hard to get half as far. After graduating from Stanford, I honed my orthopedic skills at both the University of Michigan Medical Center and the Pacific Presbyterian Medical Center in San Francisco as a general surgery resident before landing a residency with Dr. Wayne Southwick, chief of orthopedics at Yale University and one of the world's leading spinal orthopedists at the time. It was a wonderful opportunity I couldn't turn down, and I ended up finding my calling, thanks in large part to the man who became my next, and greatest, mentor.

After our interview, he gave me a ride back to the train station in New Haven.

"Dr. Southwick, will being a Negro affect my chances of being a resident here?" I asked him before climbing out of the car.

"We want to get the best people we can get," was his response.

I'm sure making me one of those "best people" for the residency program at Yale burned a lot of bridges for Wayne Southwick. But he didn't care. He sent me to Sweden on a National Institutes of Health scholarship to study biomechanics. He nominated me for membership in several prestigious orthopedic societies. In short, he was the man most responsible for elevating me in a way that became a springboard for the rest of my career.

"Why'd you give me a job? Why'd you take such a risk?" I asked him one day.

"Because it seemed like the right thing to do," he said, after a reflective pause.

I had gone to medical school originally to follow the path that Tony Davis helped lay out, with an eye on practicing psychiatry. But life, as it often does, had other plans. Somewhere along the line, a magazine article proclaimed me to be "the Jackie Robinson of orthopedics." I resist labels of all kinds, but I take special pride in that particular one because it represented the barriers I'd broken down in the process and the doors I'd left open for others following in my wake, who hopefully wouldn't have to overcome the same adversity that I did.

Part of the reason I was sorry I hadn't known Tony Davis had been a fighter pilot was my own experience as a combat surgeon in Vietnam for two years, beginning in August of 1966. Subject to a special doctors' draft, I could have found alternative service but opted not to. I wanted to jump over there and do what I could. It is well known that there were many options to avoid service in Vietnam. I chose to serve for two very simple reasons. One, my function there would be to save lives and alleviate suffering, not to eliminate lives. Two, in a very real sense, people fought and died in World War II to protect my life and, at least to some extent, my freedom. This constituted an obligation in my mind.

Surgery was done in a bunker-like room with no windows, ventilated by a twelve-inch electric fan. It contained a sink, a counter on which instruments were placed, a supply cabinet, and army field-type operating tables. For light, a simple coil and socket with a reflector was used with a backup generator always on hand in case the power failed. Not on par with a typical US hospital operating suite, but more than adequate.

Out in the jungle beyond Qui Nhon City the battlefield had its own rhythm, and when something big was happening the choppers would come in one after the other bearing the wounded. You'd hear the whine of the engines and the whop, whop, whop of the rotors, bringing a rush of corpsmen, nurses, and doctors running toward the helipad and the triage unit next to it. During those periods I could be working fifty or sixty hours straight along with the other surgeons, snatching a few minutes of sleep here and there whenever we could. The rest of the time we were up to our elbows in blood.

At first it was overwhelming. No amount of training could prepare you for this. Ten or fifteen gurneys lined up with troopers straight from the battlefield, many of them with heart-stopping injuries. But within a few days I had the routine down pat. Grab a patient, establish an airway, stop the bleeding, get an IV started, take X-rays, figure out what kind of specialist you needed. In those terrible periods I'd sometimes get to feeling as if my hands were operating on automatic pilot. I might be standing there semi-comatose, my eyes glazing over, but my hands knew the debriding routine by themselves. Cutting, washing, clamping off veins and arteries, cauterizing bleeders.

The journal I kept of my Vietnam experience includes an entry in August of 1966 about treating a twenty-year-old infantryman; he had taken a direct hit from a land mine, which had blown off his left foot and riddled his leg with shrapnel and injured the skin of his right wrist. I was quite depressed and upset to witness this young soldier's plight. Although I didn't personally blame Lyndon Johnson, my emotional response was to want to grab our president by the elbow and bring him in to show him this terrified young man, writhing in pain, with his leg and arm in bloody dressings. If we could have all the world leaders spend a week in a MASH unit with a military surgeon, there would be fewer wars.

My Vietnam experience didn't stop in the operating room either. I also volunteered at a nearby leprosarium, doing the best I could to help the unfortunate lot confined there.

What was going on at the St. Francis Leprosarium made for quite a contrast with the Eighty-Fifth EVAC Hospital, where I was assigned. I saw victims who had a hole in their face where their mouth and nose had once been. And here were these Franciscan nuns running the colony, preserving human dignity at all costs. What I experienced firsthand as a result was the striking contrast between what nature can do to man and what man can do to man.

And yet amid the pain and ostracism, I witnessed so much hope and optimism. I recall gazing around the waiting room packed with leper patients, meeting the gazes of those physically unfortunate people, and feeling aware of the richness of their spirit and the depth of their wisdom, gratitude, and understanding. When I left each day, I wondered who had benefitted more at St. Francis, the helped or the helpers. I was awarded a Bronze Start for my service in Vietnam, but in my mind the residents of the St. Francis Leprosarium were far braver than I could ever hope to be.

Remember how I said to my Uncle Doc, 'We're real partners, aren't we?' while I rode with him on drives to deliver prescriptions to his customers? We were indeed, because that's what mentoring really is: an unspoken, indelible partnership between mentor and mentee. At every stop along the way of my life, I've been fortunate enough to have people like Vincent Campbell, Tony Davis, and Doc Jones around me. Getting up after you've fallen is a lot easier when someone extends a hand.

So much of what I've done in my life, I was the first person to do it. That's a reflection of, and testament to, the people who came into my life at the right time when I needed them the most, whether I realized it or not. And once I was fortunate enough to gain a measure of success in my chosen field of medical practice, I sought to do for others what my mentors had done for me. I take great pride and comfort in the lives I touched in that manner and the great success they've gone on to achieve.

Remember Dr. Wayne Southwick? Well, he asked if I'd mentor his son Steven in the 1970s.

"I'd dropped out of Yale, after spending a couple years in Vietnam, and was just looking for a job," Steve recalls. "In essence, I was floundering around. I felt like a failure. But our first meeting changed my life. I could feel your genuine desire to help and the faith you showed in me. You made me realize I hadn't really veered off my path; this was just part of that path. And you gave me a job working with you on a project to see if putting compression on fractures would help them heal more quickly. Not long after that, we published a paper together on the psychological effects of back pain. You took me on rounds to see patients; you wanted me to get a feel for medicine. That was it. I was hooked. I went back to school and became a psychiatrist. And when I was a junior attending at Yale, working in the psychiatric emergency room with drug addiction, suicide, veterans down in their lives, I went by WWGD—What would Gus do?"

Steve published a superb book in 2018 with Dennis Charney called *Resilience: The Science of Mastering Life's Greatest Challenges* that mirrors many of the themes covered in these pages.

"Most of us at some point will be struck by one or more major traumas: violent crime, domestic violence, rape, child abuse, a serious automobile accident, the sudden death of a loved one, a debilitating disease, a natural disaster or war," Southwick and Charney wrote. "If you are lucky, then, you have never encountered any of these misfortunes; but most likely you will someday. It is estimated that up to ninety percent of us will experience some of them during our lives."

*Ninety percent!*

That makes adversity a more prevalent malady than even the common cold, and a far more difficult one to treat to boot. There's no single prescription that can cure the ills or even relieve the symptoms.

But there is one well-proven treatment for adversity: our common humanity that bonds us together and instinctively leads us to want to help one another. The kind of common humanity that led the white chief of orthopedics at Yale to offer a black man a job and the kind of common humanity that led the same black man to mentor the other man's son years later. And by the way, Steven Southwick, currently inaugural Greenberg Professor of Psychiatry, Post-Traumatic Stress Disorder, and Resilience at the Yale University School of Medicine, has become quite the mentor himself.

"I love mentoring," Steven says. "It's like having a son or daughter in some ways. There's a joy to it, pride in wanting your mentees to succeed. I so much want them to feel fulfilled and enjoy the same appreciation for life that you gave me. Mentoring is as important and rewarding as anything I've ever done in my career. There was a study done in Hawaii of kids growing up in deprived situations where they weren't unconditionally loved. That study revealed that the kids seemed to do really well in spite of all these obstacles so long as they had one person who believed in and loved them, just one person. Sometimes we don't realize the impact we can have on the life of another human being."

Adversity is a matter of perspective, an appreciation of what you've already achieved that motivates you to help more people rise to your station. That's the very definition of the common humanity that we have lost track of and need to get back. I thought I'd put my own struggles with adversity behind me, able to focus on using my ninth decade of life to cement my legacy.

Then, a few years ago, I felt dizzy and a little confused after a visit to the dentist to have my teeth cleaned. I sat down in the cafeteria and realized I couldn't remember where I'd parked my car. I knew something wasn't right, was very wrong in fact. I found my car and managed to drive home. The next day I was in the kitchen talking on the phone when I dropped it, but I didn't realize I'd dropped it, and almost fell myself.

My wife called the rescue squad, and at the hospital I was diagnosed with having suffered a minor stroke that nonetheless left me with considerable weakness in my right leg. Two and a half years later, there's been no progression, but not very much recovery either. I took the very advice I've been giving my own patients for years: to try to function as close as you can to the ordinary. My strategy is to do everything I possibly can and avoid the things I can't. It takes me two or three times as long to do anything, but I come as close as I can to doing everything I want to do.

My ninth decade of life has left me humbled with a deeper respect and appreciation for those who have overcome far more than I have currently, and at least as much as I did as a boy emerging from the black South. I rely on a walker for support these days, but that walker might just as well be the broad shoulders of those who boosted me up when I needed it the most. Physical therapists helped me learn to walk again, just as men like my stepfather and Doc Jones, Vincent Campbell, and Tony Davis helped me learn how to run, both literally and figuratively. No one succeeds in a vacuum. No one makes it alone. And a truly great joy of life is celebrating our common humanity that has the potential to make each and every one of us better.

We are all so much more similar than different. Our humanness is greater than our cultural differences, our differences in status or rank, our racial differences. In the final analysis, we're all just human.

And that's what the ensuing chapters are going to demonstrate in stark fashion. You are about to meet a diverse group of people. No two stories are the same, but in a cumulative sense they offer hope through any number of ways and perspectives our humanity translates into resilience. All our subjects faced adversity and found a way to overcome it, benefitting from the bonds of our common humanity that unite us all.

Indeed, my fellow humans, as Woody Guthrie famously sang in his classic song "John Henry," *a man ain't nothing but a man.*

# 1

# Donald McNeil

"I was thinking, I hope I can wrestle again."

That was Donald McNeil's first thought after suffering an injury at a 2007 high school Memorial Day weekend wrestling tournament in Virginia that nearly rendered him a quadriplegic.

"I was lying on the mat, couldn't move or feel anything. A trainer checked me out and said it was probably a stinger."

Then a doctor who happened to be in the stands rushed down.

"Can you feel that?" the doctor asked him.

"No," Donald replied. "Are you touching me?"

At that point, the then fifteen-year-old knew something was really wrong. Paramedics arrived quickly and slid him onto a spinal board to keep everything stable before easing him into the back of their ambulance.

"They were in a rush to get me to the hospital. I could feel the urgency. I'd been hurt before a couple times but never anything like this. I don't know if I was scared, but I was nervous."

Mostly over whether he'd ever be able to return to the mat, even though at that point the odds were against him even walking again.

"A doctor waited until much later to tell me that of the ten thousand spinal cord injuries suffered every year, only around eighty people achieve a full recovery."

But Donald displayed a relentless determination to be one of those people, right from the start, never for one moment doubting that he'd not only walk but also wrestle again. It had been too much a part of his life for too long to let it go.

"I started when I was eight. I'm not a gifted athlete, so I didn't pick it up right way. I had to work. It was the first thing I was really committed to."

His dad, Andy, had been a championship wrestler himself in his college years at Brown University.

"He was never the crazy sports parent, but wrestling created a real connection between us. He instilled in me the importance of making the commitment to train, to practice. I learned to love the sport as much as he did. It was something we shared."

Call it love at first hold. Donald stresses that it's hard to understand his instant infatuation with wrestling if you haven't experienced the sport yourself, which is truly like no other.

"Gold medals aren't really made of gold," Olympic champion Dan Gable once said. "They're made of sweat, determination, and a hard-to-find alloy called guts. Once you've wrestled," he adds, "everything else in life is easy."

But it wasn't going to be easy for Donald McNeil. The good news was that even though he'd suffered a severe contusion, his spinal cord hadn't been ruptured. The bad news was that the initial tests revealed breaks in the fifth and sixth vertebrae in his neck, along with multiple dislocated vertebrae and significant compression on his spinal cord.

The day before, Donald had beaten the same opponent in a standard match, spoiling his undefeated record. But the match in which he was injured featured Greco-Roman rules, a style with which he was far less familiar and practiced. The move that injured him is appropriately called a "pile driver" in which one wrestler lifts another into the air upside down and slams him down so that his head literally breaks his fall.

"He told me he heard me scream from the stands," Donald's mother, Betsy McNeil, recalls today. "There he is in intensive care, lying in bed with all these tubes coming out of him, and I'm thinking about installing ramps in our house. It was that bad. What kept me going was Donald's attitude. It never even occurred to him that he wouldn't wrestle again, never mind walk."

Toward that end, there were early signs of hope. Betsy's aunt hailed from the area and happened to be a nursing supervisor at Inova Fairfax Hospital. She was sitting at his bedside the night of the surgery, squeezing his hand.

"Who's holding my hand?" Donald asked from the drug-induced stupor in which he found himself.

He had felt something, and something, at that juncture, was a whole lot better than nothing. Progress, though, was slow to nonexistent over the next few days, to the point that Donald overheard a nurse refer to him as a "quadriplegic."

"Tears were rolling down his cheeks," Betsy says, her own eyes growing moist. "It was the only time he thought he might not get better."

But that was before Donald was transferred to one of the finest rehabilitation hospitals in the world, Spaulding, outside of Boston.

"He was doing physical therapy with these older guys," Betsy remembers. "He was in his wheelchair and they were cheering him on from theirs. 'Kick ass, Donald!' they'd yell out. And that's what he tried to do every day."

Not right away, though.

"I was completely paralyzed when I arrived at Spaulding," Donald reflects. "But they told me I could make a full recovery if I worked at it. It was up to me. That was the first time I'd heard something positive since the accident. And the next day I moved a finger. It wasn't much, but it was a start."

Indeed. Even as the feeling in his limbs began to return, Donald had to use a motorized wheelchair, envious of his fellow patients who could wheel around manually in theirs. It was a goal he'd never imagined setting for himself just a few weeks back. Victories were still everything to him; they were just of the smaller variety now.

"I had to learn how to use my arms and legs again from scratch. I had to be taught how to walk. Everything I'd ever taken for granted had been taken away from me. I couldn't do anything on my own. Couldn't get out of bed, couldn't go to the bathroom, couldn't brush my teeth or take a shower, couldn't get dressed. When you're fifteen and have no privacy at all, that's a big deal. I remember when I was able to pee on my own for the first time after I guess it was around a month. That was one of the greatest feelings I ever had."

So maybe it was time to let go of wrestling, realize that there was no future for him back on the mat, right?

Wrong.

"I never thought I wouldn't get back. I was always set on returning to wrestling. That confidence came from doctors and rehab specialists who told me I was healed, and the rest, how much of what I'd lost I'd be able to get back, was up to me."

And Donald credits wrestling, the very sport that had nearly disabled him for life, for the fortitude that enabled him to recover.

"With wrestling, every day you're training. You're always pushing your limits, pushing yourself to the brink. You have to bring it every day, and it's hard to get really shaken by a lot in life," he says, echoing Dan Gable's comments. "It's as much mental as physical. You have to be mentally tough to be physically strong. It's you versus yourself more than the opponent."

That credo would receive its greatest test in the coming weeks and months as Donald made slow but steady progress. With spinal cord injuries, though, every bit of progress is dramatic, like moving from a motorized wheelchair to a manual one, and ultimately to crutches.

"Moving to the crutches was a big step. That's when I was sure I could come all the way back, not just to wrestle but to wrestle at a high level again. I'd just won States in my weight class before the tournament where I got hurt. I was wrestling the best I ever had and knew I could do it again."

But his mother couldn't chase the memory of Donald's initial evaluation when he arrived at Spaulding from her mind.

"They'd run both ends of a safety pin down his leg. He couldn't feel the dull side at all, and when they put the sharp end against him and asked which it was, he'd say dull."

The McNeils have no pictures from the MedFlight up to Boston because none of them wanted a record of the experience; it was just too horrible. The rehabilitation process was grueling and often agonizing, the hardest training Donald says he's ever been through. His therapists were relentless in helping him to achieve the goals he'd set for himself. They pushed him hard, and he pushed himself harder.

"The nature of sport is to keep pushing faster, further, stronger," writes disabled US Ski Team champion Sarah Billmeier in Artemis Joukowsky III's superb book, *Raising the Bar.* "This sort of eternally striving courage is a welcome label for disabled athletes, however we are often also saddled with the other connotation of courage that assumes a disabled person is brave if she lifts her head off the pillow and dares to live a life. In my experience, the only way to eliminate the latter attitude is to live the way you want and to let your actions speak for themselves."

And that's exactly what Donald did, even though his disability proved only temporary.

"I was hoping he'd never wrestle again, but I knew how much he wanted to and I knew in my heart that he would," Betsy says. "He loves wrestling with a passion. He'd done it all over the country and it was a community for him, a way of life, a philosophy of how to live.

So much of who he was is because of wrestling. As soon as he started walking again, he started talking seriously about getting back on the mat. Was I happy? No, I was absolutely terrified. It was a conversation I didn't want to have with him."

Early in that process, Donald was as awkward as a baby taking its first steps and fell almost as often. Betsy recalls him once walking toward her Frankenstein-monster style with arms outstretched.

"What are you doing?" I asked him.

"What do you think? I've got cadaver bones in my neck where they fixed it."

Donald's sense of humor never left him, even when he lay motionless in a Spaulding Rehabilitation Hospital bed with a roomful of his high school wrestling friends around him. And once he turned that fateful corner of being able to walk on his own and perform the daily tasks that were gradually returning, his wrestling coach at King Philip Regional High School in Wrentham, Massachusetts, Walter Laskey, entered the picture. When Donald walked out of Spaulding in a neck collar after a month, an incredible achievement in its own right, Laskey was waiting for him.

"He cared about me as a person," Donald says, "not just a wrestler."

Laskey would pick Donald up three or four times a week to train with weights at a local gym. They'd talk wrestling, discuss strategy. Laskey neither encouraged nor discouraged the boy from returning to the mat; he didn't have to, since Donald had already made his intentions clear. And it wasn't enough to just wrestle. He wanted to be a champion again.

"When your life has been turned upside down by a disability," says Kirk Bauer, a disabled Vietnam veteran and former executive director of Disabled Sports USA, in *Raising the Bar*, "you need successes and you need accomplishments and you need them immediately. Participating in sports rebuilds—it's both a rehab tool and a lifestyle tool available to everyone."

The disability that proved permanent for most was only temporary for Donald and Coach Laskey because it became the driving force in his expressed desire to return to the mat. Laskey was there for him at every turn, opening the gym at odd hours to allow Donald to get extra training and mat work in, dismissing the naysayers who questioned not only his starting position on the team but also the fact that the boy was trying to compete at four weight classes above his previous level at which he'd won State the year before, something virtually unheard of. But ten months almost from the day of his injury, he competed again in the state tournament after winning Sectionals in his new weight class. Not only that, but he reached the finals.

His opponent was a big, muscular football player from Tewksbury, a long-time rival of King Philip Regional, before a jam-packed crowd. The King Philip side was hooting and hollering the whole match, saving their loudest for those moments when Donald's opponent was clearly playing dirty.

"He knew I'd been hurt and kept pulling on my headgear, pulling on my neck to try and hurt me."

Wrestling is not a fluid sport. It's about grappling instead of grace, the opponents poking and prodding each other, one groping for grasp while the other twirls his supine frame like a top to avoid purchase as they search for an opening, a moment or flicker of weakness to be seized. And when that opening doesn't avail itself, opponents are left thrashing about the mat relying on practiced instinct to gain the advantage each of them desperately seeks.

And yet there is an austere beauty to the sport, its *mano a mano* nature turning that mat into a world onto itself. Just the opponents of equal weight and the referee to maintain a semblance of order. Not a second is squandered, the six minutes in which a match unfolds as arduous and intense as any in sports. No motion is spared, and most moves are short and quick. You sit in the stands knowing what happened, but not necessarily how.

There was nothing austere or beautiful about Donald's state championship match that day, though. Instead, it resembled a street fight with flurries of flailing hands turned back at every quarter. At one point, his opponent's constant pulling broke Donald's headgear. Another wrestler who was done for the day literally ran out of the stands and gave Donald his as a replacement. That was the moment he first heard the chanting.

"DON-ALD! DON-ALD! DON-ALD!"

The crowd was squarely in his corner as the tightly fought match became a true nail-biter. They knew all he'd been through, how much he'd had to overcome to get to this place today. Donald's opponent scored first with a takedown, which Donald equaled with a stunning reversal. They traded points until well into the third round, the match knotted at 3–3. As the seconds ticked down, his opponent gained control atop Donald but couldn't resist resorting to the same tactics that had defined the match, digging his thumbs into Donald's neck. Amid a smattering of boos from the crowd close enough to spot the move, the referee had finally had enough. He awarded Donald a point for the infraction and moments later hoisted his hand into the air as the match's winner, 4–3.

And state champion!

"I'd won and it didn't matter how. I was crying because I was happy, not because I was hurt. Everyone, except for Coach Laskey and my dad, thought I was crazy for doing this. Everyone who wasn't me thought I was insane to go back to wrestling. They didn't think it was in the cards. I was still in Spaulding when I told my parents how much it meant to me, that they had to let me do it. I looked up at them in the stands, and they were both crying too."

A Hollywood ending for sure, but that didn't mark the end for Donald, not even close. Following the year of this second state championship, he transferred to Wyoming Seminary Preparatory School, where he won a high school national championship. In college he attended Rider University, where he served as a two-year captain and was an NCAA tournament qualifier in addition to being named to the Colonial Athletic Association All-Conference team, as well as an Eastern Wrestling League selection in 2015, his senior year. All good—but not good enough.

"I was disappointed I didn't make All-American, never made All-American, and now my wrestling career seemed over. I thought I was done. I got involved with the Brown University program under Coach Todd Beckerman where my father had wrestled in college. I figured that it was a way to stay close to the sport, even though I wasn't wrestling anymore."

But Coach Beckerman told Donald that he should still compete, pull up his singlet again, and try his hand at the Olympic level. That was enough for him to be bit by the wrestling bug once more, and Donald started training for the international circuit, as close to professional as the sport of wrestling gets.

"That meant starting from the bottom again, taking my beatings to compete at the highest level of the sport. I had to work so hard just to compete at that level. I thought enjoying the experience alone would be enough."

It wasn't, of course. After a difficult first year on the circuit, Donald placed at the US Open matches and qualified for the international Maccabiah Games, just a step down from the Olympics and the third largest sporting event in the world, just behind the Olympic Games themselves and the FIFA Soccer World Cup. Open only to Jewish athletes, he was eligible because his mother, Betsy, is of Jewish descent.

"When McNeil learned Team USA was recruiting wrestlers for the Maccabiah Games," writes his hometown newspaper the *Sun Chronicle*, "he submitted his application, won all three of his matches during the trials in April of 2017 at the University of Pennsylvania and then began training in earnest these past few months with the members of the Brown University wrestling family."

So ten months after breaking his neck, Donald was back on the mat winning another state title. And ten years later he was ready to compete on an international level among over nine thousand athletes from eighty-five countries competing in the twentieth Maccabiah Games. How did he do?

"The 25-year-old McNeil scored a 10–0 victory over Moshe Klyman of Canada in the quarterfinals," the *Sun Chronicle* reported in July of 2017, "then a win over Israel's Pim Kadosh in the semifinal round, then scored a technical fall (10–0) verdict over Israel's Robert Avanesyan in the championship match."

His father, Andy, had participated in the US Olympic Team trials himself years before and just missed making the cut. So no one was happier when Donald returned home with a gold medal than his parents, especially his mother.

"I could say no to Andy about Donald wrestling after the injury," Betsy said, "but I could never say no to Donald. Then ten years later he wins an international championship, and all I could think of was him lying in a bed unable to feed himself. It felt like yesterday, but in that moment there was only tomorrow."

As for Donald's "tomorrow," his present and future have been intrinsically affected by his past. He's studying rehabilitation counseling at Assumption College and is currently doing an internship in that field with the Case Management Department of the very Spaulding Rehabilitation Hospital he'd been carried into, only to walk out a month later. He's thinned out a bit but still sports the close-cropped hair from his days competing, as if he'd be ready at a moment's notice if the mat beckoned him back. There's a gleam in his eye when he talks about the work he's doing today, and you get the feeling it's the same gleam his expression wore before a match. Excited and ready for whatever's to come.

"I want to make sure patients get all the services they need, but I'm more interested in the mental health aspect. I've always been a person who believes in the importance of being mentally strong, not just physically. To be able to deal with whatever life throws at you, no matter how difficult or grave. People really don't know much about spinal cord injuries. My goal is to help them make the most of a bad situation and set them up with as many resources as we can, the way people did for me."

In that role, Donald finds himself working with the very doctor at Spaulding who treated him. A nice take on life coming full circle. And what does he tell those who find themselves potentially facing the same kind of crisis, the same kind of adversity, as he was at one point?

"That it's always important to be motivated, to work toward a goal. It seems funny to say that to a patient who's suffered catastrophic injuries. But you won't be disappointed in life if you have something to work towards and look forward to. Setting goals is about always moving; reaching that goal doesn't mean you stop, it means you set another one. Today I'm going to pee on my own. Today I'm going to get dressed. Today I'm going to shower. It may not seem like much, but for someone who couldn't do that yesterday, it's a whole lot."

~ ~ ~

## Reflections

Donald McNeil's story illuminates a path to overcoming the devastation of violent trauma, the physical and emotional disruption of his life by a sudden grave injury.

Most of us may never experience this particular kind of trauma, but it's also true, as psychiatrists Steven Southwick and Dennis Charney tell us in their book *Resilience*, that most of us won't escape one or more severe traumas in our lives: debilitating illness, a bad accident, loss of a loved one, abuse in some form, depression or other deep emotional distress, natural disasters, war. Ninety percent of us, they write, will experience at least one traumatic event as we go through life.

But we also have a great capacity for healing, for overcoming even the most serious ordeals we encounter. We do that in a myriad of ways. We reach into ourselves, we reach out to others. We use our minds, our hearts, our imagination, our connections, our instincts.

Most often we call on more than one available means of strength and support to regain our balance or even profit from the crisis we have experienced and emerge as stronger, more capable people.

Donald McNeil was fortunate to have the resources he did as he fought to come back from an injury that might well have left him paralyzed. He had his parents' love and commitment. He had the expert help of highly trained and encouraging therapists. As he healed, he had a close connection with his coach, an individual who cared deeply about him not just as an athlete but also personally. McNeil was fortunate to have all of that powerful support coming to him from others. But anyone who reads his story has to be struck by the inner resources he brought to his struggle to come back.

We see in his interview the hopefulness that was part of his personality, the sense of humor that never left him. He was an athlete, and the son of an athlete, and athletes are by nature driven and competitive both against opponents and against themselves, always striving to find ways to triumph. We see in Donald McNeil the spirit, courage, and persistence that are so beneficial in any endeavor, but most especially when we're faced with great challenges.

Most striking, though, was his relentless determination to remake himself into the wrestler he had been before his injury. His mother assessed that accurately when she said, "So much of who he was is because of his wrestling." For all of his good fortune in his support from others and his own innate character traits, Donald McNeil was most fortunate in that he had found at an early age an endeavor that was an outlet for something deep in his nature. Some people find a vocation, either early or late, that allows them to express who they are through what they do. Doctors who were always interested in what makes bodies tick, engineers attracted as children to all things mechanical, scientists fascinated by nature and its laws, athletes who love and need the strenuous exertion and competitiveness of sport. That outward expression of an inward self is one way a person experiences the purpose and meaning of his or her life. And having a purpose and meaning in life is one of the great drivers of resilience. Donald McNeil's young life embodied that kind of purpose.

# 2

# Ann Hagan Webb

*I* remember the sound of the rosary beads as one of the sisters brought me over to the church to meet him.

"Him" referred to the priest who systematically abused Ann Hagan Webb for several years, starting when she was five years old in kindergarten and continuing into junior high school. That was only a small part of the testimony she gave before the Rhode Island House of Representatives on February 19, 2019, about her experiences inside a West Warwick, Rhode Island, church. Ann pulled no punches that day, airing in public for the first time the details of the experiences that had remained repressed for decades.

"It brought all my demons back to the forefront after I'd long since put them to bed. The next morning, I wanted to run around to everyone's house and take the newspaper from their stoop so nobody would see the story on the front page. From the time I finally remembered what had happened to me, I always just said I'd been abused, left it as a euphemism. I wasn't sure I could do it, but on that day I knew I had to make it real so people would stand up and listen."

On the day in question, Ann and others had come to the Rhode Island State House to advocate for a bill before the House Judiciary Committee that "would extend the statute of limitations on the pursuit of legal claims against child molesters and any institution employing them that looked the other way," according to the next day's issue of the *Providence Journal*.

The issue that Ann wanted to strip from the doorsteps of her neighbors and everyone else in Rhode Island after bearing her soul the day before. The bill's sponsor was her sister, Representative Carol Hagan McEntee, a state representative.

"It is unfortunate that this bill is needed in our society because it signals that not only are our children being sexually victimized," she told the *Providence Journal* that August at a signing ceremony presided over by Governor Gina Raimondo, "but even more sadly, many of these victims will never have their day in court to face their abusers and demand accountability for the vicious childhood assaults that have haunted their lives—oftentimes for decades. It is for this reason that we need to significantly extend the statute of limitations on civil actions relating to sexual abuse."

The bill passed the Rhode Island House and Senate by a combined 107–1. So Ann and the other victims who testified about their abuse must have been convincing.

The now sixty-seven-year-old had majored in psychology at Brown University, graduating in 1974 and going on to earn a doctorate in counseling psychology from Boston University in 1982, already a practicing psychologist when the memories of the abuse she'd suffered at the hands of her parish priest came roaring back with a vengeance.

"I was about forty at the time, so this would have been around 1993. I didn't really remember third grade, when I suffered the bulk of the abuse, at all. Victims come to grips with what happened to them in their own time. The triggers for releasing all the pent-up memories are different for everyone, and they spring up when the psyche of victims like me is ready to deal with it. Something happens in your life that sends everything rushing on through in technicolor. Up until that point, I had a notion that something had happened to me, but I kept it in a box until it finally broke out. It could be a victim meets a child who was the same age as them when they were abused. The trigger could be anything. For me, it was a story a friend told me that brought it back and my children being the age I was when it started; just one incident at first, then I realized it was much, much more than that.

"It's a very special situation, when it's a man of God who's the abuser. They use their authority. When you grow up Catholic, it's in your bone marrow, and when you're five years old you take everything literally. Priests are the next best thing to God. They can wipe the sins off your soul in confession. When you're a little child, you believe whatever's happening must be your fault. You must have done something bad and this is your punishment. The idea that a man who's so close to God could do that is impossible to imagine. How can you possibly accuse him? Who's going to listen?"

Ann grew up in the 1950s, when our sensibilities couldn't conceive of such a thing, much less lay blame at a priest's doorstep. But here are the facts as we know them today, according to the advocacy organization CHILD USA: "One in four girls, and one in six boys, will be sexually abused. Child molesters on average will abuse at least 150 children and child sexual abuse costs the federal government over $9 billion each year. The trauma of sex abuses often leads to depression, PTSD, alcohol and opioid abuse, and many physical ailments, frequently delaying disclosure. The average age for disclosure is 52 years old."

Ann knows those facts all too well.

"The first thing I say to patients who've suffered abuse is that I believe you. It's so important for them to be believed when maybe they haven't been their whole lives. They don't always start with their specific stories. They hem and haw for a while. They beat around the bush, and sometimes it takes weeks and weeks for them to get to their story. I say to them that the reason you were referred to me is that it happened to me too. I get it. They breathe a sigh of relief at that, because they've lived alone with this for decades."

That said, Ann didn't always specialize in treating victims of sexual abuse, even when her own repressed memories began spilling out.

"Here's the deal. I worked on my own stuff for ten years. I was in therapy myself two or three times a week working through it. I treated a few victims before I remembered, but I wasn't the best therapist for them because I was missing stuff, which was my own brain protecting me. So I had to work on my own issues before I made this my life's work. And once I went public, people started contacting me for help from everywhere. 'I saw your name in the paper,' they'd say, 'and I think you're going to understand.' They'd avoided the triggers that would cause them pain for years by that point. Facing it all finally is like reliving the experience a second time. It makes them feel small and vulnerable again, the awful torture they experienced brought into the light. So what I say to them is, 'You can live through the memory of it and I'll be right here to help.'"

Again, because Ann lived it. Not that becoming such an outspoken advocate has been easy.

"Go to the Bishop Accountability website and just click on the letters in the alphabet and you'll see the names of priests who've been credibly accused. Hundreds and hundreds of names under each letter, all backed up by fact and testimony. These are serial, prolific abusers who've abused hundreds and hundreds of kids. For what other crime is one incident not enough to take action? The church might say, has said all too frequently, 'It's only one person, so it's not credible.' For example, the Diocese of Providence refuses to call my abuser 'credibly accused.'"

To deal with that, Ann has been active in, and was originally the New England co-coordinator for, SNAP, an acronym for Survivors

Network of those Abused by Priests. She's now the Rhode Island SNAP leader.

"But there's only so much living and breathing this stuff I can do. I'll always provide a support network, though. If people want to come forward, I'll have a cup of coffee with them. They can tell me their story, person to person. SNAP is a group that's done a lot of activism. Finding other survivors, going to demonstrations outside churches, handing out leaflets. That helps others come forward and meet other people who shared the same experience, letting the world know. SNAP proves you're not alone, proves you're not crazy. This really did happen to you, and it wasn't your fault. You might think it didn't and that you're crazy because the rest of the world thinks priests are still good and holy, so you must be making this up. But you didn't, and you're not alone. I remember attending a conference in 1994 sponsored by Survivors First early in my recovery. I went into this auditorium and there were a thousand people in there. I hadn't gone public yet, and wouldn't until 2002, but the idea I was in an auditorium of a thousand people, and more than half of them had been abused, made me realize the depth of the problem.

"And none of us were alone anymore. It validates your experience. Hearing someone else tell their story, you think, 'Oh my goodness, I felt that too.' Because up until then you had doubted yourself. If the priest who hurt you was right, then you must be wrong. You must be bad inside. When I was in kindergarten, the bus driver had to drag me out of the house to get me on the bus because I was so scared to go to school. And I cried every morning. Then I stopped crying for decades and I didn't cry again until I got a twelve thousand dollar check from the church to cover the costs of my therapy. It wasn't the money; it was the admission by the church that it was their fault, that they had caused it.

"You never overcome the experience totally. But if you work on it enough, you can overcome it for the most part and find a way to live with the rest. When you break a leg, it heals. Then years later, when it rains or you get older, the pain comes back from arthritis or just age.

That's the way it is with sexual abuse. There's still some leftover pain. It helps me to help other people. I'm a person who wants to give back. I'm really lucky I survived the way I did with a loving family that provided a lot of the advantages of life. Now I want to give back, because I have a lot to give back to the world."

Interestingly, Ann doesn't treat a lot of young adults or even victims in their twenties.

"Most survivors don't come forward for many years. Young people who address their experience early have a much harder time. Our psyches are designed to protect us from pain. But people who try to deal with the trauma as teenagers or young adults often don't have the emotional distance or equipment to address it. Too much has been taken away from them."

The problem, though, stretches far beyond the Catholic Church. The Jerry Sandusky scandal at Penn State taught us that much. Then came the case of Larry Nassar, a doctor who treated University of Michigan athletes for more than forty years, during which he was a serial abuser, ultimately accused by more than 150 women. That was followed by Dr. Richard Strauss, an Ohio State University team doctor, accused by 177 former students of the same kind of systematic abuse, only with young men.

The Catholic Church, though, boasts no rival when it comes to the length of time it has turned a blind eye to the actions of its priests, leading to scores and scores of ruined lives at the hands of those entrusted by local communities to be conduits of God. The church has shown a constant reluctance to own up to its responsibility for enabling these thousands of pedophile priests—repeatedly reassigning them, refusing to acknowledge the problem or their guilt, and becoming willing accomplices or accessories in the process. Ann is at loss to explain that dichotomy as much as anyone.

"I wish I had an answer for you. I believe in the basic good in people, but I don't get it. I guess it comes down to absolute power corrupting absolutely. The church doesn't see that telling the truth would work. Hide the truth instead, cover it up. They've never stopped believing that they have the power. 'We have the power so what we say is gospel.' And they really see themselves as the people who tell the rest of us how to live. I've stopped trying to figure out or change the Catholic Church, but I've helped expose them. I held a mirror up to them in the hope they would change and fix things because it's the right thing to do, but I've given up on that. Continuing to focus on exposing the church is the best I and other survivors can do, because otherwise they're not going to change."

The BishopAccountability.org website is a testament to those efforts. The site's home page is laid out in tiny print because there's so much content that needs to be squeezed on. Scroll down a bit under "Major Accounts of the Crisis" for a sampling of the terrible tragedies akin to those Ann's patients tell her every day. Take this one from the *San Jose Mercury News* in August of 1987, an article entitled "Priests Who Molest."

> *At a time of heightened national awareness of the problems of child abuse, the Catholic Church in the United States continues to ignore and cover up cases of priests who sexually molest children, according to court records, internal church documents, civil authorities and the victims themselves.*
>
> *Church officials insist that a notorious 1985 Louisiana case in which a priest molested at least 35 boys has taught them to deal firmly with the problem. But a three-month Mercury News investigation reveals that in more than 25 dioceses across the country, church officials have failed to notify authorities, transferred molesting priests to other parishes, ignored parental complaints and disregarded the potential damage to child victims.*
>
> *"The sexual molesting of little boys by priests is the single most serious problem we've had to face in centuries," said Father Thomas Doyle, a Dominican priest and canon lawyer who tried for two years to force the U.S. Catholic Conference to deal with the issue.*

Ten years later, a February 1997 article in the *Indianapolis Star* reported this in an article entitled "Faith Betrayed:"

*In the heart of Indiana lies a Roman Catholic diocese tainted by priestly sins, dark secrets of lust and betrayal that have wounded scores of victims.*

*Even more painful, for some, has been the church's response.*

*Instead of compassion, they found cover-up.*

*Instead of justice, they watched their abusers go free.*

*The Rev. Ken Bohlinger, who masturbated with boys, now sells luggage in Arizona. The Rev. Ron Voss, who sexually abused male teens, moved to Haiti. Monsignor Arthur Sego, who fondled girls, was retired to a Missouri rest home.*

*Other priests of the Lafayette Diocese are back in their pulpits after they were accused of sexually exploiting vulnerable adults. Some priests pursued relations with parishioners or fellow priests. A few lured teens with alcohol and pornography.*

*One priest had sexual relations with a teen who went on to become a priest himself. After donning the collar, that victim also became a sexual predator, abusing male adolescents, His name: Ron Voss.*

And this, another ten years later, from an article that appeared in the *Providence Journal* in December of 2007 entitled "The Abuse Files:"

*The church fought to shield its files on 83 priests who have been accused over the years, but earlier this year, the Rhode Island Supreme Court ruled against the diocese. Last spring, the plaintiffs' lawyers got their first glimpse of the files, though under a court seal. In recent weeks, some of those documents have entered the public domain as exhibits or in motions in the current cases.*

*What they have found, the lawyers say, is the best evidence yet of a litany of sexual abuse—and a conspiracy to hide it.*

*In one document summarizing a church lawyer's conversation with an accused priest, the lawyer, William Murphy, wrote that he told the priest not to say anything about "misconduct" that Murphy would be obliged to report to the authorities. Instead, Murphy wrote, the priest should tell then-Bishop Louis E. Gelineau, in a private conversation analogous to confession, because "that would provide some significant measure of protection."*

*"I told [the priest] pointedly that if there were such details, I did not want to know them," Murphy wrote.*

That's the kind of backdrop Ann Hagan Webb has been dealing with both as a psychologist treating victims of sexual abuse for more than twenty-five years in her practice and as a victim herself.

"After a new cardinal was named to lead the Boston archdiocese to replace Bernard Law, we formed a working group, throwing out ideas we could present to him. We developed a strategy for change in the diocese that could address the crisis, hoping to advise the new leadership. On the day that Cardinal O'Malley arrived to his new job in Boston replacing Cardinal Law, I went to the residence early in the morning. It had been announced that he would be meeting with survivors the first day. I had high hopes for change and a real attempt to help survivors, and I knew I could be a voice for many survivors. But they threw me off the property, saying that only the press was allowed. I learned later that only handpicked 'loyal Catholic' survivors would be invited to the meeting with the cardinal that afternoon, not outspoken advocate/survivors like me, despite my being the New England SNAP coordinator.

"A few weeks later, twenty-five Boston survivors, still believing in Cardinal O'Malley's promise to meet and talk to survivors, met and developed a document advocating for change in how the abuse 'crisis' could be handled. Two of us tried to deliver the document to the cardinal's residence. We were turned away at the door, and they would not take our document. We mailed it and faxed it. It was returned unopened. The church tried to make it look like they wanted to listen to survivors, and that's as far as it gets."

Lip service and sometimes not even that, continuing to this day even as the same abuse keeps repeating itself in a never-ending cycle, claiming more and more victims who show up in Ann's office. She remains more cognizant than ever about what parents should do if they fear their child may have suffered sexual abuse.

"Make it as easy as possible for the child to talk. Take them to a therapist who may try something like play therapy. Openness is the most important thing. Don't be afraid to talk freely about sexuality, about things going wrong. But that's a tough one because so many perpetrators know how to control their victims by threatening them. 'You tell your parents and I'll kill your puppy.' Or: 'This is just between us. If you tell, then we won't be able to see each other.' And this one: 'If you tell, no one will believe you.'"

Ann stops there, then quickly resumes, speaking of a hurt she knows all too well herself.

"But if they don't tell, nobody *can* believe them."

Apparently, though, somebody's listening, hopefully a lot of somebodies.

"I'd like to thank Ann Hagan Webb," Wayne Smith of Warwick, Rhode Island, wrote in a letter to the editor of the *Providence Journal* in January of 2020, referencing a commentary Ann had written, "for helping people like me better understand the disappointing and tragic hypocrisy of the Diocese of Providence. The issue is also personal because I was a Tyler School student and served as an altar boy and a choir boy at the Cathedral of Saints Peter and Paul. Fortunately, I have many beautiful memories. I am truly inspired by the writer and her courageous colleagues who are only seeking justice. I believe their actions will save children and/or help prevent future victims of childhood sexual trauma. I am with them 100%!"

~ ~ ~

## Reflections

"It isn't neglected truths, but those that are frustrated of their proper expression, that take the most drastic psychological revenge."

Gregory Dix, an Anglican priest and scholar, was referring here to a phenomenon in religious belief, but the insight applies to unresolved psychological trauma as well. The abuse Ann Hagan Webb suffered took place from kindergarten through at least seventh grade. It wasn't until she was forty that she came to grips with what had happened to her, and when she did, the memories unleashed a storm of emotion that took another decade to resolve.

Webb speaks here with the authority of an experienced clinical psychologist with special insight into the trauma of sex abuse. Anger, frustration, and the demand for justice flow through her account. The reader may be taken up with her insistence on the accountability of the Catholic Church. The phenomenon of priestly sex abuse has had an enormous impact on Catholic faithful, including Webb, and it has affected non-Catholics as well. But what's significant for us here is not the enormity of the phenomenon but the path to healing conveyed in Webb's telling.

The pathway she describes begins with recognition. She tells us that up until the point when something triggered her memories, she had "had a notion that something had happened to me, but I kept it in a box." Enlightenment philosopher Baruch Spinoza's dictum about suffering only being relieved once we have "a clear and precise picture of it" seems to convey exactly what happened with Webb. After thirty-plus years she finally had a clear, concise picture of what she suffered as a little girl. For all that time, the memories had been so brutal that as a defense mechanism her mind had suppressed them.

For Webb, the suppression of memory was not the kind of post-traumatic stress reaction that may accompany, for example, combat experience or a bad car accident. Because her abuser was a priest, the shock of the experience was exacerbated by guilt, which further bottled up her memories. Psychiatrists Southwick and Charney tell us that accepting the reality of a situation even when "that situation is frightening and painful" is of primary importance in overcoming a life crisis. It's only by seeing a causative event clearly and accepting its reality that we can begin to heal. Webb tells her own patients "you can live through the memory." In other words, it's possible to bear the pain of bringing their demons into the light (at least in a safe setting), where dealing with them affords the potential for understanding and empowerment.

In Webb's case, recognition and acceptance were therapeutic in several ways. She says about her sex abuse patients that telling their stories enables relief "because they've lived alone with this for decades." For Webb, too, acceptance and sharing relieved the constrictive hold on her emotional life that was an effect of isolation. Recognition and acceptance also enabled her to deal with the guilt she had lived with for so many years, either subconsciously or consciously.

Webb's relentless demand for justice echoes through her account. The need for vindication and redress are natural reactions to being wronged. But here we are likely seeing sublimation at work—anger and a desire for justice transposed into activism and support of others.

Effective sublimation is often considered a means toward achieving closure. But because sex abuse in the church is ongoing, closure may not be a relevant psychological category for Webb. But it's also possible that deep trauma doesn't easily resolve into closure under any circumstances, that feelings of hurt and anger may be compartmentalized but that they have an ongoing life beneath the surface of even the most resilient personalities.

# 3

# JOSH PERRY

"**W**e knew something was wrong as soon as I gave birth to Josh," Connie Perry recalls of that day in 1979. "The nurses wrapped him up and took him out of the room. When the doctor came back in, he explained that Josh wasn't normal, that he had Down syndrome. But Josh didn't look any different from our other kids. We didn't even know what Down syndrome meant at the time."

Josh's first pediatrician thought he did.

"He told us that Josh should be institutionalized, that there was a nice place right down the road that would take care of him and train him. That's all I needed to hear. I wrapped Josh up in his blanket and out we went."

And it's a good thing she did. Forty-one years later, Josh is among the most recognizable and successful actors with Down syndrome, having forged a remarkable career highlighted just recently by his winning Best Supporting Actor at the Hollywood Divine International Film Festival for a film he did called *The Christ Slayer*. He and his mother flew to Pennsylvania from Louisiana, where Josh was able to accept the award in person.

"I was so excited," Josh recalls of hearing his name announced as the winner. "I did it! It was wonderful. It's important that people see I'm a good actor. I want to live my dream and do it right—I mean, do my part right. Do my job. Learn my character and know my character. Prepare for the role. Live inside who I'm playing."

*The Christ Slayer* was unusual for the fact that the part wasn't written for someone with Down syndrome. It was a straight part, and the producer and star, DJ Perry (no relation), decided to take a chance thanks to a gut feeling about Josh, for which he was well rewarded. Josh normally has only a handful of pages to learn when he takes a role, but in *The Christ Slayer* he was on screen for eighty of the script's pages. He showed up for the table read having memorized all of his lines. He knew his part completely, reinforcing and affirming the instincts that led DJ Perry to hire Josh in the first place.

"It was challenging, more fun. I got to act more."

And the response to that?

"Probably the brightest spot of this film's cast is the awesome idea to cast a special needs cast member in a role that doesn't over-emphasize his condition," wrote Box Office Revolution in a review of the film. "Treating him as a regular actor is a huge step forward for disability rights, so this creative team's decision to do this shows a deeper care for inclusion in the arts."

"Albus is beautifully played by Josh Perry," Dove.org proclaimed in yet more stellar coverage of Josh's performance.

"Josh Perry's portrayal as Longinus' servant is a delight to watch and gives some laugh-out-loud moments," a poster said on the Internet Movie Database (IMDB) site.

"I want to define me, not let detriments define me," Josh says, forever passionate about being an actor, not just an actor who happens to have Down syndrome. "I want to be a good actor. I am a good actor and I want to be better."

For all its accolades, *The Christ Slayer* didn't allow Josh to do much of what he does best, which is comedy. He and his older brother Scott, a successful actor in his own right, started taking advantage of that proclivity in sketch comedies he and Josh would do together. Think Laurel and Hardy, Abbott and Costello, even Red Skelton, Jackie Gleason, or Carol Burnett. Scott started his own YouTube channel, and that marked the beginning of Josh's acting career. He hasn't looked back since.

"Scott has always been able to pull things out of Josh that are unbelievable," says their mother, Connie, from her home in Lafayette, Louisiana, where Josh and Scott were born and raised. "He knows how to get him to perform."

"People think because you're labeled a certain way, you need to act that way, which is so limiting," Scott says, elaborating. "I was on the set with Josh when he was filming an episode of *Shameless* [starring William H. Macy for Showtime]. Someone in Production kept coming up to me, asking 'Does he...' or 'Can he...' Asking me those questions instead of Josh. So I said to him, 'Dude, ask him!' I pulled the director aside and said this isn't the right guy to be the liaison because he's not getting Ponce. He's an actor like everybody else. You can just talk to him."

"The Ponceman," or simply "Ponce," are Josh's beloved dual nicknames. The origins date back to when he was a young boy and had put on some baby fat. His father, Al, called Josh "my little ponce" and the name stuck because, even though it wasn't meant as something positive, Josh embraced it in his typical fashion; he doesn't let anything hurtful change his outlook. Instead he takes ownership and never looks back.

For that episode of *Shameless*, he acted opposite the great Joan Cusack playing a woman disabled by her agoraphobia, an affliction that's even more debilitating than the Down syndrome of Josh's character. It's an interesting mix and kind of profound in that respect. After the table read for the episode, William H. Macy himself came up to Josh to shake his hand and congratulate him on a job well done. Josh has also worked side by side with Val Kilmer, the late Peter Falk and Rip Torn, Diane Ladd, Joseph Gordon-Levitt (*Looper*), John C. Reilly, Seth Green, and Doug Jones (Abe Sapien in the first two *Hellboy* films) and has enjoyed his experience working with all of them, sometimes in films where his reviews outshine theirs.

"Josh Perry's casting is particularly notable given he has Down syndrome," the *Bible Films Blog* said in its coverage of *The Christ Slayer*. "The role feels like it could have gone to any actor; there's nothing about it that indicates that the character has the syndrome or anything like it. At the same time, though, because the story setting is in a world before such a label had been created, it's perfectly plausible that someone with a similar condition could have been a servant for a man who was himself vision-impaired. I love that the film makes nothing of it. It doesn't feel like it's trying to make a point and yet it does."

But there were no such accolades or stars in Josh's first role in film that was actually for a short Scott was making. He played someone who vomited.

"Working with my brother was the happiest moment in my career. And I was a very good puker!"

With that, Josh was bit by the acting bug that had been nibbling at him for years.

"We'd watch old movies and television shows," Scott recalls, "and Josh would fill these notebooks with his favorite lines, actors, titles, and moments. There must be boxes of them at our house."

To that point, Josh is a walking encyclopedia of filmdom, able to quote lines from just about any film out there. And his tastes run the gamut from Monty Python to Stanley Kubrick, from *Die Hard* to *Dirty Harry* to *Dr. Dolittle*, from *Grease* to *Arsenic and Old Lace*. Though that old classic is his most recent favorite, Josh says the role he'd like to reimagine the most would be Danny Zuko, famously played by John Travolta in *Grease*. And don't get him started on Travolta's Vincent Vega character in Quentin Tarantino's *Pulp Fiction*.

"He'll go from the Marx Brothers to Hitchcock," relates brother Scott. "And he really gravitates to something like *Strangers on a Train* because he'd love to play a killer, the badass. He doesn't see it as strange or weird to be playing a character like that with Down syndrome because he doesn't see himself that way. And he's drawn to strong performances of all kinds."

Not surprisingly, Josh is also a fan of great physical comics like Dick Van Dyke and Lucille Ball. And he's just as comfortable being the straight man as the funny man, no stranger to, or fear of, self-deprecation.

"He doesn't let his limitations define him," Scott says. "We always hear about the struggle to be comfortable in your own skin. Josh doesn't think like that. He likes himself. He's comfortable in his own skin. The roles that are usually offered are some sort of mentally disabled character. But I absolutely don't think he is limited to playing those characters."

"Never give up. Never quit dreaming. Always look forward to the next movie," Josh says, summing up the way he looks at things, looks at life.

But there was a time when Josh was looking in another direction altogether.

"He came home from school one day," his mother told Brandon Hardesty for the terrific documentary he and filmmaker Kenny Johnson made on Josh, "and said, 'Some kids at school called me retarded. I'm retarded. What's retarded?'"

Scott and Josh's approach to this, once their work debuted on YouTube, was to use the word as much as they could, to mock and make a parody of it, to take the sting out. Along with Mediocre Films, they created a sketch show called *The Retarded Policeman* in which Josh plays a traffic cop prone to pulling over people to meet his quota. The idea sprang from an idea the brothers had about having Josh play a Dirty Harry–type character, combined with Mediocre

Films' notion of him being a traffic cop. Origins aside, the series is laugh-out-loud funny.

"Ninety percent of people get exactly what we're doing," notes Scott, "but that leaves ten percent who are convinced Josh doesn't know what he's doing. Sometimes they confront me at festivals or showings and I say to them, 'How could he be doing the joke if he doesn't know what he's doing?' It's exasperating."

Exasperating to the point where the network tried to add a disclaimer to their sketch comedy that has gone viral on YouTube.

But it never aired because the creative team, primarily Josh and Scott, wouldn't allow it.

"The reasoning being," Scott says, "why would an actor who has taken a role, memorized it, performed it, nailed it, have to put a warning before the piece that he is the star of to inform the audience that the actor actually knew what he was doing? If Tom Cruise doesn't have to do that, then Ponce doesn't have to do that."

*The Retarded Policeman* episodes have been viewed over 173 million times. Some of them are drop-dead hilarious, including one where Josh pulls over an ornery African-American man named Cosmo. What follows is a classic comic exchange featuring machine-gun-quick retorts in a fashion best befitting the likes of Larry David's *Curb Your Enthusiasm*. And Josh plays it straight the whole time, never appearing to be in on the joke.

"We're proud of you, son," Josh's YouTube parents tell him in another segment. "You're the most retarded policeman ever."

It's ribald, it's irreverent, it's mocking, and it works like all great parodies do by succeeding in making us laugh with someone instead of at them. Combating the stereotype by becoming the stereotype and playing to that 90 percent instead of the 10 who are never going to get it, or Josh, anyway. Suffice it to say, *The Retarded Policeman* is not politically correct, but that's the whole point. It's classic sketch comedy. You know what's coming, the formula hardly varying, but you can't wait to see what comes next anyway so you can laugh at it. As an actor, in Josh's mind, that's the greatest gift he can give.

"I love making people laugh. It makes them feel good."

But there's a serious side to *The Retarded Policeman* in Scott Perry's mind, as he alluded to in an interview with Brandon Hardesty and Kenny Johnson in that superb documentary they made for the Supporting Actor Spotlight series called *Josh "the Ponceman" Perry*.

"*The Retarded Policeman* highlights Josh's biggest strength as an actor, which is his ability to simply be in a scene. Underplay and understate his role, but also be a ham when the moment calls for it. The word 'retard'—people can't even say it, so how can we talk about it? Words have power. But Josh wanted to take back that word and make it his."

Define it on his own terms, in other words, and YouTube, the Wild West of video entertainment that was just getting started at the time, offered the perfect forum to do so.

"There are no boundaries on what Josh can do," Connie Perry said proudly in Hardesty and Johnson's thirty-minute documentary.

Scott isn't so sure of that or, at least, has a different perspective.

"Ponce is smart enough to know that he's not smart enough. I see that frustrates him. I'd love it if he acted more. He lives with my parents, and they've been great, incredibly supportive. When he lived with me out in Los Angeles, he was firing on all cylinders, getting a lot of work. It's harder back home in Lafayette, Louisiana. There just aren't enough opportunities.

"I remember this short film I made in 1999 or 2000. Up until then, Josh hadn't done a film, just the YouTube stuff. We needed an Elvis impersonator. Ponce loves Elvis and loved impersonating him. So he got the role, and he's wanted to keep performing ever since then. He has this natural timing, even in drama, and solid instincts for an actor. He did a great job in that film with the kinds of things you can't teach."

Something else you can't teach is the example Josh sets for others with disabilities who share his dream of acting, because he's not alone. Deaf actress Marlee Matlin won an Oscar for playing a deaf person in *Children of a Lesser God*. RJ Mitte, a young actor with cerebral palsy, played a young man with cerebral palsy in the groundbreaking TV series *Breaking Bad*. Tom Sullivan forged a stellar career as an actor despite being rendered blind by a medical mistake shortly after birth, going on to live by his "Sullivan's Rules," one of which was: "any negative can be turned into a positive."

Scott Perry takes that one step further when reflecting on what others suffering from disabilities can learn from his brother's experience.

"His career really proves that nobody really knows anything. Anybody who tells somebody they can't do something without even knowing that person—I mean, what gives them the right? They start with an opinion, a preconceived notion about somebody they don't even know. Most of our original content doesn't mention that he has Down syndrome in any way, shape, or form. We don't make Down syndrome a part of his character at all. The TV series we did for Fuel TV, *Stupidface*, was a sketch comedy show. We did three seasons of that show and never once referred to Ponce as having any sort of handicap whatsoever. He was just a badass DJ, DJ Ponce, who was also hilarious."

That's why Chris Burke, another actor with Down syndrome who forged a great career as a working actor on shows like *Life Goes On*, hates the very term, preferring to call it "Up" syndrome.

"I have a motto on my bedroom wall," he once said. "'Obstacles are what you see when you take your eye off the goal.' Giving up is not my style. I just want to do something that's worthwhile."

Sounds like something Josh would say. So is this Burke quote:

"Having Down syndrome is like being born normal. I am just like you and you are just like me. We are all born in different ways, that is the way I can describe it. I have a normal life."

"I didn't know anything was wrong with me when I was growing up," adds *Breaking Bad*'s RJ Mitte. "I thought everyone went to occupational and speech therapy, I thought these were common things. I thought I was quite normal until I went to school and someone told me it wasn't normal to have a disability. A lot of people don't want to hire disabled actors. They think you're going to take twice as long over a shot, or they don't want to have to put up a ramp for disabled access. They think, 'Why would I do that when I can just hire an able-bodied actor to play the disabled character?'"

*The Ruderman White Paper on Employment of Actors with Disability in Television* sums up the problem this way:

*Although people with disabilities make up nearly 20% of our population, they are still significantly under-represented on television. What compounds the problem is the fact that even when characters with disabilities are featured on the small screen, they are far too often played by actors without disabilities. We found that more than 95% of characters with disabilities are played by able-bodied actors on television. While streaming platforms had a better percentage, they also had a lower overall count of characters with disabilities. This lack of self-representation points to a systemic problem of ableism— discrimination against people with disabilities—in the television industry. It also points to a pervasive stigma among audience members against people with disabilities given that there is no widespread outcry against this practice. This is nothing short of a social justice issue where a marginalized group of people is not given the right to self-representation. We must change this inequality through more inclusive casting, through the use of Computer Graphics (CG) to create ability, through the media holding the industry responsible, through the avoidance of stereotypical stories, and ultimately through the telling of stories that depict people with disabilities without focusing on the disability.*

With that in mind, Josh has worked toward expanding the mold instead of breaking it, continuing to take roles in which he plays characters clearly written for someone with Down syndrome while also seeking out opportunities where his character isn't defined by that at all. That process got jump-started by a film called *The Bridge*, which he wrote and directed in California himself in 2013 to take more control of his character, further bucking the stereotypes associated with Down syndrome. The well-made short, swerving in and about the streets of Los Angeles, climaxes on the bridge of the title, which is more metaphorical than anything, representing not only the various bridges Josh has crossed but also the ones he's built so others may follow in his path. Toward that end, *The Bridge* bears a simple dedication in the credits:

*For all the artists because art has no limitations, just like me. Rock on.*

—Ponce

That appears just after a title card that reads, "Written and directed by Josh 'the Ponceman' Perry."

Expanding on that, he was featured in a film shot in Michigan called *Lost Heart* in which he plays Chip, the brother of a woman who returns home for her father's funeral, and the film follows him helping her come to terms with his death. It's a straight dramatic role that allowed Josh to cry on cue. As is his custom, he nailed it on the first take.

"That was fun," he recalls.

He says his favorite role was probably in *Coffee Town* in which he got to play opposite Josh Groban and actually sing Bonnie Tyler's "Total Eclipse of the Heart" with him at the wrap party.

Groban told his co-star that he had the better voice, and the Ponceman didn't argue.

~ ~ ~

## Reflections

Josh Perry's challenge isn't the kind of trauma that can engage a person's will to overcome. Josh's limitation is a permanent, severely limiting condition. There is no cure for it, no way to heal it.

One way of dealing with such a circumstance is "acceptance"—a realistic coming to terms with the fact that the situation confronting us is not changeable, no matter what resources from within or without we can bring to bear on it. Think of someone suffering a terminal disease, a permanent physical injury, or some other unavoidable condition of life. The patients at the leprosarium Dr. Gus White worked with in Vietnam fell into that category. What struck him most about them was their tranquility, a serenity he found "almost spiritual." Leprosy is a slow-moving disease that gives its victims plenty of time to come to terms with what is happening to them, time to search for and find a level of inner peace.

Southwick and Charney often refer to the Holocaust survivor and psychiatrist Viktor Frankl, whose book *Man's Search for Meaning* launched a psychiatric movement and has sold over ten million copies. Frankl, who barely survived the Auschwitz death camp, wrote, "We may also find meaning in life even when confronted with a hopeless situation, when facing a fate that cannot be changed." Acceptance, he says, "may lead to spiritual growth, that is, to giving meaning to even the most circumscribed life."

Josh Perry's response to his condition is the polar opposite of acceptance. "I want to define me," he says, "not let detriments define me." Scott adds, "He likes himself. He's comfortable in his own skin." That's evident from his tone, his sense of humor, his upbeat personality. The psychologist George Bonanno makes the point that there are many pathways to resilience. One is repression, in clinical terms "repressive coping." Repressive copers, he says, tend to avoid unpleasant thoughts and emotions. Traditionally, repressive behavior has been thought of as denial, a personality maladjustment. Not necessarily so, says Bonanno; repressive coping "appears to foster adaptation to extreme adversity."

Bonanno is a leading researcher in this field, though he has no lack of critics. Whatever the academic debates, Josh Perry's life allows us to reflect on the rich variety of coping mechanisms that make for human resilience. His refusal to dwell on his limitations has also enabled him to stretch the envelope of possibility for individuals with Down syndrome. Others have broken through our stereotypes of people with disabilities, including the autistic professor of animal science and best-selling author Temple Grandin, Academy Award–winning deaf actress Marlee Matlin, the actor RJ Mitte who has cerebral palsy, and the blind singer and actor Tom Sullivan. In this regard, of course, we know about towering figures such as Beethoven, Stephen Hawking, and Helen Keller. But they seem somehow beyond the norms of human experience. Josh Perry isn't that. Instead, he teaches that common resilient coping mechanisms like commitment to a vocation, hard work, and the desire to better oneself can change and expand the parameters of life for those with disabilities, just as they can for the more normally "abled" among us.

# 4

# Jim Pantelas

*My wife was six and a half months pregnant on the day I was diagnosed with stage 3B, non-small-cell lung cancer. That was eleven years ago, and I've been dancing with NED (no evidence of disease) for the past ten years. But dancing doesn't necessarily mean having fun.*

Words from Jim Pantelas in a post for the Lung Cancer Alliance in April of 2017. Nearly three years later, he's just returned from Washington and the National Lung Cancer Advocacy Summit, the purpose of which was to train activists on how best to approach their own congressional representatives and other politicians to advocate for more research dollars.

"I learned how to talk to congressmen here," he tells me. "I introduce myself as a thirteen-year survivor of lung cancer, but I also tell them how it breaks your heart to live in a community where we lose a friend every week and 432 people in total per day, a fact that pretty much flies under society's radar. Then I'll ask what their lung cancer story is. It almost always turns out they have a friend or relative with the disease, so they can relate. Everything gets so much more personal and poignant when it's about them than when it's about me. I want it to be about their story, not mine, about someone they love who's dying or has died. If you have lungs, you can get lung cancer—that's the overriding point.

"I had surgery where doctors took out most of my right lung. Because the cancer had metastasized, that was followed up by both radiation and chemotherapy treatments. Our daughter Stella was born the day of my second infusion."

Life does pile on at times, but it wasn't done yet with the Pantelas family. Their newborn daughter had been home for only five days when she suffered a brain bleed that resulted in her experiencing seventeen seizures over the course of the next twenty-one days.

"I spent most of my time in between treatments at St. Joseph Hospital and at Children's Hospital at the University of Michigan. That's when Stella was diagnosed with cerebral palsy that left her a quadriplegic."

But Jim doesn't consider himself the victim of tragedy, or even any more courageous than anyone else.

"I don't think there's any courage involved. I had to live because I couldn't die. I think of life as a strange journey along parallel roads of science and faith. When you go through something like this, when the life you were expecting and planning for changes, you have to re-create yourself with new parameters. You get the opportunity to be resurrected, to live every day the way you want the world to see you and become the person you want to be."

Jim's analytical approach to the tragedies that came to define his life was born during an earlier career with the National Security Agency (NSA), where he worked on big data projects.

"I've been around big data all of my life, so I tend to think of life in terms of iterations. I have stepsons who are now in their mid-forties. How do I teach them how a man dies—because that's the job of a parent. That's not an issue of courage; that's an issue of responsibility, just like taking care of my family was.

"Lung cancer is a strange disease. People blame you for getting it because of the smoking stigma. It's strange when you think that, for all the great work that it's done, the American Cancer Society has perpetuated that myth by relentlessly associating smoking with lung cancer. More than anything, those warnings on cigarette packs have left society judging you as a victim of an addiction you may never have had. I'm talking about the myth that lung cancer is a smoker's disease when there are far more sufferers who contracted the disease from radon, asbestos, or other environmental factors. And there's a ton of people out there who never smoked who are getting diagnosed in their twenties, thirties, and forties, thanks to genetic mutations we're just starting to understand."

And he's putting his data analytics skills to good use in that regard.

"I do a lot of advocacy work, and some of that work revolves around reviewing and overseeing studies as part of an institutional review board at the University of Michigan. We jokingly have a saying in my family: forever forward. You don't have an option. You either go forward or you die. You get out of bed in the morning and go forward and, if you get the chance, you do it again tomorrow. I don't fear death. I don't think death is the enemy. What happens when you die? You go back from whence you came. It's all about going home."

Jim was diagnosed after being sick for a year. He'd been running his own company for fifteen years with offices in California and Michigan, where he lives. The company served as a recruitment process outsource, working with companies that were trying to grow but hadn't found the right people yet to position them for that growth. Those companies would outsource all their hiring to Jim's company.

"I was tired all the time and had to curtail my workload. Ultimately, I closed my California office in San Ramon, and with the reduced workload came a drop in income. When I got diagnosed, I had to think about how I was going to pay what were sure to be six- or seven-figure medical bills, even with good health insurance. The problems that you think are important are still important when you get diagnosed or are going through any trauma. You just end up with additional shit to deal with, but the day-to-day stuff doesn't go away. You still have to deal with all the things you dealt with before. It's not that they suddenly become unimportant; they just become secondary."

In addition to dealing with lung cancer, Jim found himself having to deal with a child who was going to need round-the-clock care for her entire life. Some people wear their feelings on their sleeves. Jim seems to be the type who internalizes things, including his own pain. No two people dealing with this kind of adversity do so in the same way; instead, each finds their own coping mechanism. And for Jim, that coping mechanism, more than anything, was volunteering.

"So what does a workaholic do with his life when he can no longer work?" he wrote in a post for the Lung Cancer Alliance in April of 2017. "He volunteers!" He continued:

*I began volunteering ten years ago—first at the children's hospital that took care of my daughter, and then more and more in support of lung cancer funding, legislation and research. And that involvement is now a major part of my life. It started with assignments to review multiple research proposals as a peer reviewer for PCORI (Patient Centered Outcomes Research Institute). I represented the non-scientist and patient perspective on an oncology IRB (Institutional Review Board) at the university I volunteer at. I also sat on an IRB for my local Veterans Administration Hospital, and I participated in two IRB meetings for the NCI (National Cancer Institute) where I'm also a regular board member. I followed up on two research efforts that I helped to develop and worked on a draft for a research project I want to pursue. I sat on a Pediatric Ethics Committee, chaired a Patient Experience Board, was a member of a Cancer Council and partici-pated in a Quality Panel for the hospital where I receive my care.*

*Disagreements in care, cessation and end of life issues, treatment options—those all come before the ethics committee. I found myself in situations with families going through so much more than we were and, in my role as advocate, I was able to give a voice to people who were neither willing nor able to provide one for themselves. I started going on consults just so families could see another parent in the room directly involved in their care. I was also invited to give lectures and talks. I'm typically asked to talk about families experiencing trauma because that was the way the administrators saw my story. And I found telling my story to a roomful of people could be a pathway to healing. It's overwhelming to walk into a room where a child is dying.*

Some might read that and believe Jim's doing all this because he wants to escape, to find excuses to busy himself with something other than his daughter's chronic care and his own illness. He scoffs at the mere notion of that, finding it absurd.

"Why do I do all this? Mostly, I'd say because it all matters. Maybe it's because I'm still alive, and this is my way of paying the universe back for allowing me to continue breathing. But in reality, it's also because I love what I'm doing. The work I do has value to my lung cancer community, and it has value to my family. I took care of myself from the outset because I didn't want any distractions from what Stella needed. Everything she and my wife needed came first, and maybe that's why, I tell people, that's why I've survived: because I don't have to think about myself. I drove myself to every chemotherapy and radiation treatment. I didn't ask anyone to step up or in to help me because I wanted the focus to be on them helping my family instead, even though there were times I was too weak to even walk up the stairs to the nursery to help my wife with Stella."

Jim may have spent his career in data analytics, a cause-and-effect guy, but he's also a great storyteller with a keen notion of the human condition and the smallest gifts that loom so much larger when received at the most opportune of times.

"It's real hard for cancer patients to ask for anything for themselves. On my Facebook page, I have a heart made out of sentences, out of words. Look closely and you'll see it's a primer for things you can do for someone that's suffering. The treatments for my cancer extended into the winter, and it happened to be a winter where we had a ton of snow in Michigan. But every time I came home, the driveway would be plowed and cleared because a neighbor of mine took it on himself to do it. I got home from surgery to find another neighbor mowing my lawn. People who knew what I needed just did it, without being asked or prompted. I never asked them to do anything, but they did it anyway because that's the way people are when you give them a chance. These days, when I go and see someone who's sick with cancer, I'll buy a bunch of stuff for them that I think might taste good. I'll ask them how they're doing, if there's anything else they need. Then I leave, because I don't want them to feel like they need to use their strength entertaining me."

Taking care of a disabled child with a myriad of challenges would be enough for any single person to face on its own. But he isn't just up to the task; he's taken it on with the humility and commitment that defines who he is.

"We have an eye gaze machine on order that will allow Stella to communicate directly with us for the very first time," he says, truly excited by that prospect, and for good reason. "It's going to be fairly rudimentary, pretty much just yes and no, but for Stella, just to be able to say no would be huge for us."

The machines were designed primarily with ALS (amyotrophic lateral sclerosis, a.k.a. Lou Gehrig's disease) patients in mind. These systems rely on eye movement to pick out various letters on a computer screen to allow the patient to form a word or entire message, requiring only the capacity to make upper, lower, and lateral eye movements. Since Stella lacks the cognitive skills to manage more than basic communication, starting with yes or no will be a game changer for her, Jim, and the entire Pantelas family. But the strength and confidence he exudes occasionally belie the kind of thoughts that sometimes keep him, and virtually all lung cancer survivors, awake long into the night.

"What scares me? Damn near everything. I get a headache and the first thought is brain metastasis. I still get 'scanxiety,' fear of what's coming in the next test, every year before my annual. And I'm dreadfully afraid that I'll live longer than my funds will hold up and that I'll be worth more to my family dead than alive. I'm afraid that I won't be around to see my girls graduate from junior high, let alone high school or college. And I'm afraid that someone else will end up being considered their dad by then. Mortality? Shit, I don't know. I'm sixty-six years old. My dad died of small cell lung cancer when he was sixty-seven years and forty days old, and his was a brutal passing. As I approach that age, I wonder if I'll live longer than he did. And I wonder if my name will pass anyone's lips a year or two after I'm gone. I do what I do because I want to try to make sure my girls don't ever have to deal with the disease that will have killed their father and the grandfather they never knew."

In spite of those occasional difficult times, Jim lives his life on an incredibly even keel. After all he's been through, nothing seems to roil or rattle him, his approach and manner the polar opposite of someone whose shoulders break under the weight that life piles on. When he talks about Stella, though, there's a different tone to his voice, as he speaks straight from the heart.

"We were vacationing on Mackinac Island a few years back," he recalls, a reflective smile flashing thinly, "which is a small island, maybe eight miles around, tucked between two peninsulas of Michigan. Mackinac's claim to fame is that no cars are permitted. You get around by carriage, bicycle, or horseback. It was Fourth of July weekend, so the island was packed. I tell my wife Kathy that when we're on vacation, I take care of Stella so she and our other two daughters can go off and spend money. I was standing in the lobby of the Chippewa Hotel with Stella when this woman came up to me and asked me if Stella was tube fed. She asked a bunch more questions, and it turned out she lived on the island and had a daughter named Olivia who'd passed away. Stella reminded her of Olivia, and she told me that the carriages on the island are now outfitted with wheelchair lifts because of her advocating on her daughter's behalf.

"She also had a special bicycle made for Olivia that was basically a bike in the back with an electric motor on the rear wheel and a wheelchair in the front. She told me all about it. We were actually staying on the mainland, and the next day she called me and asked if I could be around the ferry stop for the boat's 2:15 arrival. I said I could and when the ferry arrived, she got off with the custom-made bike in tow, the very last thing she has of her daughter's. It hadn't been run for six years, and she thought Stella was the perfect person to have it. I researched the bike when I got home; turned out it was manufactured in the Netherlands at a cost of around fifteen thousand dollars. I got it fixed up, and it holds a charge for thirty miles. When summer rolls around, I take it over to Stella's school and let them keep it to use for the summer months. Teachers take pictures every year of kids getting a ride. You can tell how happy they are, how much the ability to experience something we would never think twice about changes their lives. And we send those pictures to Olivia's mom so she can see that her daughter's bike is being put to good use."

Jim's ten-year-old daughter, his youngest, is already an accomplished equestrian who rides American Saddlebred horses in competitive meets all over the country. And his middle daughter, who's twelve, dances competitively and is headed for Nationals this year.

"These are the things," he says, "that get me out of bed in the morning."

The equestrian academy where his youngest daughter learned to ride, only four miles from their home, was actually founded by a woman who lost her son to cancer at the age of fifteen. Jim met her at the Michigan hospital where he does the bulk of his volunteering.

"It's all about community."

~ ~ ~

## Reflections

What is grit? Angela Duckworth, a distinguished psychology professor at the University of Pennsylvania (and a MacArthur "Genius" Award fellow) has taken the lead in understanding this concept from a social science point of view. Grit, she writes, has two essential components: perseverance and passion. By "perseverance" she means sticking it out regardless of failures along the way. By "passion" she means a relentless determination to pursue a goal until you've achieved it.

Jim Pantelas stood up to two disasters that hit him at exactly the same time: cancer and a newborn afflicted with cerebral palsy that required a lifetime of intensive care. His explanation of how he warded off despair? "I don't think there's any courage involved. I had to live because I couldn't die." This is a man with grit at the center of his character. "You don't have an option," he says. "You get out of bed in the morning and go forward…if you get a chance you do it again tomorrow." In other words, you simply do not give up.

Marcus Luttrell, author of the best-selling *Lone Survivor*, remembers his SEAL instructor telling him, "You're going to hurt… That's a big part of becoming a SEAL. We need proof you can take punishment… Don't buckle under to the hurt, rev up your spirit and your motivation." Can you cope with unfairness, another instructor asked, with setbacks "and still come back with your jaw set, still determined, swearing to God you will never quit"?

That part of grit is a trait, an inborn disposition not to give up. Pantelas embodies that disposition. He also has "passion," a goal of overmastering importance: staying alive in order to care for his daughter. "I had to live," he said. But for Pantelas, staying alive wasn't just a matter of a hardheaded, built-in refusal to give up. It's *how* he stayed alive that's so revealing to anyone interested in understanding resilience.

When your life stops taking the course it originally embarked on, he says, when that comes to an end, you need to re-create yourself. "You get the opportunity to be resurrected, to live every day the way you want the world to see you and become the person you want to be." That's the way he puts it. You have to change your habits and desires to fit new parameters. "The most fundamental principle of all," wrote Joseph Soloveitchik, one of the great modern Jewish sages, "is that man must create himself." In Pantelas's case, he must *recreate* himself.

For Pantelas, that meant putting himself back together out of the same pieces that made up his former life, but in a different way. So, as he put it back in 2017, what does a workaholic do with his life when he no longer can work? "He volunteers!"

But Pantelas doesn't volunteer to distract himself from his troubles (which would by itself be a coping mechanism). He does it in a way that matters to him—at the children's hospital that is taking care of his daughter and then more and more for cancer research where he can bring to bear the skills he developed at the National Security Agency working with big data projects. In short, he is doing something that is meaningful to him. He has found a different, but related, vocation, i.e., a purposeful life.

In the course of Pantelas's work with cancer studies, he also discovered an affinity for talking with and comforting cancer patients. He found that sharing stories was healing for both those he was visiting and for himself. Having a purpose is expansive. A purpose is almost never static. It evolves and enlarges, and in the course of doing that it transforms, in sometimes profound ways, the individual living a purposeful life. We see in Jim Pantelas's experience not just that it is possible to emerge from a crisis whole, but that adversity may make us stronger, more capable, and richer in those elements by which we measure our lives.

# 5

# Claudia Thomas

*The popularity of motorcycles in Maryland kept us busy that summer of 1980. When a rider flies off a bike, he "rag dolls" against any obstacle he meets. As a rule, arms and legs are ripped apart, and the pelvis is often fractured. The most gruesome motorcycle injuries I saw in a person who wasn't DOA occurred that July, during the first month of my trauma fellowship…*

—From *God Spare Life*, an autobiography by Dr. Claudia Thomas

So how does Dr. Claudia Thomas feel about being the first African-American woman ever to become an orthopedic surgeon?

"I didn't even know I was the first until Dr. Charles Epps, chair of orthopedics at Howard University, told me after I'd finished my training. It means my parents did the right thing. I can remember sitting at the kitchen table as a three-year-old calling out flash cards my mother had cut from a cardboard box. The letters A through Z were printed on one side of the card, and she had drawn pictures from apple to zebra on the other. That was my Head Start program, my exposure to early education. This was the 1950s, a time in America when people of color had to work harder and be more prepared in order to make it. My mother had dyslexia but was never diagnosed and ended up failing second grade twice. She wasn't going to let anything like that happen to me. And my father loved math, the clarity of it. He taught me numbers, which gave me even more of a head start. Without the typical barricades in front of us, my sister and I excelled from our first day in school. We followed the path laid by our parents.

"We lived in a little brick bungalow in Queens [New York], when it was common to finish the basement so you could have more space. I remember laying down a tile floor, hanging knotty pine walls, and installing a drop ceiling with my father while my mother and sister ran in the opposite direction. He taught me carpentry, how to use a saw and a drill. My love of math filtered down to geometry, then solid geometry which is all about angles and measurements. And so much of what my father taught me back then I was able to apply to orthopedics, from setting a dislocated hip, where it's all about angles, to performing a full hip replacement using manual instruments, before power tools were in common use. I remembered all my father taught me.

"When I learned I was the first black female orthopedic surgeon, I knew I sure wasn't going to be the last. You've got to extend your hand back down to people coming up after you. Being the first doesn't mean much if you're the only."

Claudia tells the story of standing on an emergency room gurney to put a patient's hip joint back into place after it had been dislodged in a car accident. She wasn't on duty in the ER that day but was summoned when a pair of two-hundred-pound male doctors couldn't manage the task. Angles again. Solid geometry.

"Every program I applied to, I would have been their first female orthopedic resident. I wasn't sure I wanted to go into orthopedics during the initial process of choosing my medical career. I was considering other specialties, but orthopedic surgeons had totally different personalities than other doctors. They seemed genuinely happy with what they did, and welcoming too. Their attitude was: let us share what we do with you."

"Going into orthopedics was an evolution," Claudia told Theresa Campbell of *Lake and Sumter Style*, a magazine based in the area of Florida she now calls home.

She went on to tell the magazine about being invited into the operating room during her second year at Johns Hopkins Medical School to see the reshaping of a femur bone in a young man who had a condition that caused his hip to be deformed.

"I scrubbed my hands, put on a gown and gloves, and was being taught by an enthusiastic orthopedic surgeon who clearly loved what he did. He showed me how to put the hardware in the bone to hold the femur in its new position. He let me use the drill. He let me put a screw in the bone, and I thought, 'This is it. Solid geometry. Carpentry. This is my field.'"

Claudia was blessed with very long arms and legs, which enabled her to use those limbs as a lever just as effectively as big, strong men do. She had found her calling, and nothing was going to get in her way.

Until it did.

"They found a cyst on one of my kidneys, and I had to have surgery to remove it. I knew there was a chance they'd have to take the whole kidney, just as I knew you can live a perfectly normal life with only one."

Claudia was already no stranger to adversity, having stared down the likes of Hurricane Hugo after moving to her husband Max's native St. Thomas in 1985. On September 17, 1989, the storm attacked the island with unprecedented ferocity, wind gusts reaching as high as 250 miles per hour. The storm struck after dark, battering their home and threatening to literally tear it apart with Max and Claudia huddled inside.

"I knew we could die. The storm could tear the roof off like a piece of paper and take us with it. I dropped to my knees and began to recite the twenty-third psalm, 'The Lord is my shepherd,' and that calmed me, got my pulse rate down."

But Claudia remains convinced it was that experience that started her kidney failure and set her on the road she found herself treading a few months later. She picks up the story in her autobiography, *God Spare Life.*

*I awoke with no concept of time and no memory of the recovery room. I was in a hospital bed on my right side, in horrible pain from my rib cage to my pubic bone. My throat felt raw and parched.*

*"Claudia." The voice was familiar. I opened my eyes to see Dr. Light, my surgeon, standing before me.*

*"Dr. Light," I whispered. My eyes closed slowly.*

*"Claudia, I have disappointing news." I opened my eyes. Dr. Light came into focus. "You had cancer. In both your kidneys."*

*I was still groggy from the anesthesia, but I understood Dr. Light clearly.*

*"I took out both your kidneys. You can't get a transplant until we know that the cancer hasn't spread. We're going to have to start you on dialysis."*

Back to the present.

"The first thing I thought was, 'Praise God!' Because I was alive and I knew I was going to make it. I'd been walking around with cancer for a while. What if they hadn't found it at all? The church was always an important part of my life growing up. I remember listening to the radio during dinner one night when a news report came on talking about a plane that had lost its landing gear and was circling Idlewild Airport, near our house. My father stopped the meal and we went into the living room, held hands, got on our knees, and prayed for those people. The plane landed safely on its belly, and in my heart of hearts, I believed our prayers had saved those people, just as I knew prayer could save me when I needed God the most."

*The blood supply to half the pelvis and a leg had been torn away, which left no options for repair. Faced with a situation that required my immediate clinical attention without the luxury of empathy, I quickly defined the goal as saving life, not limb.*

But Claudia's treatment wasn't the more traditional dialysis proce-dure most of us are familiar with, when blood is "washed" three or so days a week. This was more about exchanging the fluids in Claudia's body to assure as proper a balance as possible of electrolytes, such as sodium and potassium. And that meant she had to have the treatments two or three times a day instead of per week. Her mother learned how to perform the procedure at the hospital, becoming a virtual expert, which was good because the nurses dispatched to Claudia's home weren't familiar with a treatment that had literally just been approved. The good news was that Claudia's sister turned out to be a transplant match. The bad news was that Claudia would have to remain cancer-free for at least a year before the operation could be scheduled.

And it turned out to be a difficult year indeed. At one point, Claudia retained too much fluid. She developed a blood pressure spike, which caused a grand mal seizure. She ended up in a coma for four days, suffering from bleeding on the brain on top of every-thing else.

"How did I make it? I can't explain it, any more than I can my mother, an ordinary person with no nursing experience, being able to master a dialysis treatment that nurses couldn't. The months passed and I was finally deemed cancer-free."

Claudia was approved for a transplant. End of story, right?

Wrong.

"When I had my kidneys removed, I was given blood that con-tained an antibody that would have forced me to reject my sister's kidney. I'd been switched to hemodialysis, the gold standard, and my weight dropped to ninety-eight pounds. I was so frail I knew my body wouldn't be able to endure much longer. I was losing hope, back home in Baltimore praying for a miracle. One day, a young man named John who delivered medical supplies to my home came by and was carrying boxes to restock my dialysis equipment."

"'John, did you hear? I can't get a transplant,' I told him."

"'Doc, the Lord already took care of that,' he said out of nowhere. John carried the boxes without losing a beat as he blurted out the affirmation."

Claudia's life became a waiting game. She and her sister Cathi made regular visits to the Johns Hopkins histocompatibility lab, awaiting the moment when the antibodies that had ruled out a transplant were no longer present in Claudia's blood. Weeks passed, then months, with no good news, leaving Claudia to question John's sudden pronouncement. But she never lost faith, even after several visits to the emergency room, including one during which she needed to be resuscitated. Then the miracle she'd been praying for happened.

The lab was finally able to definitively identify Claudia's problematic antibody as one that would actually *not* force her to reject her sister's kidney. Surgery was scheduled for September 29, 1991. Claudia had her miracle. True to John's pronouncement, the Lord, it seemed, had really had this taken care of all along.

*Within the golden hour, I controlled the bleeding and completed the amputation that the accident had started, by cutting through the tissue still connected to the damaged portion of the pelvic bone. That half of the pelvis was disposed of, with its nonviable leg attached. The colon and bladder were severed from their orifices and were surgically diverted to empty through openings in the abdominal wall.*

The kidney transplant ended Claudia's career as a surgeon, but not as an office-based orthopedist or as a teacher. She decided to make the most out of the second chance she'd been given and forged a new life for herself as a diagnostician, instructor, and something more. At an age when many are considering retirement, Claudia relocated to a practice in Florida and began anew.

"That experience, the cancer, made me a doctor who was more able to interact with people on a spiritual level in dealing with whatever was afflicting them. It made me express things differently to patients and be more open with my spirituality, share that with them. Sometimes somebody needs a hug. Sometimes it's not back pain that's the problem; it's something going on in a patient's life that's tearing them apart. You can't give anyone faith, but you can tell them what happened to you and give them hope."

The firm grasp that had once held surgical instruments now holds hands instead.

"I had a patient in my office recently. I don't remember what he came to see me about, but his spirit was in the toilet. He was Jewish, and he told me he didn't believe in God because of the Holocaust. I wanted to give him something to take from our meeting, more than just a diagnosis of what was causing his pain but what was breaking his spirit, because I felt that's what I really needed to relieve. I wanted him to believe in something bigger than himself, so I told him this story about a man who climbs up on a roof to escape terrible flooding. Another man comes by in a rowboat and offers to save him.

"'I'm waiting for God, thank you,' the man says.

"Then a man in a motorboat comes by and offers to help him get down from the roof.

"'I'm waiting for God,' the man says again.

"Finally a helicopter drops down from overhead and offers to lift him to safety, but he says the same thing a third time, and you know what? He ends up drowning. So he goes to heaven and says to St. Peter at the Pearly Gates, 'Why didn't God come to save me?'

"'He sent you two boats and a helicopter,' St. Peter tells him.

"I told this patient that story in my office because I wanted him to know that sometimes we're waiting for something that we don't recognize we already have. I knew I had to heal his spirit before I could heal his body."

Not that Claudia doesn't miss surgery. This is a surgeon who welcomed the sight of a bone sticking out of the skin because she knew she could fix it and give the patient their life back. She still does that, just in a different way. And she's also done it by becoming a mentor, an homage in part to those who'd helped her become the first female African-American orthopedic surgeon in history, going all the way back to her childhood in Queens, New York.

"My pediatrician was an African-American female named Dr. Pearl Foster. Seeing her in that white starched coat told me this was something I could do, someone I could be."

Dr. Foster inspired and encouraged Claudia, a great gift to any child, which lingers to this day. She went to college at Vassar, where she majored in black studies instead of math, though becoming a doctor was nonetheless never far from her thinking even then. At the end of her junior year, Claudia elected a premed minor. A dream is a dream. But she had other things on her mind as well, specifically the inequities of how the college was treating its minimal number of African-American students.

"We sought accreditation of the Black Studies program and a degree that would make it possible for students to declare Black Studies as their major," she writes in *God Spare Life*. "We demanded funding for the program and an increased presence of full-time Black faculty to accommodate the expanded Black Studies program. We asked for immediate renovations to the community-based Urban Center, and a bus to transport students to and from the center. We also asked that the 'experimental' status of the African American Cultural Center, 'the Black House,' be dropped and that permanent Black housing be provided for large numbers of students. We cited statistics—that Blacks made up only forty-two students out of sixteen hundred, a pitiful two percent of the student body. We demanded that the college make an effort to recruit more of us. We petitioned for a Black counselor who would assist students with career placement."

When those efforts fell short, on October 30, 1969, Claudia was one of those who led thirty-four female African-American students in an occupation of Main Building, where Vassar's administrative offices were housed. In doing so, they risked expulsion, physical harm, and arrest. In Claudia's mind, though, the injustice could no longer be tolerated, so she took a stand that lasted three days and ultimately resulted in negotiations that gave birth to Vassar's now esteemed Africana Studies program. That program celebrated its fiftieth anniversary in 2019.

"We were doing it for future generations," she explains. "We risked our educations, risked being expelled, and the struggle goes on. Racism is as bad as it ever was. Sexism is as bad as it ever was."

The same fighter mentality accompanied Claudia throughout medical school, her residency, and her professional career. The term "give up" isn't in her vocabulary; she's always the last person standing and has never relinquished her relentless approach to any task she takes on, all with unyielding support of the aggrieved while displaying righteous indignation toward their aggrievers.

"When I was serving as chief resident of orthopedics at Yale, I noticed a pediatric resident being berated by her chief resident, who had a reputation for embarrassing those under him for the slightest mistake. The young lady ran off in tears. I grabbed her by the arm and took her into a supply room.

"'Don't let them see you cry,' I told her. 'Don't you ever let them see you cry. Once you break down and become the weak person, you become the joke, you get picked on. I don't care what you're feeling; don't let them know they got to you.'

"I guess I was her mentor," she finishes.

Claudia describes another doctor as the mentor who did the most for her career and on whom she models her own efforts.

"He said he wanted me to be the best. He gave me the precious opportunity to write papers with him. Nobody else was offering me publication opportunities, and somebody has to invite you into that coveted arena. He took me in a direction that led me to becoming a professor at Johns Hopkins. That mentor was you."

And Claudia can recite stories of mentoring others herself going all the way back to elementary school, though it was an epiphany sometime around 2007 that set her on her most recent path. She was a member of the board of directors of the Gladden Society, named after Dr. J. Robert Gladden, who became the first black board-certified orthopedic surgeon in 1950 (the year Claudia was born), and a discussion ensued about the lack of those following in his path still to this day.

"It all goes back to losing African-American males, our boys, as early as middle school. So I challenged our executive committee to start mentoring middle school boys."

She had come down to Florida to join a practice that had six black surgeons, including former mentees of hers. Between the six partners, they've been able to mentor forty young men each year who fit the bill, encouraging the boys to succeed in their schoolwork and in life. In April of 2015, Claudia herself led a four-day trip to Washington, DC, for seventeen boys.

"I want them to know they stand a better chance of being like me than being like Mike. These boys had never been on an airplane or in a big city before. They'd never had that opportunity, had never seen X, Y, or Z. I wanted to do something positive for them to broaden their horizons. Mentoring just comes naturally for me. One of my mentees back at Johns Hopkins is the founding partner at the Florida practice. You do what has to be done to make a difference."

*As devastating as those injuries were, there was reason for triumph. Each young man survived his traumatic hemipelvectomy, an injury previously reported in the medical literature as fatal. Although I could never feel good about the loss of a limb, I rejoiced at having saved two lives.*

~ ~ ~

## Reflections

"How did I make it?" Claudia Thomas asks herself about how she recovered in a hospital from a four-day-long coma. "I can't explain it."

Thomas, a groundbreaking orthopedic surgeon, expert at the mechanics of her profession, the forces involved in mobility and weight bearing, the molecular structure of bones, the leverages, the geometry, and the science of it, does not have a scientific explanation for her recovery. She believes it was a miracle.

That wasn't the only miracle Claudia Thomas experienced. In 1989, when Hurricane Hugo tore through St. Thomas where she was living with her West Indian husband, Max, the winds tore at their house and threatened to rip it apart. The terror was overwhelming. Thomas fell on her knees and prayed. They survived. God had spared them. Other events Thomas considered miracles occurred throughout her life. She entitled her autobiography *God Spare Life,* a West Indian expression meaning "God willing."

In this book we will encounter several other interviewees for whom faith figures largely in their stories of facing and overcoming adversity. Tom Catena, whom you will meet in an ensuing chapter, in his Nuba mountain hospital draws strength from prayer and sees the spark of God in everyone, giving him an unshakable moral sense of shared humanity. But Thomas is different. She believes in God's direct intervention. Her belief has sustained her through near fatal surgeries and drastic medical complications. In many ways, faith has framed her life.

Each of these interviewees draws on faith differently. The common denominator is that belief in God allows them to tap into a source of strength greater than themselves. They understand that the circumstances they face are overwhelming and the resources they themselves can muster are inadequate. Belief in God empowers them.

For believers, the power of faith can hardly be overemphasized. And faith is plastic—it can conform itself to the needs and personality of the believer. But in whatever form it takes, faith and spirituality have been shown to enhance hardiness and endurance. "Scientific research," Southwick and Charney tell us, "supports the relationship between faith and resilience." Claudia Thomas's life attests to that.

Thomas's life teaches other lessons as well. Her physical problems—cancer, kidney failure, major surgeries—forced her to leave the practice of orthopedic surgery, which she loved and considered her vocation. Like Jim Pantelas, she was forced to call a stop to the life she had built and create a different life for herself. Also like Pantelas, she embraced that challenge.

Unable to perform orthopedic surgery, with its rigorous physical demands, Thomas refashioned herself not as a surgeon but as an orthopedist—that is, a diagnostician, teacher, and counselor. A surgeon's role is usually short term, her expertise centering on the operating room. As an orthopedist, Thomas has the opportunity for closer, more intimate interaction with patients. In that setting she's far more than an expert technician; she's able to share her own experience, even her spirituality. She is able to reinforce hope.

Thomas's story illuminates the power of religious belief, but also the important role that empathy plays in providing a strengthening, sustaining life purpose as a counter to the trauma of loss.

Claudia Thomas's resilience drew on the love and commitment of family, on the critical support of mentors, and on a courageous, unafraid, and empathic nature. But the essential element at work here is, without a doubt, her faith in a personal God whom she trusts to watch over her.

# 6

# Mangok Bol

*It took Mangok Bol 14 years to leave Africa, ultimately landing at Brandeis University. He was one of the Lost Boys of Sudan, one of the thousands orphaned or displaced by civil war and spirited to the United States.*

*—Boston Globe,* March 4, 2019

The Lost Boys of Sudan is the name given to a group of over twenty thousand boys displaced during Sudan's second civil war that spanned all of eighteen years, from 1987 through 2005. As many as half of them died, children like Mangok Bol who fled his village at the age of nine at the very outset of the conflict.

"Education wasn't really something that was a part of my life. At the age of five, my parents tried to take me to school, kindergarten, though it didn't last very long. But leaving my home, going into exile, starting a new life without my parents—I felt I was alone and on my own. I didn't know when I'd be able to go back home. I guess you could say I took refuge in education because I was a refugee. I didn't have my old world anymore, and education became about learning more about the rest of the world. Listening to teachers, learning math, geography, and English, fostered a feeling in me of wanting to know and then wanting to know more. Learning became the driving force in my life. It was an escape because it took my mind off my sadness of being separated from my family."

"His first classroom in Kenya's Kakuma refugee camp was in the dusty shade of a large tree," Leah Burrows wrote for *Brandeis Now* in July of 2013. "His second had mud brick walls and a grass-thatched roof. His third was a stuffy, overcrowded concrete room."

Her interview with Mangok was conducted in Brandeis's Mandel Center for the Humanities, the utter antithesis of the educational world from which he came. Mangok holds the position of administrator for the Mandel Center, along with being the program administrator for Brandeis's renowned international and global studies program and, in May of 2013, received his master's degree in finance from the school's equally renowned International Business School.

"Education became my driving force. Looking back, that was the dividing line in my life. That was the beginning. What kept me going for all those years was this internal desire and drive to learn as much as I could about the world."

Perhaps also to understand and better make sense of the lot he'd been cast. Mangok and two cousins he'd fled with "walked for a month across difficult terrain and unmarked roads to reach Ethiopia," according to the article in *Brandeis Now*.

"Once there, education provided hope," Mangok recalls. "I wanted to read books. I knew my village but nothing else. Open this book or that book opened up the feeling that the world was bigger. The whole driving force behind wanting to know more was that another larger world existed. I needed to find my place in it and I found hope in myself, in doing something meaningful like learning. Math wasn't my favorite subject, but I had this teacher at the refugee camp in Ethiopia who taught me the formulas and everything made sense. I became so interested, I wanted to be him, I wanted to be good like him. I wanted to teach math. He was my first mentor. He changed my whole perspective, the first person that made me see the value and purpose of education. I was thirteen at the time and maybe I didn't really want to be a teacher, but I wanted to be *something*. And when I wasn't doing math, I was reading because when I was reading, I wasn't thinking about what I had left behind."

Bol remained in that refugee camp for three years with thousands of other Lost Boys before forces of the Ethiopian army drove them out.

"It was 1991, and I think that was the time I was most scared of all. The Ethiopian regime had changed, and the new government was hostile to us. So we had to flee. It wasn't a smooth journey; we were chased the whole way. After running away from South Sudan, I finally felt secure. And then I was suddenly living again through the unknown for a second time, heading toward a destination I didn't know at the time."

With no other choice, he and the other Lost Boys fled back to Sudan, where things were even worse than they'd been when they'd fled the first time. There was no security, no safety, and, also, no schooling. Mangok's life dissolved into a steaming cauldron of uncertainty, bred by factions of the civil war like the SPLA (the Sudan People's Liberation Army), which was after boys like Mangok to conscript them as soldiers. He was hundreds of miles away from his home village and had no conception of its fate, while fearing the worst. In the four years since he'd originally fled, he'd had no contact whatsoever with his parents or siblings. The very definition of a lost boy.

"I became a Lost Boy for the second time. This time, I could make sense of what was happening because I was thirteen. I had a clear understanding. I was stranded in a small village, knowing my mother, sister, and brothers had probably been killed. When I finally tried to make it back to my village, I learned it had been abandoned. Everyone was gone. I had nothing. I had no one."

Until America came calling to almost four thousand of those Lost Boys.

"In early 2000," Leah Burrows reported in that same article for *Brandeis Now*, "as the United States, Canada and Australia began offering refuge to the Lost Boys, Bol's name was among the many forwarded to US resettlement agencies by Save the Children Sweden. After more than a year's wait, Bol made it onto a flight bound for the US—one of the last—as reaction to the 9/11 attacks effectively ended the Lost Boys rescue effort. He landed on Sept. 27, 2001, in Boston—a city randomly assigned—and found a job at Logan International Airport working nighttime security. He sent most of his earnings to his brother and mother, whom he'd managed to find still living in a Sudanese village, and put what little was left toward education. Bol started classes at Bunker Hill Community College and soon transferred to the University of New Hampshire, where he earned a BS in business."

"Life is good for now," he told a television reporter shortly after graduation, as reported in *UNH Magazine*. "But I have a lot left to do."

"After graduating in 2008," the article in *Brandeis Now* continues, "Bol met then-Brandeis anthropology professor Mark Auslander through the Sudanese Education Fund, where both served on the board of directors. Auslander, who had mentored other Sudanese students at Brandeis, suggested that Bol look for a job on campus. Bol was hired as a program administrator for the interdisciplinary programs in international and global studies and cultural production in the anthropology department."

Auslander, in other words, followed in the footsteps of that math teacher from the Ethiopian refugee camp as mentor to Mangok. And his efforts were swiftly followed by an even more influential mentor in writer David Chanoff.

"In the schools they came from, there was no such thing as analysis or critical thinking, skills we expect college students to have, so they had to make a tremendous psychological transition in the way they learned," Chanoff, academic adviser to the Sudanese Education Fund, a Boston-based nonprofit group that gives refugees money for college, told the *Boston Globe* in May of 2006.

"It wasn't just me," Mangok reflects. "He took a real interest in us, the Lost Boys—you know, refugees. He was there from the very beginning. He's that person that really made everything look possible. When you grow up without parents, or family really, there's a hole. David went out of the way to give us a reason to succeed here, and that filled much of the hole. He was a big part of me succeeding in America."

"I'm taken aback," Chanoff says upon hearing Mangok's words. "My wife Lisa and I felt from the beginning, when we got involved thanks to our son who was a refugee worker, that we were getting more out of this than the kids we helped were. They'd been through so much, gone through so much, yet were so looking forward to their lives, optimistic in spite of everything they'd been through. That kind of thing refreshes your spirit. It was so amazing to just be around these kids who had such hope after all the disasters they'd suffered. They are absolutely remarkable. When you look at them, you understand the resilience of the human spirit."

But why the Lost Boys? Why not some other cause?

"That's a good question. And the answer to it is that it's not that one form of needy or suffering people is any more valid than any other. Why not help cancer victims, or homeless children? I think the answer is that, thanks to our son who was a refugee worker in Africa, we had an opportunity to be engaged. But I also think the causes you champion often come out of your own background. For example, my family's Jewish. I'm of the generation that came of age after World War II, so I knew all about the Holocaust. And the experiences of these children, the Lost Boys, who came out of Africa connected my wife and me with our culture's past, even if it wasn't a past I necessarily had personal contact with."

But the new extended family Mangok nurtured at Brandeis and beyond served only to make him miss his real family all the more, family he hadn't seen since 1987. Beyond that, he'd learned that his brother and his brother's wife had been killed and his nieces and nephew abducted, back in South Sudan.

"I had no choice but to go home. I had to get them back."

That became more than a mission for him. He couldn't let those children experience what he had as a child. They were his blood, and saving them would be his way of paying back those who had helped Mangok along the way, like that math teacher. He didn't want the memories he still held from that period of his life to be mirrored in the experiences of his nieces and nephew.

"I never got back to my village because it had been destroyed. My mother and sisters came to meet me in the capital for the first time since I left in 1987. I was more than a little scared. My mother was in mourning because she'd already lost one son, but she found a bit of comfort because I came to be with her. But she was also asking herself how we could be celebrating and smiling with open arms instead of mourning my brother. It didn't feel right to be celebrating anything, not until we got my brother's children back."

Mangok's nephew was two, his nieces four, six, and eight when they were abducted. It would take more than one trip back home to find them, but he wasn't about to be denied despite initially encountering setback after setback, disappointment after disappointment. The game changer came when Samantha Power, the former professor at Harvard who'd later become the United States ambassador to the United Nations, heard about his plight and interceded, reaching levels Mangok never could have reached on his own, including pleading his case with David Yau Yau, governor of the region where the kids had apparently been either given or sold to other families.

"In the summer of 2015," the *Boston Globe* reported in March of 2019, "four of the eleven children abducted from Bol's village were rescued, including his five-year-old niece Anyieth. A few months later, his three-year-old nephew, Majuei, was found. A few days after Thanksgiving in 2015, another niece, Ajoh, was rescued. That left Abiei, the oldest, still out there, alone."

And Mangok won't rest until she's found too. In 1987, he'd walked for weeks through treacherous, blood-soaked lands just to survive. Now it was about helping others survive and find their way back home, starting with his own family.

"The reason why I want to give back is because I feel this bigger sense of responsibility to myself. When you've benefitted from someone else who helped shape who you are, the best thing you can do is help another person when you can. I've always felt that way since I was very young. Give someone a ride, tutor somebody, or edit a friend's paper, or just be a friend when they need one. I made a promise to myself when I came to the US to give everything I have to everything I do. When I was a resident assistant at the University of New Hampshire, a young woman had just broken up with her boyfriend when I was on rounds. I heard her crying and went into her room and sat down. She told me she felt like it was the end of the world. I told her it wasn't, it was just part of life. I don't blame you, I told her, because you haven't seen the kinds of things I had. I gave her my life, what I consider to be the end of the world. How I buried one of my best friends when I was only twelve years old. I told the young woman in the dorm that what she was going through was temporary, that she would meet someone else. Give it a couple days and you'll be fine. She became a good friend of mine and later told me I helped her see the light. Because of what I'd been through, I didn't lack for knowing of what other people were going through, the level of crisis in their lives.

"The world is really big, very big. One thing that very few people have figured out is how to really care for the world itself. I give a lot of credit to the United Nations agencies that helped me. This was the work of some good people that put their heads and hearts together to make good things happen for people. Being a refugee is not a life you wish to lead. It's a dangerous life, a lonely life, and it deprives you of everything you left behind. You end up missing so much, the lifelong lessons and experiences—you just don't have those. There's this huge gap between the people who need the actual help and those who are positioned to help others but haven't figured out how to do that yet, the way someone like Bill Gates has. He'd probably tell you that a lot of it is putting the right resources in the right place at the right time. And there are people like Samantha Power out there who are willing to help in any way they can just because it's the right thing to do."

Just like returning home repeatedly to recover his own nieces and nephew was the right thing to do. Nonetheless, was he scared of returning to his native country for the first time in over twenty years?

"Giving up was not an option for me. The belief was reinforced by the fact that I'd seen the worst already. In other words, the worst thing had happened to me already. Nothing, absolutely nothing, could be worse than what I'd already seen."

The memories are still there, forever lurking at the edges of Mangok's consciousness. But there are plenty of new ones that have pushed them aside and blunted the pain they once rekindled, thanks to the people who were there for Mangok and other Lost Boys.

"Sometimes the people who mean the most to you in life aren't necessarily those you have the longest relationships with," reflects David Chanoff. "You might just have a momentary interaction with someone that has a tremendous impact. Even when the Lost Boys made it to that refugee camp in Ethiopia, they had to sleep outside because the shelters hadn't been built yet. One of them would begin to cry, then others would begin to cry. And before you know it there would be thousands of these children crying in the wilderness. It's so moving, it's almost unbearable. Anything, the slightest bit of empathy, that spoke to them as individuals and gave them some kind of hope left an extraordinary impact. It's exaggerated because you're helping someone at their most vulnerable stage of life, when they need it the most, and that makes the effect you can have even greater.

"In the abstract, we all have the responsibility to help others. I once wrote a book with a woman who'd been a refugee in Siberia during World War II. She survived because people, strangers, took care of her. They had no real reason to, but they still did. Years later, that woman made a lot of money and started a foundation to help homeless mothers and children because she felt a responsibility to help others in need because of those that helped her."

For his part, Mangok defines the resilience that allowed him to overcome all the adversity he experienced as being directly related to his love of people and the sense of community, of our common humanity, that it fosters.

"I've always considered myself part of a whole, part of a group, not me alone. That's what helped me survive as a Lost Boy and helped me adjust to a new life when I came here in 2001. I've had the same friends for twenty years now, ever since I came to America. It's a priority for me to be considerate of others, to respect one another. It's good to be in a network who share much of the same thinking but offer different perspectives. You have people around you who provide a reason to go on, to look forward to something else. People who challenge you to grow. A true sense of community based on education, in other words."

It almost sounds as if Mangok's entire life since fleeing his home village in 1987 has been about rediscovering family; if not his own, then the most reasonable facsimile he could find, which he has clearly succeeded in doing even as he reunited the family he was forced to abandon in helping to rescue his nieces and nephew.

"A final niece is still out there," he reminds us. "And I won't rest until she's found."

After all he went through as a Lost Boy, he feels he owes her that much. Payback, in many respects, for all hands extended out and down to him. And, contrary to Thomas Wolfe's famed lesson, Mangok learned he could indeed go home again.

"We learned a lot of things the hard way, so when we see an opportunity, we want to go for it. When you have been through hard things, you always look for what you can do right, to try and change what happened before."

~ ~ ~

## Reflections

In the wake of two severe blows, Jim Pantelas needed to figure out a new life for himself. Claudia Thomas was faced with a similar challenge. Mangok Bol's experience is as stark an illustration of what creating a new life means as is possible to imagine.

Mangok was ten years old when disaster struck his community in a wave of genocidal violence. His village was wiped out, his family either dead or missing. He, along with thousands of other children whose villages were also gone, were set adrift into the unknown with no food, no water, no shoes, no protection from the predation of wild animals and the attacks of marauding enemy militias. Mangok and the others trekked for many weeks to safety in Ethiopia. Along the way they buried friends who died of thirst, starvation, and disease.

There were thousands of them, these so-called Lost Boys of Sudan, from many different South Sudanese tribes. But each one of these thousands was essentially alone. Everything that had held their lives together had gone up in smoke—their parents, their clans, their songs and dances, their customs. "I didn't have my old world anymore" is how Mangok remembers feeling. The world that had given him and the others their identity no longer existed.

In the shock and trauma, some of the children lapsed into despondency. Mangok didn't. Refugee relief agencies set up schools in the children's camps. Very few of the boys—there were a smaller number of girls—had any prior schooling; they all came from preliterate cattle cultures. But now learning fascinated Mangok. Numbers, letters, geography, English language. The inherent curiosity of the human mind kicked in. He began to learn about the world beyond his village—its countries, its peoples, its science, its many cultures and their accomplishments. Learning was an escape from loneliness and sadness—a coping mechanism. But it was more than that. It gave Mangok ideas about the possibilities life had to offer.

So did the teachers themselves. There was one math teacher in particular whom he liked. Mangok wasn't that good at math, but here was a role model, someone doing something with his life that Mangok could aspire to. And it wasn't just the math teacher. Mangok and the other Lost Boys saw the pilots bringing in relief supplies, the doctors, the nurses, the agency officers. "A pilot," one of his friends said. "Why can't I be a pilot?"

For Mangok, education was the driver. When he got to the United States in 2001, he was admitted to the University of New Hampshire, then to the graduate program in international business at Brandeis. Education had opened his mind, and it had given him a career. In America he had also re-created something of a family and a community, mentors who loved him and the Brandeis University community especially that rallied around him when very bad news arrived from South Sudan.

In 2005 peace had come to Sudan, and with communication possible, Mangok found that his mother was alive, along with several siblings and their families. He was in touch by phone, talking to his mother for the first time in almost twenty years. He had thought she was dead; she had thought he was.

Then came the bad news. Several years ago, in a cattle raid back home, Mangok's older brother and sister-in-law were killed and their four children abducted. Since then, his efforts to get the children back have dominated his life.

Mangok knows exactly what it is to be a lost child. He knows in his bones the longing everyone has for family and community. As of this writing (in 2020), he has succeeded in getting three of the four abducted children returned. Resilience, Mangok might say, resides in the bonds that join family and friends to each other. That and the almost unlimited creative potential of the human mind when it opens to the world around it.

# 7

# Heather Marini

Heather Marini can easily recall the play she remembers most from playing quarterback for the Monash Warriors Gridiron Club's women's team in Melbourne, Australia, in 2016.

"It was fourth down and twelve and we were on our own seven yard line. I'd just messed up a read on a read-option [a play in which the quarterback decides whether to run, pass, or hand off], so I decided to call the same play again and ended up running over ninety yards for a touchdown."

The Warriors ended up losing that game 54–52, through no fault of Heather's; she ran over six hundred yards in the game.

"That ninety-yard run was my fifth touchdown of the game. I ran off the field exhausted, thinking 'I'm not sure I have another one in me.' My legs were shot. Then I looked up and we'd given up another touchdown, so back in I went."

Elected team captain, she was ultimately named the team's offensive MVP, prior to being honored as the league's Rookie of the Year and finishing second in MVP honors. Not bad for her first year as a player at the age of twenty-five, without even mentioning the fact that she also led the league in punting.

Heather, now thirty years old, didn't quit in that shoot-out, and she hasn't since. Appropriately enough, in the spring of 2020 she was named quarterbacks coach at Brown University, making her only the second female position coach in the history of Division I college football and the only one in Division I today. That said, she resists the notion that she's a "groundbreaker."

"Governors always come in to break ground, when in reality others come in to do all the work. Somebody had to be first, or second, and it just happened to be me. A lot of women were behind the scenes doing the work that got me here."

Much of that groundwork was laid at the 2018 Women's Careers in Football Forum held at the NFL Scouting Combine, where Heather was among forty others looking to break into the game at the college or pro level.

"She stood up in front of San Francisco 49ers general manager John Lynch, Washington Redskins head coach Ron Rivera and Tennessee Titans play-caller Mike Vrabel and said: 'I'm going to be an NFL head coach and I have a question for you, Coach Rivera,'" Alexis Mansanarez wrote for the TDN (The Draft Network) Premium site in March of 2020. "Heather Marini went on to ask Rivera about a defensive scheme he used in Carolina and how, or if, he would transition it to Washington."

Among the other coaches Heather encountered there, James Perry was the most encouraging. He had just been named head coach at his alma mater, Brown University. Perry had previously coached the Bryant Bulldogs, where he'd hired two women on his staff: Phoebe Schechter, who went on to a position with the Buffalo Bills, and Sue Lizotte, who's taken a bigger job at a Division III school.

"The number one reason I was open to hiring women was that we're trying to get the best staff we can," says Perry. "So when I was alerted to the notion that women were trying to break into the sport, I looked at it as a whole new pool of talent to pull from, another way to get great coaches. Heather came up to me after I spoke and stayed in touch with me afterwards."

"You need to reach out," Heather reflects. "A lot of people out there want to help, and you never know which handshake is actually your job interview. 'Come watch film with us,' they'll say, or 'Come to practice.' You want to meet and make as many friends as you can in this industry. You can never volunteer too much, and I volunteered for ten years. Putting in those hours, doing a lot of work, was how I got the opportunities that I have."

Not that it was easy.

"Most people want to help, but the degree to which they're willing to help varies. They're more than happy to share their knowledge, but when you ask them for a job, they're not willing to go that far. So people may be willing to give you their time and, while that may not result in getting a job with them, the experience prepares you for the job, the opportunity, that's coming. Most coaches have signposted their journey along the way. They played football in high school, probably in college, and maybe even the NFL. They started out as analysts or graduate assistants. So one of the biggest challenges I had to face, as a woman and an Australian, was to convince others where I fit into that scheme. I was lucky enough to have been a head coach in Australia, but what does that mean exactly? I knew I had the skills and that I had to convince them I could contribute. The fit doesn't have to be just right, it has to be perfect, and you have to be ready when the right opportunity comes along.

"I actually coached for a couple years before I played my first game, which was strange in its own right. It was hard to take off that coaching hat—you've got to get that out of your head. At the end of the day, coaching is teaching. I was always good at taking complex things and breaking them down to seem simple. I grew up coaching players who'd never played football before, so I had to make the game accessible for them."

Just like somebody had to make it accessible for her back in Australia, starting with her then boyfriend Kieren, who was playing for Melbourne's Monash Warriors Gridiron Club when Heather, already interested in pursuing some kind of career in athletics, was just eighteen in 2008.

"I went to watch him play after we started dating, and it was the longest game I think I've ever been to. It was freezing, and it seemed like there was a penalty on every play. There were no stands, just a field in the middle of nowhere, and I was dressed way too, well, cute because we'd just started dating. My future husband was playing center, so I couldn't even see him and had no idea what was going on. After that game, I wanted to say to him I like you and all, but I'm not coming back."

Heather, of course, did come back. American football in Australia far more closely resembles the game played in college here as opposed to the pros, and at the junior varsity level to boot. The entire team staff, coaches included, were volunteers. The following week, Heather decided to grin and bear it again to watch her boyfriend compete on the same field in a playoff game.

"I got there by halftime. The sun was out and it was a much better experience. Then the spring season started and the team needed some help on the training staff, so I volunteered. The following year, I became the only strength and conditioning coach in Australian football. My goal was to set a new standard of professionalism, and we ended up facing the undefeated first seed in the first round of the playoffs. It was blistering hot, and we outran them up and down the field. We were the fitter team by far and went on to win the championship, for which I received far too much credit. The coaches, which included my husband who was a player-coach, asked me if I wanted to become more involved, and I thought, if I'm going to do this, I should learn more about the game, so I got accredited."

Coaching assignments weren't divvied up the same way they are here in the States, so Heather found herself coaching all of the positions on offense at various times. And in doing that, she learned the game from the ground up, while honing her communication skills.

"I had been around very strict, disciplined coaches growing up who maintained very high standards. I definitely took that approach on as a coach myself. When you're coaching teenage girls, it doesn't always go down the right way. With teenage boys, though, that's right up their alley."

But what drew Heather to the game more than anything was the people. There was something about the culture of football, the people who played and coached, that she was attracted to, and, of course, it helped that Kieren was the head coach of the Warriors before she took the reins from him in 2012. She ran the team for two more years after that, finishing runner-up for the title twice.

"In my last championship game, our quarterback tore his ACL literally as he was running onto the field. This was Under-Nineteen football, and our backup was all of fourteen years old. We put up a good fight, but…"

Among the players Heather coached was Adam Gotsis, who went on to become an All-ACC defensive end at Georgia Tech before embarking on a pro career with the Denver Broncos. Her first stop in the United States actually came in 2010 when she did a sports performance internship at Oregon State that set her on the road to making history at Brown University.

"While she was a head coach in Australia," NCAA.com reported on the occasion of her being elevated to a position coach at Brown, "Marini wanted to win games, but she also wanted to educate her players. She didn't want to have a narrow playbook. She wanted them to know what a Cover Two was, what a bubble screen was, how a guard pulls, and how a speed option is executed. Marini was adamant in her players getting an all-around schooling on the finer points of football."

"I wanted to make sure that my offense was relatively balanced but also to show enough of everything, because I didn't want to be the last football coach the players ever had," Heather explained for that article. "I wanted them to go up to the next level and be able to know what a counter or a sweep is, to say that they've seen it before. I wanted them to get a football education. I love football so much and I want them to love it too."

And it was probably the only sport she didn't play growing up on a list that included swimming, track, soccer, badminton, and a basketball-like sport called netball. She attacked each, even as a child, with an analytical mind that sought to penetrate the base layers to the nuts and bolts of every sport she took part in. Then, when the Warriors established a woman's team in 2016, she donned pads for the first time and emerged as the team's starting quarterback.

"It gave me a different perspective. It was hard as a player to get out of my own head, because I wanted to be a coach as well. That was a new experience and unique in a way that not very many people get the chance to see the game from the coach's side and then go onto the field and put your money where your mouth is and show that you understand what's going on and be able to execute.

"I was lucky when I was playing to still have a big leadership role. We were running my offense. But I missed seeing the big picture from the sidelines. Things happen so quickly on a football field, and I didn't necessarily know what had happened to the left because I was looking right. The biggest challenge was not to overthink things and just focus on doing my job. But it was the same spirit, chasing that competitive high. I just loved being involved in the sport, in the midst of it all."

Heather knew at that point football wasn't just going to be a part of her life; it was destined to *be* her life. No easy task, given the stereotypes she would have to overcome. With career goals in mind for both of them, she and her now husband Kieren uprooted their lives in Australia and settled in the United States in 2017. Heather spent two years scooping up every volunteer opportunity she could find, starting with a summer scouting position for the New York Jets. She shook a lot of those hands that were indeed essentially job interviews until her fingers ached, wrote a ton of emails, and generally stayed in touch with everyone she met as a result of the NFL's Women's Careers in Football Forum. Refusing to be discouraged over not landing a job faster, and not about to give up, Heather kept shaking countless hands at the forum in both 2017 and 2018, as well as at the NFL Rookie Coaches Clinic to which she was invited in 2018, until she finally shook James Perry's. Looking to fill out his staff with the best talent available, he found just that in Heather and hired her as his offensive quality control coach.

"You might think players might say something like, 'You never played in the NFL. Why are you telling me what to do?' But players actually figure you out pretty quickly. You show them you're there to help make them better, they're going to give you the respect they give any other coach. But when you see a *guy* at a coach's convention, it's like, 'Hey, Coach, how are you doing?' It's not that easy for a woman. People see you and they're not sure if you're a manager, a trainer, or a coach. One might say, 'I saw you in my quarterbacks meeting the other day. Do you coach?' At that stage, the challenge lies not so much in being respected as recognized."

It was both for Brown head coach James Perry, who won one Ivy League title for the Bears in 1999 as an all-time record-breaking quarterback, and then another as the team's quarterbacks coach himself in 2008. He then went on to win two more Ivy League titles as offensive coordinator at Princeton and recruited much of the talent responsible for two other titles after he'd left the school.

"Heather was super persistent to get the job. She was determined, and when we had an opening for the offensive quality coach after I got the job at Brown, I hired her. Over the course of the next few months, I wanted her to take a few of the things we were doing and just expand on them so we could do them better. How can we be better on third down; where's the data point, the analytics? Football is very data driven, and Heather's attitude from the beginning was how can I take these tasks and make us better. As a head coach, I'm looking to hire the smartest people who do the research and find the newest and best techniques. Heather's smart, she's hardworking, but the first real test she faced after being promoted to quarterbacks coach was recruiting. But so far, so good, *real* good, because she's able to connect with the mothers as well as the fathers, and in a lot of these homes the mother is the chief decision maker when it comes to choosing a school. I see Heather becoming an offensive coordinator and then a college head coach, and I don't think it's going to take that long."

She's not alone. Jennifer King and Katie Sowers have blazed their own trail to the NFL, Jennifer now with the Washington Redskins and Katie with the San Francisco 49ers. Jennifer has rejoined none other than Ron Rivera, whom she also worked for when he was head coach of the Carolina Panthers, and Katie had also previously worked with 49ers head coach Kyle Shanahan when he was the offensive coordinator with the Atlanta Falcons.

"I would love to be a coordinator," King told Redskins broadcaster Larry Michael. "I know now I'm at the bottom of the food chain, but I've been moving up and I'm learning a lot and I'm super excited to be here and work with [offensive coordinator] Scott [Turner] and his staff."

"I was embraced on day one," Sowers told *The Guardian* of her experience with the 49ers. "It's important to have someone in those leadership positions vouching for you. When you gain the respect of the influencers in the room, everyone follows, and that was huge. Kyle's not going to hire a woman to make a point. What's really cool is that I showed in Atlanta that I could add value to the team. Having Kyle recognize that helped my confidence and set me on a path to become a better coach."

"We're in a production-based business. It's all about winning, and we've got to create that opportunity to win," Ron Rivera told

247Sports. "It doesn't matter who you are: if you bring something special to the table and help us, we most certainly want you. These aren't just women who coach football. These are coaches."

Rivera wasn't necessarily including Heather in that mix, but he might as well have. While her professional experience in Australia was considerably different from Jennifer King's or Katie Sowers's here in the US, it prepared her well for ascending the Division I coaching ladder.

"Sometimes the language is a little different, just like the language is a little different if you're going to go coach in Japan," she told TDN Premium. "But trying to build up the complexities and the nuances, stuff like that, it's going to be different program to program, just like it's going to be different level to level. I coached players who had maybe never seen a football before, so being able to use my words and really explain concepts was something that was a real strength of mine. Now that I'm starting to learn more strategy and more X's and O's and stuff like that, my strength has then been to deliver it to players."

And what advice does she offer to other women looking to break into the coaching ranks?

"I'd say start at your alma mater. If you're in school, start at your school," she told NCAA.com. "I don't think there is any school on the planet that would say no to more volunteers. Everyone starts the same way. That's how you network, that's how you build trust, that's how you gain experience and your ability to see the game."

In other words, you have to pay your dues, invest that kind of time in yourself. Heather also stresses to those wanting to follow in her footsteps to be great communicators, capable of explaining things in a way that's easy for players to understand.

"For me, it was also the variety of the experiences. You have to want to keep learning and be able to demonstrate that to coaches. I did internships, I read a lot of books, I visited programs, watched films with coaches, went to a lot of practices to see how things were being done. I never stopped learning."

But she was a woman in a man's game, and casual observers might have expected the stereotypes that define football to become a self-fulfilling prophecy. It turned out to be anything but that.

"I get asked about sexism, mistreatment, microaggression, disrespect, and the like a lot. But the truth is I've had very, very few negative experiences in the thousands of interactions I've had in football; they're not even worth calling out. There was this time back in Australia when I was coaching the Warriors. The referee saw me in the coach's box and yelled at me to get back because I wasn't a coach," she adds, laughing. "Over here, I've had so many more encouraging and supportive mentors; it's just not my general experience to be around haters, and my overall experience has been nothing but positive. Exceptions don't make the rule.

"I'm a coach who happens to be a female, and I can't help but smile when one of the players I'm coaching calls me 'sir' as a slip of the tongue. It doesn't bother me at all because it shows that they look at me like all the other coaches. Having women in football is a good thing, something to be celebrated. The players can call me 'sir' if they want, or 'ma'am.' It's all the same.

"In my mind, athletes want to get better, and they're attracted to anyone who can help them do it. If you can help Michael Phelps with his stroke or Roger Federer with his serve, they're not going to care about your gender. If you can help them win, they'll listen because that's what athletes are about. At the end of the day, athletes need information and want the best people to give it to them."

And currently she's passing on a lot of that knowledge as quarterbacks coach at Brown.

"It's going to be a great experience to learn all the things I haven't learned yet. You never know when you're going to get your next experience until you're actually in it, and every experience has to be a learning experience. Especially for women coaches looking to make their mark, you have to be great before someone recognizes that you're great."

~ ~ ~

## Reflections

There's a well-known aphorism attributed to Eleanor Roosevelt: "No one can make you feel inferior without your consent." Prejudicial stereotyping always attempts to view its victims as inferior, unwelcome, not good enough. Prejudicial stereotyping is often personal, but the institutional variety is, if anything, more pernicious. Institutionalized prejudice expresses a cultural predisposition built into a profession, an organization, a business. Its most destructive form is when prejudice is embedded in the mores of society itself.

Prejudice functions to exclude individuals who do not belong to an acceptable class, religion, race, or gender. Dr. Joycelyn Elders, President Bill Clinton's first surgeon general, was a pediatric endocrinologist, but in the discussion of her nomination one senator asked, "What kind of nursing duties do you perform?" He was born and raised in an earlier time, he was conservative, he had grown up with the cultural assumption that doctors were men per se. And Elders was not just female, she was black. The idea of a black woman doctor struck at not one but two of the senator's culturally embedded prejudices.

Heather Marini is a female coach in what may be the ultimate male, macho game. Football's essence is physical confrontation and the controlled use of violence. Until very recent times, that had made it an exclusively male field of endeavor. The cultural prejudice is that it still is. Marini's breakthrough as a coach is a challenge to that prejudice. You would expect, then, that along the way she must have encountered some level of skepticism, even ridicule. Yet when the interviewer invited her comments on that, she replied, "I get asked about sexism, mistreatment, microaggression, disrespect, and the like a lot. But the truth is I've had very, very few negative experiences in the thousands of interactions I've had in football; they're not even worth calling out."

The question this interview raises is not: How has Heather Marini overcome the adversity inflicted by cultural prejudice? The question is: How has she insulated herself from it? And what might we learn from her ability to do that?

Among the resources she has brought to bear on her circumstances are elements of resilience we have seen in other stories. Most significantly, Marini was absorbed in a vocation. Her intrinsically robust physicality had led to a focus on football, which engaged her mind, her body, and her desire for connection with others. Her immersion in this vocation empowered a remarkable degree of persistence and determination, undaunted by the many years it has taken to achieve her goal. This purpose-driven endeavor immunized her in a sense against the frustrations and doubts that might have sidetracked her or at least created destructive resentments and bitterness. A second element of her hardiness is the trait optimism that has been so prominent, for example, in the experiences of Donald McNeil, Jim Pantelas, and Paul Allen (whom we will meet in an upcoming chapter).

What Heather Marini shows us is that purpose, operating in the context of confidence and optimism, can be proof against hypersensitivity to the insult and hostility that almost inevitably accompany institutionalized prejudice. Her experience stands in revealing contrast to the destructive consequences brought on when a sense of victimization and grievance predominates instead of the drive toward fulfillment and self-realization.

Jill Costello (center) pictured with her mother, Mary, (left) and her aunt.

# 8

# Mary and Jim Costello

"Everyone wants to believe their child is special," says Mary Costello. "Jim and I are no different there. But I'll tell you a story that typifies our daughter Jill's approach to life and to cancer that had become such a big part of it in that last year. For her radiation, a mold of her body was prepared for her to lie in to make sure she didn't move during treatments. When she finished her final treatment, she told the staff she wanted to take the mold with her.

"I said, 'Jill, why do you want that? I don't want to see or even think about it.'

"But she insisted that we put the mold in the car and take it with us in the drive back to the University of California at Berkeley. We parked in front of the sorority and her sisters went and got this stick with all these ribbons hanging from it. Then they turned the radiation mold into a piñata and just bashed the heck out of it, like she was going to do with cancer.

"'I'm going to take this and beat it to shit,' Jill said.

"That typified her attitude, and that's what her sorority sisters did to that body mold," Mary reflects. "Raising children, you worry about a lot of things. You worry about drunk driving and drugs and violence. But you never think your twenty-one-year-old, who never smoked, is going to be diagnosed with lung cancer."

On the occasion of *Sports Illustrated*'s sixtieth anniversary, the magazine selected its sixty greatest articles. One of these, which ran in the November 29, 2010, issue, was entitled "The Courage of Jill Costello."

"It started as a dull ache in Jill Costello's abdomen, the kind you get after a night of suspect Chinese food," the article began. "Only it didn't go away. It was June 2009, and the University of California, Berkeley crew had just returned from the NCAA championships in Cherry Hill, N.J. The Bears had finished second, behind Stanford, continuing a remarkable run of six top four finishes in seven years."

"They weren't looking for lung cancer," Mary recalls of the initial battery of tests Jill underwent. "They thought it might be orthopedic, a result of so much physical exertion. They thought the abdominal pain might be coming from cysts, or a small mass in her liver. When a body scan led to a biopsy that showed lung cancer, they couldn't believe what they were seeing."

Jill was about to begin something even more remarkable on a road that began with the devastating news that the pain in her abdomen was actually lung cancer that had spread to multiple parts of her body. The odds weren't good, and this story doesn't end with a Hollywood finish, either for the Cal Berkley woman's crew team or for Jill herself.

Or maybe it does.

"She squeezed a lifetime into her twenty-one years," her mother Mary picks up. "She affected, and continues to affect, so many people, putting a face on how lung cancer can strike an otherwise perfectly healthy young woman who never smoked. We took her to the emergency room on Father's Day in June of 2010. She was so sick, and she was in a lot of pain. I asked her what she hoped from this hospitalization.

"'A cure,' Jill told me.

"She still believed, she still fought," Mary continues, "but two days later she said she was done fighting and wasn't afraid. Jill was in control right to the end."

It was so oddly and ironically appropriate that Jill made her mark on the Cal rowing team in the crucial role of coxswain (pronounced "cox-in"), the person who's in charge of the boat from a seat in the very front facing the rowers. Setting the pace, controlling navigation and steering. The person running the show, just as Jill ran her own life.

"She was determined to succeed in everything she went into," Mary says, "and she never turned down a challenge. When Jill had chemotherapy, Jim, my sister Cathy, and I would all spend the whole day in the hospital with her. I can remember one time she brought a tote bag with her.

"'What's that for?' I asked her.

"'I'm going back to Berkeley once we're finished here.'

"'Is there something really important you need to get back to school for?'

"'Yes, my life.'"

"Lung cancer," Mary says, "was a part of her life, but she never let it define her."

Looking at Mary, it's not hard to figure where Jill got her attitude from, or her famous grin, even in the dimmest of times. The resemblance is clear, in the brightness of Mary's eyes and widening smile every time she mentions her daughter. Her expression flashes quiet reflection at times, but never sadness when conjuring memories of Jill. She left behind too much that was positive and good, so much of which has endured the years since her death. And since Jill never cried for herself, it's a safe bet she wouldn't want anyone crying for her now.

"She treated cancer like something else on her plate," Jill's father, Jim, adds, a teddy bear of a man who wears his gregariousness on his sleeve. "Something else she needed to deal with."

And that was, through the time of her treatment as well as before, a pretty crowded plate. Indeed, Jill had set three goals for herself, and nothing, including cancer, was going to change them: graduate from Cal Berkeley, serve as coxswain for the varsity boat, and win Nationals. She achieved the first two and came within mere inches of the third as well, the Bears finishing runner-up for the second year in a row.

Mary nods when we come to that. "They'd come so close, and all the girls were crying. They wanted to win so badly, for themselves, sure, but especially for Jill. But Jill was smiling, trying to cheer them up. Telling the girls there was nothing more they could have done, just as she had in her fight with cancer. They'd won the Pac-10 championship prior to Nationals, and that smile on Jill's face as she hoisted the trophy overhead…"

How she came to cox Cal's first boat that day is another testament to Jill's grit and determination, how she never let cancer beat her.

"Her first practice back was a Saturday morning in early March at Briones Reservoir, fifteen minutes from the Cal campus," that famed *Sports Illustrated* article relates. "The team began with a two-mile jog, from the boathouse to the reservoir entrance and back. Jill sat in the boathouse clutching a cup of tea and watched as, one mile out, her teammates began changing color. All fifty of them tore off their sweatshirts to reveal yellow T-shirts that read CAL CREW CANCER KILLERS. All doubts she had about her decision vanished in the cool morning air. After Jill's first practice the girls in her boat went up to [Coach] O'Neill. Jill, they told him, had been awesome. Not because she was courageous or because she had made it through practice. Rather, because she was now a better coxswain. And as the weeks went on, O'Neill realized the rowers were right. He likes to say that there are three types of coxswain: the motivator, always rah-rah; the drill sergeant, ever demanding peak performance; and the airline pilot, cool and collected. Her first three years, Jill was more of a motivator, but now she had become an airline pilot. Maybe it was the cancer, maybe it was maturity, maybe it was a combination of the two. No matter what happened—a missed stroke, a slow start—Jill did not change her tenor. It would all be O.K., she seemed to say."

It wasn't enough for her just to beat her own cancer; she wanted to beat cancer period, both Jim and Mary stress. Bonnie Addario, one of the foremost lung cancer advocates in the world and a survivor herself, remembers getting a call from Jill in December of 2009, six months after her diagnosis.

"I want to do a run," she said.

"That's great, Jill!" Bonnie said, thinking out loud that the coming summer would be the perfect time.

"It can't wait. We have to do it now."

That was Jill the drill sergeant, in other words. And, needless to say, the run happened, attracting nearly five thousand entrants on a foggy Sunday in February of 2010 and ended up raising more than $45,000. That made it one of the largest fundraisers for lung cancer ever at the time. It has served as the template for "Jogs for Jill," fundraisers that continue all over the country to this day in her memory and in pursuit of her most passionate cause. That's Jill still being Jill, in this case the rah-rah motivator.

Which brings another reflective glow to Mary's face. "Every time Jill was in the hospital overnight, I stayed with her. I didn't want her to be alone. The first morning, when I woke up she was watching something on her iPad. She smiled at me and said, 'Come here, get into bed with me. We'll watch this together.' At first, I thought how sweet that is. She really needs me. Then I realized she was comforting me, because she knew I was the one who needed it."

Jill, the airline pilot.

"I remember when Jill was maybe five years old. She was dancing and singing, really putting on a show and showing no signs it was going to end," Mary recalls. "So I told her, 'Jill, the show is over.' She stared at me and said, 'No, it's not!' For Jill, nothing was over until she said it was."

"She wanted to take Jogs for Jill international." K. C. Oakley, Jill's sorority sister, best friend, and fellow standout athlete smiles at that. "She had this quality of bossiness, but it was bossy because she knew what she wanted to get out of any situation. And she never said no to anything, always looking for new opportunities and was down for any adventure. She wasn't good at everything she did—don't get me started on her singing and dancing!—but she always tried. She was a doer, and she wanted to beat cancer not just for herself but for everyone. I'm getting married in a month, and my bridesmaids were the people who were there by her side right until the end. They weren't my best friends when Jill was diagnosed, but they became that because of who they proved themselves to be."

Her sorority sisters sponsor their own fundraising run, the proceeds going to someone who's faced some kind of adversity, not necessarily cancer, which was just the way Jill would have wanted it. Mary and Jim know firsthand that was the effect Jill had on people, leading by example.

"It would be a great consolation to Jill that her life led to helping other people," Mary says. "When she realized right at the end that she wasn't going to survive, she wrote in her journal, 'Did I make the world a better place? Yes, I did.' I think she always demanded the best of herself, challenged herself to be the best she could be. And because she was that way, she made the people around her want to be their best too. Anything else would have been disappointing to her, and second best didn't exist in her vocabulary.

"There's this huge mountain in Yosemite National Park called Half Dome, and it's a big thing to climb it. The crew team went there every year to climb to the top of Half Dome to build camaraderie. And for the first three years on the team, Jill had climbed Half Dome."

"Ran up it," Jim swiftly corrects.

"When you're on top you can see things you can't see from anywhere else, any other vantage point, just like Jill getting sick gave her a whole new perspective on cancer. 'I'm not afraid,' she'd always say, even though there was nothing more she could or that anybody could do. That final race, when Cal came in second in the Nationals, she knew they were winners because they'd done everything they could possibly do and just came up a little short in the end. Just like Jill did in her fight against cancer."

To the point where shortly before what was to be Jill's final race, the family made a pilgrimage to Lourdes in France, site of numerous purported miracles over the ages.

"It was an incredible experience," Mary recalls. "We went with the Knights of Malta, who sponsor sick people, twenty-five thousand from all over the world they refer to as *malads*. But the odds of getting to Lourdes were long at best. It's a huge process to be selected. You have to write letters, find sponsors from the religious and medical community. It's almost impossible, yet when the selection committee read Jill's letter it was unanimous. We went to Lourdes and would have loved to come home with a physical miracle, and in a way I suppose we did. No, we didn't come home with a physical cure; we came home with a feeling of peace. A strange feeling that left us believing that so many people are facing devastating challenges and they all have faith, looking for a miracle in whatever form that takes. We came home secure in the notion we were doing everything we could physically. Seeking out every doctor, every treatment, anything to keep Jill healthy. Sometimes, though, we have to realize it's out of our hands and in God's. It wasn't for us to determine Jill's fate."

In addition to that inner peace, Jill and her family came back with something else from Lourdes: a supply of the famed holy water that Jill swiftly dispensed to her teammates on the eve of the Nationals. If Lourdes couldn't deliver her wish to live, perhaps it could help deliver another one: for her beloved Bears to be crowned national champions.

It wasn't desperation that sent the Costellos to Lourdes, it was hope. Jill never lost hope until the very, very end, and that more than anything was responsible for her squeezing ten years of living into those final twelve months. You think about stage four lung cancer patients and maybe the first thing that comes to mind is how desperate they must be. Not Jill. Hope and faith proved to be the best medicine for her, even as the others had stopped working.

She spoke at Genentech, the cancer research firm that continues to develop drugs aimed at making lung cancer a manageable disease. She was interviewed on NPR as the voice of nonsmoking lung cancer sufferers. She became the national face of eradicating the stigma that only smokers contract the disease.

Mary smiles, part sadly and part reflectively. "We still go every year when Cal takes on Stanford in the penultimate race of the season. People, total strangers, come up to us and they all know Jill's story and it's influenced them so much beyond cancer. Everyone's going to have some challenge in their life, cancer or something else. Don't let that challenge consume you and become your life. Face it and go on with what's really important to you.

"That first race we went to after Jill passed," she reflects softly, after a pause, "both teams whipped off their warm-up tops to reveal matching T-shirts that read BEAT LUNG CANCER. Having the shirts say that was more important than putting her name on it, because that was her goal. Maybe not for herself, but for somebody else."

Somebody like her own mother. Since Jill's passing, Mary has been treated twice for cancer, first uterine and then breast, in 2016.

"Just thinking of her, knowing she was there with me, helped me so much when I was going through chemo and radiation, reminding me that cancer wasn't my life, just a part of my life. I never felt overwhelmed. That helped me immensely as an adult suffering from cancer, never mind a younger person. I was going to enjoy the future in a way Jill never got to experience."

As was the case for her daughter, cancer only rented space in her body; it never took ownership any more than it did for Jill right up until the end. Call that Jill the motivator again, or perhaps Jill the airline pilot, maybe even Jill the drill sergeant.

"In June of 2010, Jill was graduating college and, I have to say, that after a year of cancer, all the chemo and everything that goes with that, all the emotions, I wasn't in a party mood. But Jill wanted to have a party, and I have to think my daughter has taught me so much because she taught me what you need to celebrate, you always need to celebrate, whether there's cancer in the picture or not."

"Life is happening now," Jim adds.

"Do what you have to," Mary picks up. "Not tomorrow or a week from now, but today."

~ ~ ~

## Reflections

"The death of a child is considered the single worst stressor a person can go through," says Deborah Carr, chair of the Sociology Department at Boston University, an expert in family responses to the death of a loved one.

Most parents who have lost children can attest to that. That kind of loss may well have lasting psychological and other health effects. Even as time dampens the shock and sadness, the grief over such an event never entirely disappears.

Mary and Jim Costello's response to their daughter Jill's death seems to have taken a different path. There is no doubt they experienced profound grief when their daughter died, but their ability to process her death reveals two factors in the resilience dynamic whose power is sometimes underestimated. There is a celebrative tone in their memories that may be fairly common when we consider the passing of individuals who have lived full and accomplished lives but is much rarer when we think of those who have died young, with their lives still in front of them. That is especially so for parents, for whom the loss is all the more grievous as hopes, aspirations, and love are so unfairly crushed.

Tracing the sources of Mary and Jim Costello's strength in coping with the loss of their daughter, two factors stand out. One is acceptance. They did everything in their power to see that Jill had the best available medical treatment. Then, as people of faith, they visited Lourdes, the Catholic pilgrimage site where many believers have experienced apparently miraculous remissions and cures. Jill's cancer was not cured, but the experience left Mary and Jim with a sense of calm that they did not have previously. They came home secure that they were doing everything they could, but that in the end Jill's fate was not something they could influence further. The outcome, as they put it, "was in God's hands."

Acceptance, and the equanimity that comes with it, is a powerful coping mechanism when people are in extremis, when overcoming is no longer a possibility. Discussions of resilience most often attempt to describe the factors that help us surmount adversity. But what keeps us together as human beings with agency and dignity when recovery is no longer possible? Acceptance is the prerequisite to that end. It was a factor in the Costellos' ability to face Jill's terminal disease and then to accommodate themselves to her passing.

Acceptance is a way of absorbing the shock of loss. But the Costellos' resilience in the face of their loss went far beyond acceptance. What was the driving force behind that?

Pride in children's accomplishments is universal for parents. The Costellos' pride in the way Jill faced her situation and the influence she exerted on her friends is the leading theme in this interview. Jill Costello's character shines through in both her parents' and her friends' descriptions of her. She was a fighter, a leader, a caring, charismatic personality who was a role model for those who knew her.

Role models, we know, can play a galvanizing role in the lives of those they touch. What is so unusual here is that Jill was not just a role model for her friends; she became a role model for her parents as well. Under ordinary circumstances children inherit from their parents. For the Costellos, those roles were reversed. The parents inherited inspiration and ultimate values from their child. Jill's life demonstrated how a person is capable of maintaining control until the end, asserting the positive value of life even when life draws toward a close. Celebration is an expression of that same affirmation. "My daughter taught me what you need to celebrate, you always need to celebrate," Mary said, "whether there's cancer in the picture or not." The ability to affirm life in the face of suffering and even bereavement may well be the foundational pillar that underlies all the various pathways to resilience we are tracing in the lives of our interviewees.

# 9

# Tom Catena

The Antonov An-26 approaches the Nuba Mountains in Sudan with a whine that swiftly builds into a roar. A speck that is the cargo plane turned retrofitted bomber by the Sudanese Air Force quickly grows into a metallic sheen speeding across the horizon, sending Nuba schoolchildren scurrying from their lessons into foxholes in which they spend this terror-inspired version of recess. Crude barrel bombs dumped from the plane's belly lay waste to the nearby landscape, coughing up huge plumes of dust, smoke, and flames, the ground left burning and scarred.

When the smoke finally clears, adults rush the children wounded by debris and stray shrapnel to nearby Mother of Mercy Hospital, where Dr. Tom Catena stands ready to receive them. Watching him and his small staff swing into action makes you think of what you might see at Mass General or Mount Sinai hospitals, even an episode of the old TV hit *ER*. But this is not Boston or New York. It's the

Nuba Mountains, where Dr. Tom is the only doctor for four hundred square miles.

"How he came, I don't know," Bishop Macram Max Gassis, Bishop Emeritus from the Diocese of El-Obeid, told filmmaker Ken Carlson in his brilliant documentary *The Heart of Nuba*. "From where he came, I don't know. We call it a miracle."

"The lives here matter as much as any in the world," Dr. Tom says a few scenes later. "Everybody's life is valuable, and we can't lose sight of that or lose our humanity."

After another long day at Mother of Mercy, he walks by flashlight from the hospital through a corrugated steel door that brings him to a small chapel lit by candles, where he will pray for his patients, the natives who've become his people, and maybe even himself, asking God for the strength he needs to keep doing what he's been doing for over a decade now, selflessly serving a population that relies on him for their very lives.

For that decade-plus, the man known affectionately as "Dr. Tom" to the tribes who call the Nuba Mountains home has been on call twenty-four hours a day to serve the near million civilians who have been mired in civil war for years. Patients have been known to walk for up to seven days to receive treatment for injuries from bombing attacks and ailments varying from bone fractures to malnourishment, cancer, malaria, and, of course, wounds suffered from the dreaded Antonovs or the even more fearsome Soviet fighter jets that flash across the sky at supersonic speed. It's estimated that during the war, Dr. Tom treated five hundred patients per day and performed more than one thousand operations each year. Always at the risk of his life and never even considering abandoning his post as the only physician in the entire war-torn region. Keeping track of the war wounded in a handwritten ledger instead of a sophisticated computer database. At the time of *The Heart of Nuba*'s completion in 2016, the number of war wounded had reached 2,176.

"There have been innumerable occasions when fifty to eighty wounded would come to our hospital after a battle. Being the sole surgeon at the hospital, I am responsible for each one of these casualties. Sometimes we're up all night operating on the wounded, and we know there is no other option. We keep working until all of the wounded are treated. Giving up is not an option."

Dr. Tom does it all without microsurgery, laparoscopes, or CT scan machines under a single overhead light that has to be adjusted constantly through the course of each operation. The hallway lined with cots passes for a recovery room. There's no ICU because the entire hospital is effectively an intensive care unit.

"This place is like home to me," he tells Carlson. "There's hope in this place and these people. That's why these lives matter as much as any in the world."

The devastation that Dr. Tom has born witness to came at the hands of the nation's now deposed dictator, Omar Hassan Ahmad al-Bashir. Al-Bashir cared nothing for the people of the Nuba Mountains; he wanted them dead or gone in order to exploit the land for its vast mineral wealth. His bombs scorched the earth of the fertile mountain lands, the villages and crops left smoldering, as the char-riddled, shell-shocked residents fled to caves to enjoy a lifestyle that barely qualifies as primitive. Which suited al-Bashir just fine, since it was their abandoned land he was after.

Dr. Tom, in blue scrubs draped over his thin frame, looks at Ken Carlson's camera with the same compassion with which he greets his patients. "I know if I left, people would die. If I left, I'd be saying that my life was more important than other people's lives, but that's not true. I don't believe it. I had to stay."

When the war started in June of 2011, all of the hospital's meager security personnel fled, along with the rest of the ex-pats staffing Mother of Mercy, leaving only Dr. Tom and two other staff members. That left him the additional role of training locals to replace them, an arduous task made possible only by the Nuba people's pride, work ethic, and refusal to be driven from their land.

"Even the healthy would come to us for refuge, starving after walking for days," he says into the camera, the interview resuming after a delay caused by one of the dreaded Russian Antonovs buzzing the skies overhead like an iron dinosaur. "But they didn't ask for food. They asked to work in exchange for it. That's how our foxholes ended up getting dug."

And what does he think about the lofty praise he's justifiably garnered for his work, which includes being named the Aurora Prize Laureate "for rekindling faith in humanity"?

"Like many people, I'm a bit shy when praise is directed my way—sure it feels good but never fully comfortable. I hope that these kind words can be turned into tangible results and that others can perhaps follow our example and lead lives of service."

Dr. Tom (or "Catman" to the Brown University football team during his playing days in the 1980s) was one of 550 nominations submitted from sixty-six countries. The Aurora Prize brought with it a grant of $1,000,000 that Dr. Tom apportioned equally among three different charities that support bringing modern-day medicine to the Third World.

"Dr. Catena embodies the spirit of the Aurora Prize, and we extend our deepest gratitude to him and the people and organizations around the world that support and inspire him to continue his noble work despite immensely challenging conditions," says Ruben Vardanyan, cofounder of the Aurora Humanitarian Initiative and United World College at Dilijan. "We are honored to share his story with the world to shed light on the goodwill that exists in the world so that helping others becomes part of our global culture."

"We all have an obligation to look after our brothers and sisters," Dr. Tom says of his experiences today. "It is possible that every single person can make a contribution, and to recognize that shared humanity can lead to a brighter future. With my faith as my guide, I am honored to continue to serve the world and make it a better place."

Of his work in the Sudan, no less a source than Nicholas Kristof wrote for the *New York Times* on June 13, 2015, that, "He does all this off the electrical grid, without running water, a telephone or so much as an X-ray machine—while under constant threat of bombing. . . . The first time Dr. Tom sheltered, terrified, in a newly dug pit for an outhouse, but the hospital is now surrounded by foxholes in which patients and the staff crouch when military aircraft approach."

"We're in a place where the government is not trying to help us," Catena told Kristof when the reporter visited a region the rest of the world has forgotten. "It's trying to kill us."

And there's no one to help, given that the United Nations and organizations that have strived to provide support were long banned from supplying vaccines and provisions. Dr. Tom, you might say, is on an island in the middle of the mountains.

Before he became Dr. Tom and was still Catman, he made All-Ivy and was an Honorable Mention All-American his senior season at Brown University in 1985, while being named a Rhodes Scholar candidate.

"We had a very strong defensive line in those days," recalls Walt Cataldo, a two-time All-Ivy, All-ECAC at safety who played with Catena for two years. "But Tom was a key cog and, as nose guard, everything revolved around him. He wasn't a big rah-rah guy, but he showed up for every practice and every game and never took a play off. He was very humble, very focused, and came ready to play all the time. He was never after the limelight, content to handle all the ugly assignments so us linebackers and safeties could make the tackles. I remember him in the trenches, covered in mud, somebody comfortable with doing the dirty work, getting down and dirty. And he was also a great human being. He treated us very well as underclassmen. Took us under his wing and embraced us, made us feel part of the team. Tommy never had one ounce of 'What's it in for me?' in him. That's what I remember most about Catman."

After graduating Brown, Catena decided to forego the executive position at General Electric he'd been offered thanks to his Brown University engineering degree to pursue a career in medicine and enrolled at the Duke University School of Medicine on a US Navy scholarship. He entered the United States Navy in 1992, becoming a naval flight surgeon. After fulfilling his five-year Navy obligation, he completed a residency in family medicine and during his residency began his medical foray into the developing world with mission trips to Guyana and Honduras before spending six years in Nairobi and then moving on to the Sudan.

Trained in family medicine, Dr. Tom learned surgery on the job, and on the fly, while in Kenya. He gleaned from books what practiced surgeons spent years mastering, learning new things from scratch every day he was on the job, which was pretty much every day period.

"You can't know everything," he reflects, "but you can learn a lot."

The Aurora Prize is only the most recent accolade acknowledging Tom Catena's incredible contribution to humanity. In 2013, Brown University awarded him the William Rogers Award, given to a Brown graduate who exemplifies the university's mission to prepare alumni for lives of "usefulness and reputation." He was named one of twelve "Catholic Heroes for America and the World" by *Catholic Digest* in 2010. The National Football Foundation gave Dr. Tom its highest honor, the Gold Medal Award, in 2014 in recognition of building onto his stellar performance on the football field an exceptional contribution to humanity. And *Time* magazine named him one of its most influential people of 2015.

"Tom Catena symbolizes everything that our organization represents," NFF president and CEO Steve Hatchell said at the time. "He was a powerhouse as a football player who distinguished himself as an exceptional leader at Brown. He took those same skills and turned himself into a doctor, helping the less fortunate in the war-torn region of the Sudan. Many of us dream of making the world a better place. Tom Catena has given up all his earthly possessions to do that every day of his life. He is off the charts in making the world a better place."

"A truly remarkable individual, Tom Catena stands as an inspiration to us all," adds NFF chairman Archie Manning, who would be given the foundation's Gold Medal Award himself two years later, "having created a powerful path for making a difference in one of the bleakest places on earth. His role in the Sudan in providing medical care has become so critical that it has taken us more than a year to arrange to bring him back for the event, and this December marks the first Christmas in thirteen years that he will be able to spend with his family in America."

Corry Chapman witnessed the work of this modern-day Albert Schweitzer up close and personal when he worked by Dr. Tom's side for a time in the Sudan, an experience he brilliantly recounted in an award-winning 2008 article entitled "Always on Call" for *The Lancet*, England's premier medical journal.

"Those first months took a toll on Catena," he writes. "He got malaria twice. He dropped fifty pounds. He never left the compound. Surgical emergencies arrived daily, often nightly. Catena worked in an isolated region with no cities or government and no other doctors nearby. He managed a hospital that relied on solar power, pumped water, and pit latrines, its small storehouse of supplies replenished only twice a year by cargo plane from Nairobi. Everything was limited, nothing could be wasted. Catena stretched his drugs, sutures, and physical energy as far as they could go to treat overwhelming need. It nearly broke him, but the effort paid off."

Chapman writes profoundly of the incredible obstacles Dr. Tom had to overcome in being the only doctor for four hundred square miles.

"I worked with Catena for five weeks at Mother of Mercy Hospital in Sudan, in the remote Nuba Mountains, a wilderness reachable only by UN planes delivering food. It is an eighty-bed Catholic hospital that serves a population battered by fifty years of civil war. It is also the only surgical hospital in central Sudan. Mother of Mercy opened in March 2008 with a permanent physician staff of one: Catena. He is the hospital's medical director and the only one who applied for the job. He arrived on site a week before the hospital opened.

"On my first day there I saw one patient with leprosy, two with tuberculosis, and fifty with malaria. We removed a man's prostate because he could not urinate. We admitted a baby with meningitis, the top of her head bulging and tense. Over the next few weeks, I saw diseases that I see in the USA: diabetes, hypertension, stroke. I also saw bowel parasites, pus-filled eyeballs, starvation, and goat feces poked up a girl's nose to stop a nosebleed (a local remedy). We operated a lot: an emergency caesarean section when we delivered a premature baby and strapped him between his mother's breasts to keep him warm and alive, ruptured ectopic pregnancies, many urological operations, some bowel surgery, a thyroid operation. We amputated legs and fingers. Sometimes during an operation a fly would settle on exposed bowel or muscle. The anesthesia technician had to chase it around the room, trying to kill it."

"People in the Nuba Mountains will never forget his name," Lt. Col. Aburass Albino Kuku of the rebel military force told Nicholas Kristof for that June 13, 2015, *New York Times* article. "People are praying that he never dies."

Even Dr. Tom knows he can't do this forever, though.

"What happens when I get too old?" he wonders out loud. "What I have to offer is my medical knowledge and skills which have been honed over the past twenty-five years. I do believe that I have an obligation to pass on this knowledge to our Nuba staff. We are sponsoring two local Nuba men for medical school and several others in medical-related fields. I plan to continue training them when they return to the Nuba Mountains until they are prepared to take over the reins of the hospital. The work I'm doing here needs to live on."

Toward that end, his goal is to ultimately get Mother of Mercy run from top to bottom by the Nuba people themselves, both doctors and nurses. Physicians like Corry Chapman stand in occasionally, but the pace and pressure is too much to bear after a month, much less a year. Never mind the more than twelve years Dr. Tom has spent here.

"We are continuing to send our on-the-job trained staff out to receive professional training," Dr. Tom says. "Thus far, we have sent over twenty nurses, eight clinical officers [like physician assistants], four laboratory technicians, and two pharmacists to professional schools in South Sudan, Uganda, and Kenya. We currently have six in nursing school, four in medical school, and one in an MBA program. We have one of our clinical officers in an ophthalmology program in Tanzania, where he is learning how to do cataract surgery. We are planning to have the medical doctors work with us for a couple of years and then send them off again for specialty training, most likely in surgery, internal medicine, and obstetrics/gynecology. These staff members will form the backbone of the hospital and clinics for many years to come. To address the greater shortage of health workers in the Nuba Mountains, we are planning to start a school to train nurses, midwives, and clinical officers. We hope to train a total of ninety health personnel over a five-year period."

He stops and then starts again, his gaze drifting dreamily toward a future that is clear in his vision.

"My goal is to see the Mother of Mercy Hospital become a major referral and teaching hospital for all of Sudan and for the top doctors and nurses in the region to be from Nuba. The Nuba have suffered oppression, marginalization, and discrimination at the hands of the Arab elite in the north for centuries, and this has been perhaps the main root cause of civil war. Killing enough 'Arabs' will never correct this attitude or solve the problem, but it would be hard for the elite of the north to look down on someone who is treating their medical condition with competence and integrity. I don't mean to simplify a complicated and long struggle, but this could be one element which in a way will compel people to respect the Nuba."

Nuba is even more home to him now since he married Nassima in 2016, one of the Nuba women who went to nursing school. Dr. Tom decided to propose while they were apart from each other, connected only by video chats on a tablet little bigger than an iPhone Plus.

"He's got nothing, but he's got everything," Tom's father, Gene, reflected in Ken Carlson's superb film.

The wedding was conducted by Tom's brother, a Catholic priest who made the trip across the world to preside.

"It was a big day, attended by five to ten thousand people," Dr. Tom remembers. "We had to move the wedding date one day back as we feared the Khartoum government had heard about the wedding and would come to bomb the celebration. An antiaircraft gun was parked nearby just in case, but things went off without a hitch. My life has changed dramatically since our wedding day—all, of course, for the better. The days here are long and very stressful with many frustrations and challenges. During my single days, there was really no one to talk to about these daily problems, and I would just stay at the hospital until late with no reason to go back to my solitary room. Now there's someone to share both the good and bad of the day, and I can look forward to some company in the evening. My wife is very good at calling me out when she sees me getting irritated. She'll quietly pull me aside and tell me that I have to keep calm for the sake of the patients and staff. She says that my happiness is very important for the well-being of the patients and conversely, my bad moods had a negative impact on their recovery."

And there are many days when Dr. Tom has every right to be in a bad mood.

"In late November 2017, we got word that the donors who normally provided the money for staff salaries would be withdrawing their support in 2018. Bear in mind that we have two hundred and thirty-two employees and 2018 was just around the corner. We had five weeks to figure out how we would get roughly twenty-seven thousand dollars per month to pay the staff. Closing the hospital was not an option, as there are simply no places to refer the patients. We had to stay open. Anyway, we felt that we had to reduce the staff salaries by a small amount in order to make payroll every month, and in the end we just reduced the salaries of the fifteen highest wage earners by fifteen percent."

What followed was the most difficult stretch in Dr. Tom's long, selfless tenure in the Nuba Mountains.

"As you can imagine, the announcement did not go over very well, and the staff turned against me and made it very difficult to get any work done. It was the most difficult five months of my life, even including the times of heavy fighting when we didn't know if we'd survive from one day to the next. For the first time since coming to Nuba, I felt like leaving and going somewhere else. In the end, my wife and I decided we had to stay and ride the storm out because so many depended on us. If we had left, many innocent staff and patients would suffer and we felt that as missionaries, it was our duty to stick it out and do the right thing. As Christians, we are obliged to forgive even those who have wounded us deeply."

As of this writing, a ceasefire has been signed and for the first time in over thirty years, according to Dr. Tom, "there is some hope for a solid peace. Still lots of baggage and many obstacles, but at least some light in the usual darkness."

Like the light Dr. Tom has been providing for the people of Nuba for more than a dozen years. Given the number of wounds and innumerable other ailments he's treated, a Muslim paramount chief named Hussein Nalukuri Cuppi summed up his feelings to Nicholas Kristof this way.

"He's Jesus Christ," Cuppi said.

The chief elaborated to Kristof that "Jesus healed the sick, made the blind see, and helped the lame walk."

Pretty much another day at the office for Dr. Tom Catena.

~ ~ ~

## Reflections

Benjamin Mays was the charismatic president of Morehouse College from 1940 to 1965, the man Martin Luther King called his "spiritual mentor." In his once-a-week talks to the Morehouse students, Mays conveyed the moral force of his convictions. "Every man and woman," he told them, "is born into this world to do something unique. What is it that *you* were born to do?"

Some of us do find what we were born to do. Others, not many, seem to be born knowing. Tom Catena almost certainly falls into the latter category. Mays was talking about a vocation, a calling. He didn't mean necessarily a moral or spiritual calling—he meant any calling, to be a musician or a furniture maker, an engineer, a doctor—any endeavor that brings together one's particular talents and passions. Catena's uniqueness isn't in being a physician, as good a physician as he is. His uniqueness is that he is a humanitarian. He is a personality that embodies humanitarianism. "You care about the other person," as he so simply puts it.

It is that motive—to "care about the other person"—that has given him the toughness to bear up under the years of devastation and cruelty that have immersed him and the hundreds of thousands of people who have been in his care. When his burdens seem intolerable and he feels overwhelmed, he tells himself, "Just do your job." That is the core of his resilience. The "job" is who he is.

In this interview we see other elements of resilience at work. He has goals: he wants to turn his threadbare hospital into a teaching and referral medical center. He wants to send his helpers for professional training as nurses, technicians, and doctors. One way he copes with the present is by focusing part of his attention on the future, not on what he is doing, but on what he needs to do.

Faith also plays a large role in his resilience. Catena, a practicing Catholic, draws strength from prayer. His faith guides him, he says.

"We all have a spark of God in us," he once told an interviewer. "We share a common humanity." Faith can play such different rolls in the lives of people. For Catena, it reaffirms and reinforces his belief in the value of every life. "We are all," he says, "brothers and sisters."

In this book we are looking at the factors that enable individuals to overcome traumatic ordeals. Catena's life offers an array of elements that bear reflection in that regard. But it's not those elements of his own character that are most relevant when we reflect on his life; it is the effect Catena has on those who find out about him in one way or another, those who know him or those who read about him. He is one of those extraordinarily rare individuals whose very presence attests that human beings are capable of both immeasurable good and unbreakable toughness. Individuals such as Mahatma Gandhi, Martin Luther King, Albert Schweitzer, and Nelson Mandela. They refresh our spirit, and in doing so they enhance our own fortitude and will to overcome the great adversities we can all expect to encounter in the course of our lives.

# 10

# Krystal Cantu

*I remember the tires popping. I remember my arm flying out the window. When I pulled it back in…*

Krystal Cantu is describing her blurred memory of the 2013 car accident when she was twenty-three that changed her life forever amid the shattered glass showering her. Her arm was hanging out the window, and neither she nor her boyfriend, Daniel, realized the extent of the damage until he came around to the passenger side to help her out.

*"That was rough, wasn't it?"* Krystal wrote in a letter to herself the day after her arm was amputated above the elbow. *"I know you probably won't believe this right now, but you were prepped your entire life for yesterday. Yesterday was supposed to happen to you. It was planned all along, you just never knew it. Nobody knew it, except for the big guy upstairs. Today is not the start of a new life, but better yet, a new chapter in your life."*

That wasn't just lip service either, or someone forcing a positive spin on an indescribable tragedy. Krystal not only meant it, she lived it in her relentless desire to get back to the CrossFit training that had become her passion.

"I come from a big Hispanic family, and the thing that brought me the most strength in addition to my family was fitness. It gave me back the confidence I lost that day. My first thought was I didn't know how I was going to do CrossFit anymore. My next thought was I had to. And it came to me so easily because I wanted it so bad, because I wanted to be normal again. I was willing to do anything it took to be good at something again. And when I saw I could do it with one arm, I went from good to great."

So fervent was her intent to get back to the gym that Krystal spent only three days in the hospital, including the day of her amputation. She was back working out at CrossFit a month later and entered a competition three months to the day after her accident. Today there are pictures and videos of Krystal hoisting a barbell overhead in what's known in lifting vernacular as a clean and jerk—not an easy move with two arms, never mind one.

"Dealing with the loss of my arm and getting back to the gym was the easiest thing I've ever done in my life. I was that determined. My whole family came up from the Rio Grande Valley in a caravan of cars, and they were with me in the hospital right from the start. They're my glue. They're what makes me who I am. I don't ever want to show them weakness. I got out of bed the day of my amputation. The surgeon came into my room to check on me and couldn't believe it. 'What are you doing?' he asked me. 'I wanted to get out of bed,' I told him. Then he asked me if I'd speak with another patient who wasn't doing as well after her amputation."

That ended up being the first of many she's interacted with since. A coworker coined the phrase KRYSTAL STRONG, and Krystal herself took it from there, using the phrase as a hashtag and a motivator, backed up by a pair of flags emblazoned with what has become her motto hanging in whatever gym she's working out in.

"I made the phrase my own, used it for my own mental health to remind me I could still make something of myself. I could get through this and be better, not just as good as I was before. Every time I look at one of those flags, it was a reminder to put excuses aside and get to work."

She did that and more, never missing a beat at the grueling, bone-crunching workouts that had already defined her but in the wake of the accident filled her with a purpose and resolve rare for an athlete of any level. Krystal had something to prove and she was determined to do it, perhaps in the Paralympics, throwing the javelin.

"I never felt any regret, I never felt bad for myself. I just wanted to get back to the gym. I always tell people that physical strength is an offshoot of mental strength. You need to be mentally strong, first and foremost. Physical strength is an added bonus. The main priority is your mental health and how you're able to exercise your brain. Train your mind in a specific way and you'll be able to train your body in a specific way. I wasn't scared after the accident because I was too focused on getting back. I had a goal and as long as I stayed focused, I never felt anxious or scared. Never fixated on what I'd lost and focused on what I still had, still could do, instead.

"And that's strange because I'm a very anxious person, a very fearful person, by nature. Put me on an airplane and I'm shaking and crying because I'm terrified of flying. I'm claustrophobic. I had to have an MRI done on my neck, and they needed to fit this cage-like helmet over my head to keep me from moving it. I didn't last even five minutes. What got me through this, and what got me to where I am today, is a no-excuses attitude. I can fail and fail and fail because in the end I know I'm going to succeed, as long as I do the work. That's why I believe this accident was always meant to happen. Something was preparing me for it, getting me ready, instilling in me what I needed. That's why I was able to take it so much in stride.

"As the years have gone by, I've realized this happened to me for a reason; everything happens for a reason. At a certain point, you stop believing in coincidence. Everything happens for a reason, and this happened to me because I need to help other people, mostly via social media, a great outlet to reach people on a global level. I always ask them how bad they want something because if you don't want it badly, it's not going to happen. 'I told you what you had to do. When you want it bad enough, when you're ready, come back and see me.' I have a no-bullshit attitude because I know from my own experience that if someone is willing to work hard enough, they eventually can and will get where they want to go. At the end of the day, I know that to be the truth, and I know how the world works."

But the world wasn't done with Krystal yet. The added pressure of hoisting all that weight on her spine, with only a single arm to manage the required leverage, led to a herniated disk in her back in 2015.

"I couldn't walk, couldn't go the bathroom on my own, couldn't get in or out of bed on my own. It was horrible, horrible, horrible. I was out of training, out of competing. It took months for me to be able to stand up straight again. Because I'd set my mind on needing to be great, I started having panic attacks as I was lying in bed doing nothing. I was freaking out. I didn't know what to do with myself. In my mind, I was a failure.

"Since I wasn't training, my boyfriend Daniel and I thought this might be the perfect time to have a baby, something we'd been talking about for a long time. I wanted a baby and I wanted to be happy again. So I got pregnant and felt thirty times worse—not because of the pregnancy, but the anxiety I was feeling. I wasn't going to let that beat me down either; I had to conquer it. I did everything I could to get better, get back to where I was before, to manage the anxiety that was trying to control my life. Now that I was pregnant, I especially wanted to manage that without medication. I needed to train my mind, retrain my mind actually."

Finally, two weeks before her son Joaquin was born, the anxiety that had been roiling Krystal lifted, like a cloud passing to let the sun shine in. Then came something else.

"I gained all this weight after my son was born. I listened to people who said eat whatever you want, you're a new mom, it's okay. That was not okay for me, not what I should have been doing. I'd let the mentality of being a new mom get the better of me too much. But there was no time for excuses anymore. I knew myself well enough to know that not being active and overeating wasn't going to make me happy, and I knew exactly what I had to do. It was no time for excuses anymore. This was just something else I had to overcome. So I lost all that baby weight and more. I got into the best shape of my life."

Krystal dramatically altered her workouts in the gym. Gone were the superheavy weights and herky-jerky weightlifting movements difficult for an athlete with two arms, never mind one. Dumbbells and kettle bells replaced straight bars that bent at the tips from all the weight loaded on them. Krystal began doing more resistance training with bands, more reps to replace the lost weight, focusing on her form and technique.

"Becoming a mother was a huge, huge change in my life. It humbled me to the fullest and showed me the full meaning of life. Before Joaquin came, it was all about proving myself and my worth to the world by being the best CrossFit athlete anywhere. Putting my body through hell over and over again. Lifting weight with one arm most people couldn't lift with two. That took its toll. Even after Joaquin was born and I lost all that weight, I went right back to what I'd been doing before. I figured I'd recovered from every injury I'd suffered before and got right back at it. But then I couldn't get out of bed when I heard him crying over the baby monitor, couldn't go to him, couldn't lift him out of the crib.

"*When are you ever going to be enough?* I asked myself. *When are you going to be okay with who you are and where you're at?*

"That did the trick. I realized I had nothing to prove anymore. I started training for the long run, not for the moment. Suddenly, I could pick up Joaquin without feeling like I was going to break. And the amazing thing is that I'm in better shape now than I was when I was lifting all that weight. It's about being careful and being smart. I never would have seen that if it wasn't for having a child. That washed away the need to prove myself to anyone but myself. I wanted to be healthy. I wanted to be me. And it took a little kid to get me to that place."

It goes deeper than that, almost like Krystal was displacing into the future all the anxiety and pressure she'd avoided upon losing her arm. So when injuries and weight gain struck and threatened to derail the goals that had become *everything* for her, all the stress and tension that had bottled up inside her since the day of the accident spilled over. Imagine holding your breath for three years; essentially, that was what Krystal was doing until she let all the breath out at once. And now that she's done that, she can approach her goals with a new attitude.

"It's always been when I have my mind set on something, nothing's going to get in my way. Setting goals motivates you, inspires you. And I still have the same goals; I'm just working toward them in a different way. The most important goal in life is getting to the place of knowing what you want.

"I tell other amputees who reach out to me that you have to find it within yourself to get up and continue living your life. Go for your goals; don't let what happened stop you, don't let *anything* stop you. I had no idea I was going to lose my arm. But I had to keep going for the same goal I'd set before that. You have to stay strong and mentally positive. You're going to break down physically if you're not okay mentally."

*"This chapter doesn't consist of rainbows and butterflies, but when has your life ever been about those things?"* Krystal posed in that letter to herself the day after her amputation. *"This chapter, instead, consists of strength and resilience. You just lost your dominant arm, and now it's time to learn everything with your left. Things won't come easy for you, but that's okay. You were born into a life where nothing ever came easy for you. You worked hard to accomplish everything in your life and the same thing will happen now. You will work your ass off to become independent with one arm."*

What else does she tell those who reach out to her for help?

"The first thing I do is start with a question: What do you want in this life? What do you want more than anything? If I'm going to help you, I need to know what you want and, more important, you need to know what you want. When you find what you want out of your life, that's your goal, and you need to do whatever it takes to reach that goal. Sure, you're going to fail. But failure is just practice to help you get where you want to be. If you want something bad enough, you'll get there just like I did. What's your purpose? What's the reason you're here? That hasn't changed because something bad happened to you.

"But just because something worked for me doesn't mean it'll work for someone else. Everyone is different in the way they need to do things. I help them more with the what than the how. They need to know who they are as individuals. I tell them you need to find out what works for you first. You need to know *you*, need to know who you are. I succeeded because I didn't listen to people who told me what to do, like stop doing CrossFit, stop lifting heavy weights with your only good shoulder. People kept telling me what I should be doing, but everyone needs to learn that on their own. Some amputees I work with try to imitate the way I do a dead lift, but their amputation is different from mine, so what works for me may not work for them. What you can do and what I can do aren't the same, and my success doesn't equate to your success, but you're going to succeed, too, in your own way."

Krystal has never used or tried a prosthetic. Faced with a choice of an extension of her arm that ended in a hook and a strictly cosmetic limb, she decided against either. A high-tech, state-of-the-art prosthesis wasn't covered by insurance and didn't seem to make a lot of sense in her case.

"If it's not something that's going to help me, I don't want it. Is it going to help me do CrossFit? No. Help me do lifts and other exercises? No. So I never got fitted for one."

During her brief stay in the hospital, no one could believe Krystal was doing so well. Her doctors never even recommended physical therapy.

"My surgeon and everyone else were blown away, to which my response was, isn't that the way it's supposed to be?"

Krystal has been writing a blog and, more recently, started a podcast aimed at helping others going through the kind of adversity she's overcome, or any adversity for that matter. She recently took the next step in her outreach by speaking to a group of middle school girls, an experience she wrote about in a blog post called "How I Empowered Young Women."

"I'd gotten an opportunity to host an Own Your Power event, sponsored by Athleta Fitness, for a group of young women. My initial idea was to make this an intimate and fun gathering with a group of friends and their daughters, but then I thought, let's really go above and beyond for this. So I reached out to one of my best friends, whose husband is a principal at a local middle school, and ran my idea by her. I confirmed the school, event date and time, and a total of fourteen girls. I still wanted to keep this a very intimate setting with a group of eighth-grade girls who the school felt needed this the most."

The results exceeded Krystal's expectations, not that she knew what to expect at all.

"I did a couple exercises with them. First, I asked them to write down the one thing that's been hurting them internally that someone had said to them and promised that they'd never be read out loud. I told them I wanted it gone from this world. Put it down on a piece of paper to get it out of you. I put them in a box and brought them home. Daniel warned me I was going to regret reading them, that it was going to be bad. I told him I needed to know how bad. But I couldn't believe how nasty these quotes were, and a bunch of them were said by parents! I was blown away by the things these girls had written down, taken aback and really saddened by the things that I read.

"But I also did a more positive exercise. I asked them to write down proper words of affirmation. 'I am great, I am successful, I am loved'—examples like that. The girls left that day with a story in mind, something positive in mind; that's what I wanted them to take away. And I also wanted them to take away the fact that looks aren't everything, because a girl with one arm had gone out and done all these things. And she has a kid. She did all that with one arm and she's confident in herself. That means something to girls like that. In their eyes you're not perfect, you don't look perfect, but you seem perfect to them."

At least as close to perfect as possible, something Krystal knows all too well.

"I need to win, which for me is now becoming the best version of myself I can be. I get off the path at times, but I always get back on. It's been quite a ride."

~ ~ ~

## Reflections

CrossFit, the physical competition Krystal Cantu was addicted to, may not be on everyone's radar screen. It consists of a series of exercises including weight lifting, gymnastics moves, aerobic performances, agility tests, and other movement and strength activities—all carried on in competitions meant to judge who among the competitors is fittest. The competitions are local, regional, and national. Like super-marathons and Iron Man contests, CrossFit appeals to people with an abundance of physicality who are driven by a highly competitive psychology.

Krystal's reaction to her accident and the amputation of her right arm above the elbow is reminiscent of Donald McNeil, the teenage wrestler who sustained a spinal cord injury. Both athletes were propelled by an unrelenting desire to return to a sport that embodied so much of who they were. "My first thought," Krystal says of her accident, "was I didn't know how I was going to do CrossFit anymore. My next thought was that I had to." Both Krystal and McNeil overcame horrific injuries, driven by the need to rebuild themselves and by a mental attitude that epitomized determination. But Krystal's story took a different turn.

Back on the training circuit, Cantu lifted so much and so vigorously that she ended up with a herniated disk, so painful that she was unable to get out of bed. When this injury stopped her from training, she decided (with her boyfriend) to have a baby. Unfortunately, being pregnant made her feel "thirty times worse." But, she says, she wasn't going to let that beat her down either. She needed to train herself to deliver without medication. Then, after giving birth, she set herself the challenge of losing the accumulated "baby weight." Then her body gave way again, so she had to train herself differently.

What's going on here? We've seen in many of our interviewees— McNeil, Mangok Bol, and others—how determination to achieve a goal wards off the destructive consequences of tragedy, how purpose generates optimism and anticipation in place of distress and fragility. But Cantu's life seems to be a pendulum of achievement and failure, a repeated cycle of striving and collapse.

One conclusion might be that while goal orientation may well play an important role in resilience, it is also potentially dangerous, fraught with possibilities for failure and a retreat into despair. Another might be that goals must have sufficient depth if they're to be sustaining. But it seems to us that Cantu's story illuminates an element of the resilience dynamic that we simply have not seen before. There's something in her that recalls Sisyphus, the Greek mythological figure sentenced by the gods to pushing a boulder up a mountain, but never successfully, so that each time the stone rolls back down and he has to try all over again. The myth is usually interpreted negatively, suggesting the absurdity or meaninglessness of life. But it also describes man as the striver, imbued with a primal need to contend, in whatever circumstances, against whatever odds.

Cantu says at the conclusion of her interview, "I need to win...I get off the path at times, but I always get back on." The ancient Greeks called that kind of person *agonistes*, someone engaged in struggle, in contention. We usually think of "striving" in terms of endeavoring to reach a goal. But striving is different from pursuing goals. It's the motive force behind the pursuit, a trait woven into the fabric of our makeup. Cantu's story suggests that the will to keep fighting is a deep feature of our humanity, weaker in some, stronger in others, triggered in different ways from one to another, but common to all of us.

# 11

# The Goldbergers

"Kevin doesn't see himself as disabled," Mike Goldberger says of his now forty-year-old son. "Anything that makes him different, he doesn't like acknowledging."

Kevin was born two months premature and, as a result, developed a myriad of neuromuscular issues that somewhat mimic cerebral palsy.

"Eventually," Esther Hess wrote for the Center for the Developing Mind website, "most families come to terms with the diagnosis of their child and they learn that although this journey that they are all on is exceedingly different than the one they were supposed to take, it offers, if they can allow it, a rich tapestry to their lives."

Mike and his wife, Kathy, agree, but their particular tapestry has changed. Kevin uses a wheelchair much of the time these days, which hasn't stopped him from being a fixture at Brown University men's lacrosse and women's field hockey games. In fact, the field hockey venue is now called the Goldberger Family Field.

"That doesn't happen if not for Kevin," his father, known as "Goldie" to his friends, says, "if not for his love of those teams that happens to be reciprocal. Kevin has focused his life around the most important thing: people. He'll never have a job, he doesn't have a real concept of money. But he knows who his nieces and nephews are, he knows the players on the teams he follows. And if you want somebody to model your life after, he's the guy. He's taught my wife Kathy and I so much about what's really important. People will say to us things like you're such good parents, you're so good with Kevin. But it's the other way around. Kevin's the role model. He's never done a mean thing in his life. He's always kind, always thoughtful, a model for how we try to live our lives."

Special needs or not, Goldie wonders out loud what kind of world it would be if everyone was like Kevin, sharing his attitude to focus not on what he can't do but on what he can. After several years at Meeting Street School, which is devoted to young people with disabilities, he entered the Barrington public school system at age six until graduating with his class. Since his condition required him to be placed in special education, he was self-contained and didn't get a lot of social interaction until the system expanded its mainstreaming efforts. And, thanks to a supportive faculty and principal along with an innovative Peer Buddies program, Kevin was able to attend regular classes. There was no college after that, but he's experienced college for the twenty-plus years since, thanks to his association with Brown athletics.

"There hasn't been a whole lot we've needed to change in our lives because of Kevin," says Goldie, "beyond setting up our schedules so one of us is always there. Kevin has an aide, Ana, who's been with him for fifteen years and is a part of our family. When she leaves at three o'clock, either Kathy or I are always home. It's natural for parents to hope their children enjoy as full a life as possible. Find the right job, find the right partner, have kids of their own. You ask yourself when they're young, will he be this or will he be that? But none of that is important to Kevin, so it's not important to us. We don't have that kind of dream for him and that's fine. It doesn't bother Kevin, so why should it bother us?"

Kathy offers another perspective. The oldest of four kids, she had a brother with Down syndrome who never lived at home.

"He spent the first twenty-nine years of his life in an institution," Kathy reflects, "and then the last fifteen years in a group home. Going to visit him when I was a kid meant standing outside his window and waving. We had no physical relationship, and Steven really had no concept of who we were. He spent thirteen years in bed because, in those days, they didn't think someone with Down syndrome could think, learn, and develop. So when Kevin was born in 1980, I said no way what happened to my brother was ever going to happen with him. Put him in a group home when he was ten, like somebody suggested? Over my dead body!"

Even before Kevin entered the Barrington school system, Kathy ramped up her own advocacy efforts.

"I got so much out of talking to other parents who have children with special needs. I got a master's degree in counseling and ended up specializing in the disability area. I wanted to help people the way I had been helped, connecting with parents who were facing the same challenges and issues that I had. I landed an internship at the Trudeau Center [located in Warwick, Rhode Island], where I ran support groups in their early intervention program. I wanted people to talk to each other and be more open with each other. To this day, I remember my grandmother coming home from the hospital with my mother, with no baby, and saying, 'We're not going to tell anyone about Steven.'"

Kathy also led a group called the Friends of Zambrano to advocate for positive change and better conditions at the very institution where her brother had spent the first twenty-nine years of his life. She joined the board of directors of the RIARC (an advocacy group for the disabled) and, later, became a transitions counselor for families that had sons or daughters with special needs who were leaving high school to face the rest of their lives, landing a job maybe or continuing their education in some respect. She did parent training, providing information and resources, all aimed at preparing families for life after eighteen or twenty-one.

Goldie is no stranger to activism either, having played a leadership role with the Rhode Island Special Olympics for twenty years. He was the State Games chairperson, a volunteer role that left him with the responsibility of coordinating and organizing the entire annual June weekend of competitive events for more than a thousand participants, some of whom went on to become national Paralympians.

You don't get any sense of regret or remorse from Mike or Kathy, no indication that they see meeting Kevin's considerable needs as a burden or bemoan the trips they can't take and vacations they can't go on. It's a matter of adapting, taking advantage of what Kevin can do and enjoy, as opposed to what he can't.

"Part of me," Kathy says, "is the typical Jewish mother. You know, 'my son the doctor' or 'my son the lawyer.' But sometimes it's not going to work out that way. You get to be a parent; you don't always get exactly what you expected. With Kevin, who knows what the future will be? When you're a parent, you love your child unconditionally. You encourage them to be the best they can be."

"Last year," Goldie adds, "Kevin and I visited every town in Rhode Island to have breakfast, every single one. We kept a chart, like sticking pins in a map. It became like a mission. It was an example of knowing you're going to enjoy doing something and enjoy who you're doing it with. Kevin doesn't ask for much. He never complains. He's a joy to be around."

Before he embarked on such adventures, Goldie enjoyed a great career at Brown University. Following a stint as the school's director of admissions, he moved on to become director of athletics before retiring seven years back. It was just time, he says, but the decline in Kevin's mobility also required more attention as any semblance of independence first waned and then pretty much disappeared. That's part and parcel of raising a special needs child who grows into a special needs adult.

"Early on in our experience of raising not one but two children with disabilities," says John Susa, cofounder along with his wife, Connie, of PLAN RI, a support group for other parents faced with that same responsibility, "we were given advice by Dr. Siegfried Pueschel, an internationally recognized developmental pediatrician and father of a son with Down syndrome. He told us that the best thing we could do for our child with multiple disabilities was to help him to live as normal a life as every other child in our family. Not focus on the *dis* part of the word, but on the *ability*. If we limit our child's life and experiences, the outcome is that he will have a limited life. Instead, it's vital to expose children to all of life and all of its opportunities, so their lives can be as full as they can possibly be. A message of hope and expectation is always better than fear."

John and Connie Susa bring another perspective to the table, showing how the vast strides in medical care have allowed even children with serious disabilities to grow into adults, something very rare indeed until relatively recent history.

"In the 1920s," John says, "children born with Down syndrome lived an average of nine years. In the 1950s, it went up to twenty, and now it's sixty or seventy."

But that creates a dilemma, a supreme challenge for the parents of children with disabilities who might now outlive them or, at least, outlive the parents' ability to care for them. That's where PLAN RI comes in. Modeled after an award-winning organization in Vancouver, the nonprofit organization is an acronym for Personal Lifetime Advocacy Networks and was formed to answer the question, *Who will care about my loved one when I no longer can?*

"It's a big issue," Goldie agrees, "something Kathy and I think about a lot."

Brown Athletics made a video in 2015 saluting Kevin for his lifelong loyalty to the teams he sees as family and calling him the "quintessential role model for perseverance."

"We love Kevin," says Lars Tiffany, then head coach of men's lacrosse, who's since gone on to win a national title at Virginia after taking the Bears to the Final Four. "He's been part of Brown lacrosse longer than any of us. He was here before I became the head coach. He's a perennial presence. He's on the bus, on the sideline in the pouring rain. He's a forward-looking guy. He travels with us and as soon as one road trip ends and we're getting off the bus, he's already asking about the next road trip."

Which suits Goldie just fine.

"In Kevin, I have a constant companion who loves to do all the things that I love to do. I'll ask him, 'Hey, you want to…' and his answer's always, 'Sure.' The lacrosse and field hockey teams have given him a great sense of community. And in Kevin they've got somebody who, no matter what the result of the game might be, is going to care about them just as much all the time. Somebody different, somebody who may not have had the advantages they had. I think he's a kind of grounding influence on them, helping to keep things in perspective."

"That's one of the things we love about him," Lars Tiffany adds. "There's always a tomorrow."

Five years later, though, it's a different tomorrow. In that 2015 video, Kevin was still getting around on his own. The wheelchair is now a staple of life, and the Goldbergers have adapted their home with grab bars and a walk-in shower with a seat so Kevin doesn't fall victim to his declining mobility.

"He doesn't have a lot of control over things everyone else takes for granted," Kathy explains. "Like walking, talking, and he gets ornery over that. Recently he told me I have to ask permission to come into his room. I don't blame him. He wants to have some measure of control over his life. He wants to make his own decisions."

But the wheelchair, coupled with attrition on the Brown Athletics' training staff and COVID-19, has put at least a temporary end to Kevin's part-time job in the equipment room, doing whatever he can to help out no matter how menial the task.

"To me," says Goldie, "Kevin has always been just like his brother Brian, each with their own special talents and their own deficiencies, just like all of us have. The key is to focus on the strengths and make the weaknesses stand out as little as possible. Focus on love and kindness, give everyone a chance to follow what they love. For Kevin, that's people."

"He's an amazing person," Brian, Kevin's younger brother, adds. "He plays the set of cards he's been dealt. He's always upbeat, always making jokes. He even took relying on a wheelchair to get around in stride. Kevin's never spent a lot of time around other people with disabilities, so that's not how he sees himself. If anything, the wheelchair has made him even more determined to do the things he loves. He's going to get to those Brown lacrosse and field hockey games no matter what."

That is, until the coronavirus, COVID-19, resulted in the cancellation of the 2020 spring sports season, left the fall season in jeopardy, and has upset the applecart in other ways as well.

"We've been furloughed from babysitting Brian's children, Kevin's niece and nephew," Goldie explains, referring to his son Brian's one-year-old daughter and two-and-a-half-year-old son. "Kevin doesn't think that's right, and he's been strident about it. He can still do it. There's nothing wrong. We just don't want to put him at any risk."

"The virus has been tough on Kevin because it's forced new limits on him," Brian reflects. "It's awesome for my kids to be exposed to someone less fortunate and who has special needs. That will hopefully shape their lives the way it did mine. Make them better people who'll volunteer for the Peer Buddies Program and the Special Olympics, just like I still do. Having a special needs person in the family makes you appreciate what a blessing it is to have healthy kids. It gives you a different perspective, makes you want to reach out and give back to those who aren't necessarily blessed with the same opportunities."

A number of the friends Brian grew up with continue to visit Kevin on a regular basis. Even with the wheelchair, they take him out to lunch or to catch a Providence Bruins game. It's a bit more complicated these days, since Kevin developed diabetes. According to Mike and Kathy, it's a battle every day to give him his shot of insulin, and having diabetes is also among the main risk factors in catching the coronavirus. What, though, if one or both of his parents caught it? That's where PLAN RI might come in.

"The best predictor of a high-quality life," Connie Susa explains, "is the number of people that know, care about, and are committed to that person. PLAN RI is designed to ensure our members continue to enjoy a good life because of the engagement of their personal support networks."

"What's important for PLAN RI," John adds, "is avoiding the isolation and loneliness that come into a disabled person's life after their family is gone. How much time does that person interact with someone who's not paid to do it? Some adults with special needs spend their entire lives around people who are paid to take care of them, and the relationships have to be qualified by those limitations. The end result is that many people with disabilities enjoy virtually no contact with anyone else outside of whatever facility they're living in. PLAN RI is all about making sure that doesn't happen. It could range from something as simple as fifteen minutes a week of interaction over a cup of coffee to helping that individual through a court hearing to reestablish lost benefits or something like that. PLAN RI helps identify those people and build that kind of support network for a person who may not be able to form or maintain such a personal team on their own. That gives the parents peace of mind because they know their child will be taken care of. And it's not random. Kevin has interests, so our goal in his case would be to find other people with interests that match up. The idea is to make sure that he's surrounded by people who know him, have an interest in him, and care about him. But we go even further than that by providing a facilitator to make sure all those people who know someone like Kevin also know each other. That creates a safety net through which no one should slip."

Goldie agrees.

"Having a special needs child requires the family to come to a vision for the future. From my experience, families that don't come to grips with that common vision experience a lot more strain and stress. I wouldn't trade Kevin for anybody. I saw him as a gift right from the start. Not everything's going to go great, but it makes us more capable of accepting and understanding the challenges of life. Every family has them, and they come in all different packages and forms. As parents of a special needs child, we've become very aware that everyone is experiencing something. That's made us more able to cope with our challenges and helped us to keep everything in perspective."

"A lot of people believe that families who have children with disabilities have higher marital stress and a higher divorce rate," John Susa points out. "But all of the research hasn't confirmed that. It's a myth. My experience is that the family actually forms stronger bonds. It makes you more resilient if you can ascribe meaning to the disability. It's like what Mike said about spending a year having breakfast at every town in Rhode Island. Before I lost my vision, my son Mark and I would go leaf peeping every year in the fall. Once, I looked over at how happy he was, beaming at all the trees, and I realized how lucky I am. I'm a father and I've been able to parent my son for forty-six years when, normally, being a parent in that respect lasts not even half that long."

Of course, John doesn't mean to make it sound easy.

"Some families become consumed with focus on the disability and all of the associated problems and negative life experiences. And they become overwhelmed as a result."

That appears to be the exception, not the rule.

"Out of necessity," Terry Mauro wrote for the Verywell Family website, "parents of children with special needs are often more flexible, compassionate, stubborn, and resilient than other parents. While it may not be something you had hoped for or expected, it is important for your child that you try to do your best. You can take comfort in the fact that you're not alone, so feel comfortable reaching out for support."

That said, Goldie offers another perspective.

"We're prepared for Kevin to decline. We don't know where he'll end up or how bad it will be—nobody knows. But that doesn't bother Kevin, and he knows we're there for him. He's got a doorbell in his room and when he rings it, either Kathy or I come. He's going to need help in the morning getting from his bedroom to the bathroom. He used to be able do it alone and he still can, but it's harder. If he falls, he gets up, just like everybody else."

~ ~ ~

## Reflections

In these chapters we've talked a good deal about empathy as one of the pillars of resilience. The ability to enter into another person's life, to feel a compassionate affiliation and understand and respond to that person's needs, enables us to see beyond our own adversity, our own trauma and burdens. Tom Catena's entire career, for example, speaks to a deeply embedded love for others that has sustained him in the most traumatic of circumstances.

In a way, empathy is a younger sibling of love. The empathic personality is open to emotional connections with others. We think of love as something similar, but more specific, more individual and intimate. We love certain people in our lives; that's different from being sensitive to emotional connections. Yet love and empathy have in common our fundamental desire for close connection; they spring from a primary psychological substratum we share with all our fellow humans. Love is rarely mentioned in studies of resilience, yet getting a close-up look at love may help us better understand how it is that deep caring for others works to counter trauma.

The Goldbergers' interview is in essence a love story. It draws attention naturally to other stories of parents and children: Mary and Jim Costello and their daughter Jill, Jim and Kathy Pantelas and their daughter Stella. The Goldbergers' relationship with their son Kevin has in common with the Costellos' relationship with Jill that in each case the parents find in their children qualities that fundamentally impact their own outlook and sense of values. In the Costellos' case, Jill's affirmation of life in the face of death is an ongoing inspiration. The Goldbergers have found in Kevin's condition the ability to focus on the most fundamental elements of attachment.

Kathy Goldberger tells us that part of her is the typical Jewish mother. "You know," she says, "'my son the doctor' or 'my son the lawyer.'" Mike Goldberger adds, "We don't have that kind of dream for him and that's fine. It doesn't bother Kevin, so why should it bother us?"

Instead, he and Kathy treasure those things Kevin can do that make him happy, and they treasure the personal qualities they and others see in him. "You don't always get exactly what you expected," says Kathy. "When you're a parent, you love your child unconditionally." This is love pared down to essentials. It's the embrace of intimate attachment with all the constrictions that may come with a relationship.

The other dimension of intimate attachment so prominent in the Goldbergers' story is the enduring nature of it. This is not something for a day, a month, a year. "I realized how lucky I am," says Mike. "I'm a father and I've been able to parent my son for forty-six years." This is an attachment, for the Goldbergers and the other parents who appear in this story, that is ongoing, to the end of life and beyond in their efforts to ensure comfort and support for their disabled children after they are gone. It calls to mind most readily the traditional marriage vows: "for better or worse, in sickness and health, till death do us part." Husbands and wives, of course, do grow apart and separate. But essential love, as evidenced here, does not admit that. It endures. The psychiatrist-philosopher Gregory Fricchione writes in his book *Compassion and Healing in Medicine and Society*, "Compassionate, altruistic love . . . is the synthesis of self-affirming with self-giving. He who loses his life in self-giving love will find it in true self-realization."

For all the dimensions of resilience we've encountered, it is, perhaps, the ability to affirm the value of life in the face of profound trauma that registers most forcefully. We have seen it in other stories, but nowhere more dramatically than in this story of the protective and redeeming power of love.

# 12

## Bobby O'Donnell

*Boom! The terrible, percussive sound of the first explosion drowned out every other noise in Boston, both literally and figuratively. The horror of that sound on a sunny Monday afternoon, April 15, 2013, was just the start of the chaos. Boom! Twelve seconds later came another. Bewildered and terrified, I stood near the finish line of the Boston Marathon on Massachusetts Avenue, stopped by police officers who seemed equally perplexed. Then thousands of screaming spectators came running towards me from the direction of the finish line.*

—From *Running Wild* by Bobby O'Donnell

Bobby O'Donnell wasn't born to run marathons. In fact, his decision to enter the ill-fated 2013 Boston Marathon came nearly two years earlier, not long after the 2011 version had been held when he was seventeen years old.

"It was one of the most superficial things ever. I was with family celebrating my father's birthday, just walking around Boston sightseeing.

And I saw a bunch of people wearing these flashy looking incredible Adidas windbreakers. I found out all those wearing them had just run the marathon."

"'I want one of those jackets,' I told my parents.

"'What are you going to do, run the Boston Marathon,' my father said.

"'Yes, that's what I'm going to do.'"

At that point, Bobby wasn't even a runner; he'd never entered a race. He went online, though, and got into a lottery to run a seven-mile road race in Falmouth on Cape Cod, for which he was ultimately accepted.

"I got addicted to the energy and community races bring right from the start. It was such a positive environment. Everyone was there to accomplish the same goal; thousands of people gathered together wanting to do the same thing, while not wanting anyone else to fail."

That supportive atmosphere was something Bobby carried into the Philadelphia Marathon in November of 2011, his first ever. He didn't finish at the top of the heap, but he did finish, enough to give him the final spark he needed to try for Boston several months later. The problem was his time in Philadelphia wasn't nearly good enough to qualify. The only alternative was to enter the race as a fundraising sponsor with at least $5,000 in pledges, and Bobby found the perfect organization to support in Boston Children's Hospital a year later, in time for the 2013 Boston Marathon, after missing out in 2012.

"I could not have had a more profound motivation to train and fundraise than those children and the people who care for them," he wrote in *Running Wild*. "My running was no longer about a marathon jacket. It was about something much more meaningful."

Except for one small problem.

"It was stressful, a nineteen-year-old college kid trying to raise $5,000, but my experience at Children's Hospital was never far from my mind. I was resolved to do whatever it took to raise money for them, and promised each donor that for their contribution, I would cross that finish line on April 15th. People could not have been more generous. By the second week of April 2013, after the first annual 26.2 for Children Golf Tournament, we had raised $7,589."

Then came April 15, 2013, a beautiful day dawning over the city of Boston and perfect for running. Bobby was a half mile from the finish line on Boylston Street when the first blast sounded. He was still standing there in shock when the second bomb went off.

An agonizing stretch followed. With no phone on him, he couldn't reach his parents who were waiting for him at the finish line. As word of what had happened began to circulate, Bobby felt the cold grasp of fear over the possibility his parents had been injured in the dual blasts, or worse. He borrowed a phone from a reporter and called his mother, but she didn't answer. A bit later, he thought he'd try a text message instead and borrowed another reporter's phone.

IT'S BOBBY. WHERE ARE YOU? ARE YOU OKAY?

Minutes passed with no response, Bobby holding on to a stranger's phone for dear life. Then finally the phone buzzed with an incoming message:

OH MY GOD. MEET US OUTSIDE OF YAWKEY WAY NEAR FENWAY. WE ARE OKAY.

Bobby ran faster to Yawkey Way outside of Fenway Park than he had during the entire marathon itself, at least the twenty-five-plus miles he had covered. His parents were fine. He was fine. His dad, a firefighter-paramedic, had been at the finish line helping the injured. He'd taken charge of the scene, helping to triage, directing others to tie tourniquets and apply pressure to bleeding wounds. The reunion should have been the end of the tortuous experience. Instead, it proved to be just the beginning, as he writes in *Running Wild*.

"My anger and frustration only intensified when the nightmares began weeks later. Again, I didn't feel entitled to the trauma and pain, but the terrors that plagued my sleep were incessant and I couldn't will them away as much as I tried. There were horrible nights when in my sleep I would see the bloody and broken bodies of the ones I loved amid the twisted metal on Boylston Street; a broken cell phone in my hand; the constant horror that it was my fault they were there in the first place. Night after night I would awaken tangled in my sheets, drenched in sweat. Why had these images implanted themselves so firmly in my unconscious? My family were among the lucky ones."

Bobby was suffering from post-traumatic stress disorder, but he didn't know it at the time. The nightmares became his secret, the stress and anxiety they were causing multiplying almost by the day. He needed a release, a vent, but had no idea where to look. Everything became a trigger for the then sophomore at New Hampshire's St. Anselm College, the most basic of enjoyments and routines denied him.

According to the American Psychiatric Association, "Posttraumatic stress disorder (PTSD) is a psychiatric disorder that can occur in people who have experienced or witnessed a traumatic event such as a natural disaster, a serious accident, a terrorist act, war/combat, rape or other violent personal assault. PTSD has been known by many names in the past, such as 'shell shock' during the years of World War I and 'combat fatigue' after World War II. But PTSD does not just happen to combat veterans. PTSD can occur in all people, in people of any ethnicity, nationality or culture, and any age. PTSD affects approximately three-point-five percent of U.S. adults, and an estimated one in eleven people will be diagnosed with PTSD in their lifetime."

That translates into somewhere around fifteen to twenty million people at any given time.

"People with PTSD," the same article continues, "have intense, disturbing thoughts and feelings related to their experience that last long after the traumatic event has ended. They may relive the event through flashbacks or nightmares; they may feel sadness, fear or anger; and they may feel detached or estranged from other people."

That description cast Bobby as a textbook sufferer, but he still hadn't put a name to what he was feeling. Following in his father's footsteps, he was working to become a paramedic at the same time as he was taking a heavy course load. But the ambulance runs that were a staple of his training became exercises in terror, triggering flashbacks of ambulance sirens screaming in a constant blare in the aftermath of the explosions from that fateful April 15, 2013. Nothing, including seeing a counselor, provided any relief. He was getting no better and probably worse. Bobby could only look forward for an answer, to one thing in particular:

The 2014 edition of the Boston Marathon.

Run that, he figured, and he'd slay the demons that had haunted him for months. Maybe the solution to his anxiety would be as simple as crossing the finish line, something he hadn't been able to do the year before.

"I put a lot of hope in that in terms of finally gaining closure. And that was after I almost changed my mind in the weeks leading up to the race. I was living 'Boston Strong' every single day of my life, listening to everyone say, 'You're gonna go back, right? You're gonna finish it.' Of course, I'm going back, I thought. Why would I not do that? That's what is expected of me, to go back. I ended up setting my expectations too high, that I could then get back to being the old Bobby. Cross the finish line and it'll reset the clock. Well, I ran horribly but it was one of the best experiences I've ever had, seeing the city so united. I loved being a part of that. But the first inkling that the race hadn't really changed anything was on Boylston Street, when I moved over to the right side of the street because the year before the bombs had gone off on the left. Why was I having those thoughts? I shouldn't have been thinking like that."

But he was, and the PTSD that had so roiled his life was still haunting him and not going anywhere by all indication. What Bobby had hoped would be the end turned out to be only another beginning. He was back at square one, the figurative starting line. And, as with any marathon, the finish line was nowhere in sight, and he had no idea where to turn next.

"I wanted so much to get back to being the person I was before the bombing. But I realized no matter how much I wanted it, I was never going to be him anymore. I had to change things, had to completely change my life, do something entirely different."

That moment of change came, at least as a harbinger, the following fall when he was one of the featured speakers at an event in Columbus, Ohio, where he'd been asked to share his story in front of upward of a thousand people. Though racked by anxiety initially, Bobby's presentation became cathartic for him, the floodgates opening for all the pent-up emotion to spill out. He talked about fear, of not letting it prevail, not letting it become your master. He had returned to run again a year after the bombing to help bring home the point that the terrorists hadn't won, that we as a society would not be defeated.

The PTSD, though, was still beating him. The time had come to find a way to turn the tables, a process that began when he signed on to a medical mission trip to Nicaragua as a paramedic, traveling there with his father. Getting out of the country for the first time proved to be a tonic, his experiences at long last spiriting him away from the thoughts and memories that had become so pervasive in his mind.

"Each day," he writes, "I ran on the beach at sunrise as the waves gently lapped against the sand. Here I could once again appreciate the motion as something primitive, pure, and beautiful. Just running. No more, no less. I felt my love for it beginning to creep back; a small glimmer that burned slowly brighter with every mile."

The healing process had finally begun. Bobby not only had discovered the right formula, he ultimately developed a bold and bracing plan to take his healing to the next level. He followed up Nicaragua with a trip to Australia during summer break from St. Anselm, where he seemed to spend as much time diving beneath the waters near the Great Barrier Reef as he did on land. On that same trip, he journeyed to Katoomba to take part in his first international race, a fifty-kilometer monster known as the North Face in May of 2016.

He ran along dirt roads and down slippery rock faces, dodging roots from trees that rimmed both sides of the trails with the sound of a rushing river often bubbling in his ears. He didn't run particularly well or fast, but the sense of beauty and life around Bobby was overwhelming. The roller coaster nature of the course was an apt metaphor for the direction his life had taken those past three years and, when it finally leveled off, he was struck by a sense of fulfilment and completion. The final stretch of the course, appropriately enough, was an imposing hill called the Furber Steps, another metaphor for all the struggles he'd endured. In the race's aftermath, he realized he was never going to forget April 15, 2013, but that was okay; he didn't have to.

"The marathon bombing will always be a part of me, but it does not have to define me."

He had found the means to redefine himself. Indeed, Bobby had gotten his mojo back. Not all, but enough for him to set off on a grand adventure, a quest not so much to reclaim the person he'd been prior to the bombing as to carve out a new path into the future. He had found the formula for that in a combination of travel and running or, essentially, traveling to run. Almost like a journey in search of destination.

After Australia came battling the challenging winds and elements in Antarctica's White Continent Marathon (January 2016). Next came the Reykjavik Marathon in Iceland (August 2016), and the Coast Trail series in South Devon, England (February 2017). Then there was, of all things, the Mt. Kilimanjaro Marathon in Tanzania (February 2017), which was followed by the Ultra Trail Torres del Paine in Chile (September 2017) and Ireland's Dublin Marathon (October 2018).

Bobby was like a prizefighter, flattening every opponent to the mat and emerging stronger on each continent as he conquered one marathon after another. But it wasn't the landscapes or courses he remembers the most; it was the people. The lifelong friendships he formed, the constant comradery of people united by a common pursuit. The further out he ventured, both figuratively and literally, the further he drew from Boston 2013. He had been renewed by a common spirit and common humanity that restored and refreshed him. Adding the Everest Marathon to the mix (November 2017), the so-called "highest marathon in the world," meant that he had run marathons, or ultramarathons in some cases, on all seven continents, and it's Everest he speaks and writes of with the most devotion.

"I met two of the closest friends I have in the world there, Tom Power and Fiona Smith. I was a twenty-three-year-old paramedic, Fiona was a thirty-one-year-old reindeer herder from Scotland, and Tom was a forty-three-year-old ballistics expert from Dublin. In what other circumstance could three people like that meet and become such good friends? It was all about the experience we shared, doing the same thing every day. Everything was so positive we all wanted to maintain that friendship. That opened me up to the world again. Running was the vessel that got me where I needed to be, but it was all about the people I met because of that, all these experiences we'd shared."

So many of them, it almost sounds like Boston 2013 was shoved straight out of the pile. Well, almost.

"Will it ever go away? I hope so, but probably not. That's okay, though, because the dreams outweigh the nightmares now. And every year the gap widens more."

And, you might add, with every marathon.

"The important thing for me to realize is that this journey doesn't have a linear path. It's still a roller coaster, and there are going to be good days and bad days, more good than bad now. A lot more. I was speaking about this at a middle school in Florida when a kid asked me, 'If you could go back and erase what happened on April 15, 2013, would you?' In the first two years after the bombing, I wouldn't even have had to think about it. My answer would have been yes. Now I realize it took the worst day of my life happening to make me the person I am. No matter how much I wanted to go back to being the old Bobby, I was never going to be him again. But if it wasn't for the bombing, I wouldn't have a lot of the best things, and friends, I have in my life today."

As a licensed paramedic, Bobby is articulately able to compare the trauma he faced with what the country is facing with COVID-19.

"I think people might be able to find COVID [a blessing in disguise] too. The Boston Marathon bombing undoubtedly was the worst day of my life. But if it didn't happen, none of anything in my book would have occurred. I would have never traveled, never experienced the world the way I did. It took having this terrible thing happen to me to have all the wonderful things that followed occur. When I face tragedy or adversity, what I've come to realize is I need to decide where I want this to go from here."

And what advice does he have to offer in a COVID-19 and post-COVID-19 world?

"This crisis has disrupted every aspect of everyday life. Everyone's going to feel anxiety. It's okay; don't be afraid to talk about it. The most important thing is to have an open dialogue with people, to maintain a sense of community with sports and other reasons for gathering gone. All that traveling I did, years of it, I only ran for a total of forty-four hours, a small fraction of the time spent. It was the people, the experience as a whole. After the bombing, the world became an incredibly scary place for me. I finally overcame that fear by seeing all the good that's in the world, and that's where I hope COVID leaves people who are traumatized by it."

The Everest Marathon may open the most eyes, but it's the Mt. Kilimanjaro Marathon that's especially relevant given that Ernest Hemingway's famed story, "The Snows of Kilimanjaro," among his best works, is set there. Bobby, after all, has the looks and sensibility of the kind of rugged individualist Hemingway was so fond of writing about. And now he's an author as well.

"After I'd written *Running Wild*, it was actually a difficult decision to publish it. Once you put it all out there, there's no taking it back. I'd been trying to figure out all these things on my own, and now someone else would be reading my story. But the whole thing, all my experiences, would be worth that, if it helps someone else. Think about it. Had the marathon bombing never happened, I never would have written the book, never would have escaped from my comfort zone to see what a beautiful place the world really is."

~ ~ ~

## Reflections

Looking back over the stories of resilience our interviewees have told, we see a variety of factors at work. Some played important roles in one or two of the lives we've been privileged to look at. Others emerge as recurrent themes as people struggle to overcome the traumas they've suffered. We've seen these common factors time and again: faith, grit, empathy, purpose, mentors, role models, and others—a core of elements that appear to define resilience, but also outliers that expand our understanding of the psychological strengths people bring to bear in the face of major trauma.

Bobby O'Donnell's struggle with post-traumatic stress illuminates one of these outliers.

To alleviate the nightmares and anxieties that haunted him, O'Donnell talked his situation through with a counselor. When that had little effect, he faced the trauma head-on, running in the following year's Boston Marathon. But despite his expectations, even a successful finish in the supportive atmosphere of Boston Strong left him suffering the same fears and agitation.

The break from the mental disorder that was creating such distress came as a surprise. On a trip to Nicaragua with his father, he ran on the beach each morning at sunrise. Something about being far away from the site of the bombing eased his mind. Running along the beach, experiencing the beauty of the sun rising over the ocean, provided an unaccustomed sense of peacefulness.

As soon as his schedule allowed, O'Donnell followed up his Nicaragua visit with a trip to Australia's Great Barrier Reef, where he spent his time diving, and then ran a fifty-kilometer ultramarathon in the

Blue Mountains of New South Wales. Understanding by this time that he had found a strategy, O'Donnell embarked on a series of marathons located in unusual and striking settings—Antarctica, Chile, Ireland, Mount Kilimanjaro, and then Mount Everest, a marathon on each continent. Along the way he met people who became his best friends.

"Running," he says, "was the vessel that got me where I needed to be, but it was all about the people I met because of that, all these experiences we'd shared."

The factors that contributed to O'Donnell's recovery present a picture of something very like holistic therapy, closely associated with integrative medicine. Holistic therapy, like integrative medicine, takes into account the physiological, emotional, spiritual, and environmental circumstances of a patient's life. It attempts to balance, or rebalance, the factors that affect an individual's health. O'Donnell may or may not have been familiar with the holistic approach, but he came to his own version of it, immersing himself in an environment that altered the way he functioned in multiple ways. The settings of his marathon runs were different, striking. Kilimanjaro, Australia's Blue Mountains, Antarctica, Everest—the interplay between himself and the aesthetic power of the places he traveled to was new and restorative. "Primitive, pure, and beautiful" is the way he described his runs along the Nicaragua beach. It would have been interesting to hear his descriptions of the other places he experienced.

It's not too far a reach to say that these settings affected, or rather enriched, the spiritual side of his nature. At the same time, marathon racing affected his physiological functions—cardiac, vascular, muscular, hormonal, etc.—in ways extensively documented by medical researchers. Aerobic exercise, we know, stimulates the production of endorphins, with the accompanying feelings of well-being. Investigators have found that regular aerobic exercise is comparable to medications and psychotherapy in reducing anxiety and depression.

Beyond the physiological and psychological effects O'Donnell experienced were the personal bonds he developed, the especially close camaraderie he formed with some of his running partners. "It was the people," he says about his marathon racing, "the experience as a whole."

In effect, O'Donnell created a different mind, body, spirit, and interpersonal landscape for himself. This is a kind of in-depth self-therapy that we haven't seen before. Integrative medicine has become an accepted if not quite mainstream therapeutic approach in contemporary medical practice, but it ordinarily centers on a close partnership between doctor and patient. Bobby O'Donnell, though, arrived at this approach himself through experiment, creativity, and persistence. The course of his recovery indicates nothing so much as the capacity of the body and mind to heal themselves. But it also reminds us that human resilience is a complex phenomenon that ordinarily operates over time and with varying degrees of success. Bobby O'Donnell's endeavor to heal himself did not eliminate his post-traumatic stress. But it shunted the trauma into the background, where passing time has continued to diminish its hold on him.

# 13

# Paul Allen

Paul Allen vividly remembers the day he lost his sight forever as a nine-year-old boy. He was halfway across a busy intersection, walking hand in hand with his mother, when he decided to break away and cover the rest of the distance on his own.

"I'm going the rest of the way," he announced, tearing free before his mother could react.

In the next moment, she watched a car miss the traffic signal and strike Paul flush, projecting him through the air. He landed on his rear end and slid across to the other side of the street he'd been so determined to reach on his own. The small of his back slammed the curb and jerked Paul backward, the back of his head striking the concrete pillar of a viaduct. Amazingly, he bounced up and ran to his mother.

"People were aghast that I was okay after flying through the air over several lanes of a four-lane street. We waited until the next day to see a doctor, who checked me out. Not surprisingly, he found severe bruising on the back of my head, but nothing else. He even examined my eyes and said everything looked good."

Only everything wasn't good. Far from it, in fact.

"Over the next seven days—riding a bike, going to school, just doing the usual things—I realized my vision was narrowing, like it was bleeding out at the periphery. But when you're a kid, you just think it's normal. I was struck by the car on June 28, 1958. On July 4, my family went to a circus that had three rings set up in this stadium. As the sun went down, I realized I couldn't see two of the rings anymore. I told my mother, and she said we were going back to the doctor tomorrow.

"At the end of the night there were fireworks, something I've loved all my life. And these were massive and gorgeous. Pinwheels, glitter bombs, sparkler showers, comet-looking sprays—the colors, the magnesium discharges of white. It was all just great. We were sitting in the middle of the stadium and when I turned to go down the stairs, I completely missed them and fell down the whole flight. I couldn't see anything at that point. Instead of waiting until the next day, we went to the emergency room right away, where they diagnosed that there was insufficient light for my retinas to discern what was around me. I was admitted then and there, to be prepped for surgery first thing in the morning.

"It turned out I was born with genetically weak retinas, something called Stickler syndrome that involves the formation of connective tissue and collagen, and that my retinas completely tore when I'd been hit by that car and struck my head on the curb. After surgery, I had to lie in bed on my back for thirty days to prevent me from moving. I was literally sandbagged into place so I wouldn't be able to move my head, my arms placed in restraints to keep me from twisting my body. I felt like a prisoner until they took the sandbags away and removed the bandages.

"'Can you see this light?' a voice asked me.

"'Is it on?' I asked him.

"That first night I learned I'd be blind for the rest of my life, I dreamed of those beautiful fireworks on the Fourth of July. I still love to go outside on New Year's Eve or the Fourth of July and listen to the percussion, remembering fireworks were the last thing I ever saw. Up until that point, I'd basically lived my entire life within nine square blocks. Now my life had gotten even smaller."

Paul's simple, comfortable home in St. Louis featured one of those old-fashioned cabinet radios, this one made of walnut, that had preset buttons that were labeled with different stations. It lacked a tuning dial, and now he could no longer tell which button was which.

"I quickly learned after I lost my sight that the first button was Chicago, and so on. So after a couple days I memorized what each of the thirty—two rows of fifteen—was, the same way I did with piano keys. Listening to that radio made me want to see the world. I'd hear voices on networks like the BBC. I didn't understand everything the voice was saying, but I knew I wanted to travel there.

"I knew what my house looked like. I knew the colors of the Oriental carpet. I could picture the drapes and the black-and-white tiles in the kitchen. I knew all of that stuff, as well as how the furniture was arranged, so I thought I could walk confidently around the house without banging into things. But knowing where things are in your head isn't an accurate depiction in time and space. You think you know where you are, but it takes time to accept that what's in your head can't be tricked into reality."

Speaking of reality, in August Paul and his mother went to see Sister Lorenzo, the nun who ran the Catholic school he attended, to see if any accommodations could be made, like obtaining books in braille or allowing a teacher or another student to read to him. Her reaction shocked both of them.

"We really cannot help you here. God has clearly punished Paul and turned his back on both of you. Try praying."

In those days, Paul relates, disabled children were required to go to a school that specialized, or was at least trained to deal with, their particular disability. So not only did he lose his sight at the age of nine, he also lost his friends and his elementary school. And, because all the schools he was eligible to attend were residential, he also lost his family three weeks later. Suffice it to say he didn't exactly fit in too well at what he calls, less than affectionately, "the blind school."

"You were literally being molded based on someone's concept of blindness centered only on what was available to you. 'You're blind. Learn to be blind. You cannot be or do something that the world will not let you do or be.' A blind teacher told me that, and it pretty much summarized the school's philosophy. Many of the other kids, most even, had been born blind. See, there was a tendency in those days to give oxygen to babies who were born prematurely, which had the side effect of burning out their retinas. And other kids at the school weren't just blind; they were also suffering from some degree of mental retardation—they still used that term back in 1958. Aside from that, many of my classmates had significant learning disabilities. I didn't feel I fit in at all and lashed out as a result. The staff there labeled me a troublemaker, a ringleader. A nine-year-old blind boy! All because I had too much time on my hands."

Paul spent four years at the blind school before his mother learned of an innovative middle school in San Diego that was experimenting with blind students as part of their transition to "mainstreaming" children with disabilities, which didn't exist at the time. A single parent, she uprooted her life to move to San Diego so he could attend that school. The transition of leaving their life in St. Louis may have been for the better, but it wasn't easy, until…

"We had a blooming lemon tree in our backyard in the house we rented in San Diego. Something about that lemon tree, the way it felt and smelled, told me I was going to be okay. I was thirteen at the time, and I still vividly remember the interview we had with the principal of Roosevelt Junior High and a member of the school board. They asked all of us blind kids why you believed you were the perfect candidate for this school. Well, we'd all come from blind schools somewhere, and our answer was the same: none of us had any intention of going back. Whatever it took to succeed here, we were going to do it. The mere thought of going back to the blind school was like having a knife at your back or a gun to your head. I was the only blind student in my class of nine hundred compared to a hundred and seventy-five students in total at the blind school.

"Going to that school was exciting, stimulating, and exhilarating because I was around sighted people. I felt normal again. It was a great experience for me; intimidating, sure, but there were people who appeared in my life and gave me true gifts. One was a Navy rear admiral named Clarence Coffin, one of the kindest human beings you could ever imagine. I'd told people at the school that I'd really like to have more outdoor experiences. Admiral Coffin, who commanded an aircraft carrier group, would regularly take his junior officers through the mountains over East Los Angeles around Palm Springs for wilderness experiences. So the admiral asked a blind fifteen-year-old boy if he wanted to go hiking with his group in the mountains.

"'This will be a great lesson for my junior officers,' he told me, and I was glad and grateful to join in.

"My first hike we came to the Palm Desert Overlook, which featured a multi-thousand-foot drop-off. 'You can probably do this,' the admiral said, 'but I want it to be your decision.'

"It took me all of three seconds to tell him I wanted to. I wasn't going to make the others take me across. And that was my first mountain climbing experience ever."

One thing his blindness only served to enhance was Paul's love of music. He took piano lessons at three years old and was playing recitals soon after. He continued playing piano until the accident when, as he puts it, "The child prodigy became the blind child freak." He played hundreds of songs from memory. Paul continued to listen to music, though his preferences changed from classical to rock and roll. He also developed a strong interest in jazz and Broadway musicals.

"I found there was a whole world of music I could pick up by ear. I didn't need to see the music. I picked a song up the first or second time I heard it."

One of his music teachers at the San Diego high school got him an audition to play in a bar. He got the gig on one condition: no drinking.

"'If I catch you with alcohol, you're out,' the owner told me. I was making twenty dollars an hour when I was sixteen years old. Music became how I supported myself. I could play any of four or five thousand songs people would request. I couldn't read the musical notes on a piece of paper, but I could picture them in my head."

Thanks to being mainstreamed, Paul had been "turned loose in the real world." He had a mentor in the Boy Scouts who got him interested in ham radio, and he met Hugh Lynn Cayce, son of the renowned Edgar Cayce, with whom he formed a lifelong friendship. Then Paul went from that San Diego high school to the nearby California Western University.

"It was a beautiful campus, but spread out over hundreds of acres. Vast with no sidewalks, and these curvy roads. No one told me where the cafeteria was or, once I found it, where the utensils or trays were. Everyone else, of course, could see where everything was. The world was so far behind back then when it came to considering the needs of disabled people. Someone at the school told me I might fare better in Europe, where colleges were known to be more advanced and tolerant."

Paul found that to be true, but only to a point.

"My dream was to become a psychiatrist. That meant attending medical school, and there was no path for that for a blind person even over there. I came home devastated."

But Hugh Lynn Cayce inspired him to study hypnotherapy, which gave birth to his interest in a potential career as a psychotherapist, for which he'd only need a master's degree. A different kind of psychotherapist because, of course, he was blind. Not so fast, though.

"I think there's a lot of implicit bias when you become disabled in some form: mental, physical, or emotional. We maintain assumptions of how things work that are simply not true. What would life be like if I got a cancer diagnosis and was given only six months to live? What if I couldn't hear? I don't know if I was a better psychotherapist because of my own personal suffering. One of the advantages surfaced when I did some in-patient work with newly disabled people. They respond differently when a blind person walks into the room. No one knows what they're feeling in that moment, and I've always been very careful about presuming what I know and what I don't. What's most important is to ask them what they're experiencing.

"After graduating from United States International University, I was living in London for a time at a boarding hotel in the early 1970s. I was surprised to hear a wheelchair coming out of the room across the hall from me. And the young woman was shocked to see a guide dog coming out of the room with me. She was a beauty pageant winner who'd been injured in a float accident when the chassis collapsed under her and she broke her neck. We'd go for walks in Hyde Park. Once, I lashed my dog to her wheelchair to do the pulling while she did the steering.

"'When was the last time you remember racing?' I asked her.

"And I started rushing down this path. It was the most exhilarating feeling. I remember feeling her hair blowing in my face, we were going so fast downhill. It was the first time I'd experienced anything like that in a very long time, and it happened because a blind person was pushing a paraplegic's wheelchair. I could feel people staring at us, probably shaking their heads, thinking we were crazy. I could hear their conversations go quiet as we passed them and imagined what they must have been thinking, a guy pushing a woman in a wheelchair with his guide dog lashed to one of the armrests. But we were having fun. We were acting like normal people."

Paul returned home to get his master's in psychology at the United States International University, part of the same international system as the school he'd attended in London. The difference lay in the incredible array of international professorial talent the school was able to attract for single semesters, sometimes even just days. Those speakers opened Paul's eyes further to all the good he could do for people as a psychotherapist, a career he believed could render the adversity of his blindness moot.

"If you can help people change and grow, they're not going to care you can't see."

Paul did several internships to learn the ropes and establish his street creds before opening his own practice after no existing one would bring on a blind therapist. He had no real idea whether potential patients would, in fact, not care that he was blind. One of his first patients was a gay man in his late fifties who was battling aging, one of those wars nobody wins.

"'I don't know if I can help you there,' I told him, 'but I can help you with your decision making, because you're making decisions that are counterproductive to what you're telling me you want to accomplish.'

"'You're just saying that because I'm gay,' he said to me.

"'No,' I told him, 'I'm saying that because you're human. The label *gay* is not relevant because nearly all humans who crave a good relationship want it to be healthy, caring, and enduring.'"

Against all odds of a blind therapist building a practice, Paul soon had a figurative line out the door comprised of lesbian, gay, newly disabled—all people who wanted to achieve something in their lives that had little to do with the labels they'd been stigmatized by. Dealing with the label was not foremost on their mind; getting on with their lives was their paramount issue. Word spreads fast among those looking for help, and his initial assessment had been right: they didn't care that Paul was blind because he was able to help them.

But how does a psychotherapist overcome not being able to see body language—a patient squirming, frowning, even tearing up?

Many practitioners would even tell you what they see is more important than what they hear.

"When people get anxious or nervous, they withdraw, and that's something you can actually hear. I used to place office toys within easy reach; my whole desk that patients sat in front of was littered with them, things I never used myself. After the session was over, I'd reexamine the desk surface to check the order—what had been moved and where. I also practiced a form of Carl Jung's sandbox therapy where patients would select objects from a bookshelf lined with toys and place them in a sandbox to create a scene based on the kind of questions I was asking them. Something like, 'When you think of your future, what does it look like?'

"I had a patient who was a fourteen-year-old girl. She really didn't want to be there, and she had no damn clue as to what she was feeling. I asked her to set up a scene in the sandbox so I could feel it. She took to the project instantly. I could hear her rummaging around the shelves, picking up certain objects and building whatever she was building.

"'Do you have any cigarettes?' she asked me.

"'You can't smoke in here,' I told her.

"'No, I mean for the sandbox.'

"So I gave her my pouch of pipe tobacco.

"'Do you have any liquor bottles?'

"'Can I give you another bottle that will represent that?' And I gave her a coffee carafe to stand in for the liquor bottle.

"I felt what she had built in the center of her design: cigarettes, booze, pills, a set of keys, a stack of money, and she'd also put in a pair of dice, an ironically revealing play on the word 'paradise.' This was how she viewed her maturing process into the world of adulthood with all its temptations, decisions, anxiety, hopes, and fears. She knew her parents had the same concerns she did, but they were attempting to control her decision-making process more than they wanted to help her learn decision making for herself. But she'd also placed the figurine of a Buddha in the sandbox facing the center.

"'That's you,' she told me.

"'Are you willing to help me figure out this stuff with you?' I asked her.

"'No, I was hoping you could help my parents get it. I want to be the best person I can be, and I want their support, and I want your guidance; I just don't want to be told what to do and how to think.'

"I'd never seen such honesty in a patient, and it had nothing to do with words. I was suddenly and forcefully returned to the blind school and how I felt when teachers told me I couldn't do or be what was important to me. I could also tell if a patient is uncomfortable or nervous because when they're squirming I could hear their chair squeak. I could tell when they're leaning back, crossing their legs. I could read their mannerisms. I could detect even the subtlest changes in their breathing. I relied on the ability to listen and discern the meaning of what I had just heard. See, verbal communication isn't just about what a person says; it's also about what they don't say. And you speculate about the dialogue going on in their minds that never comes out of their mouths. The goal is to help a person make a change they're desperate to make but don't know how to."

That said, Paul has been faced with more than his share of career challenges.

"Anyone who's been self-employed knows well the ups and downs. I was fully invested in doing what I wanted to do, to be successful, to support my family. But it was very hard. Somedays I questioned whether I should just get a job and let someone else cut me a check, but then I remembered that I'd already tried that over and over and nobody would give me that break. Did I help many of my patients? Yes. Did I fail to help some? More times than I care to recall. Some patients came because they heard about my therapy successes, and my blindness was irrelevant to them. Some cancelled their first appointment when they found out I was blind. There are many factors that go into a successful therapy. Is the patient ready to face and name whatever is holding them back? Is the patient willing to reach out for change? Is the patient motivated to carry through and make the change on their own to allow themselves to be reborn? Every day I ask myself whether I've screwed my head on sufficiently to be of help to anyone. I never wanted to be limited by my disability, but over time I came to understand my own limitations, most of which had nothing to do with my disability, eventually learning to accept and work around all of them."

So what would Paul build in a sandbox of his own making?

"Wow, that's a tough one. For me, being raised by a single mother was profound. And many of my first mentors were powerful women, and the men I was surrounded by as a child were weak and indecisive. So I guess a statue of a woman would be one of the centerpieces of my sandbox. And right next to that female statue, I'd place one of a male, only much smaller and diminished in terms of scale. Next to that, *behind* the female statue, I'd place a heroic statue of a male, Apollo or Hercules, to show I never had a strong male like that in my life. My strongest relationships by far have always been with women. But the sandbox would also contain circles of both male and female warriors to represent all the people who helped me, my mentors."

At seventy-one, blind for over sixty years now, Paul is several years removed from his psychotherapy practice and has replaced it with a second career as a medical massage therapist, touching bodies instead of minds. Using the hands he'd come to rely on far more than most, since touch had long been an indispensable tool for his perceiving the world.

"It takes time to build trust as a psychotherapist, sometimes three months of sessions just to form a mutual acceptance of each other. On the massage table, that never happens. There's no such resistance. Patients come to you to relieve their physical pain, and they can identify exactly where it is, in contrast to what's going on in their minds. And I can literally feel their pain when I work those areas. I hear changes in their breathing, like a sigh, which tells me I've hit a sweet spot."

Ironically enough, Paul sighs.

187

"I've been married to my wife for forty-three years now. When our first child was born and I held him for the first time, she could see the pain in my face when it dawned on me that I'd never see him. I could change diapers at three a.m. like all fathers, but I'd never know what my son looked like. When it comes to adversity, people have to cut themselves some slack. You need to be able to acknowledge your flaws. You learn that your reach is limited, and what you need to accomplish through self-acceptance is to turn your reach into a larger grasp. If you don't accept yourself, if your flaws are the biggest deal to you, you've limited that grasp of the future and your ability to reach toward the present. We're not alone. We all live in a world of people who are limited in one way or another.

"That said, nothing seems to make people feel more helpless and hopeless than being blind. In a recent survey, it was rated as the worst thing that could ever happen to them, including losing their hearing, losing both their hands, getting cancer—you name it. The problem is everybody wants to be special, but nobody wants to be different. All of us, though, live with some deficit we think makes us different, not because of the deficit itself so much as how we respond to it. When God closes a door, God opens a window. The problem is the window's usually on the fourth floor."

Meaning you're too far away to see what's on the other side of the glass.

"I follow the Tibetan Buddhist teachings to create space or a gap from which the impossible can emerge. Don't be so crowded in your head that you don't make room for a miracle."

~ ~ ~

## Reflections

"He's hiking up Machu Picchu. He'll call when he gets back." That's what we were told when we first tried to get in touch with Paul Allen about an interview. Machu Picchu, the great Inca building site, sits at an altitude of 7,970 feet in the Andes Mountains. It's a UN World Heritage site and attracts more than half a million visitors a year to its breathtaking setting, perched near the top of a peak, surrounded by a vast range of towering mountains. It's a must-see on the bucket list of those who want to visit the world's most spectacular places. A blind person visiting Machu Picchu doesn't quite register. It's hard enough to trek up there, and then you wouldn't see anything once you've arrived. Who would do such a thing?

Paul Allen not only did that, he did it casually, in the sense that he didn't treat his accomplishment as anything special. That was characteristic of the way he talked about himself. For many years he had been a psychotherapist specializing in hypnotherapy. He had been a massage therapist. In his younger days he had played piano at a bar; he knew four or five thousand songs. He couldn't read the music sheets, but he could visualize the notes in his mind.

In our discussions with him, there was at least as much in what he didn't say as in what he did. How did Machu Picchu impress him, since he couldn't see it? Where did he study and train for psychoanalysis? What about for massage therapy? How exactly was it that he could "see" the notes for four or five thousand songs?

In a relatively brief interview like this, Allen limited himself to touching on some of the high points. It wasn't that his training wasn't important or his musical gifts didn't deserve to be explored. They just didn't seem important enough to dwell on. He had no interest in shining a spotlight on himself and his achievements. He just wanted to talk a bit about his life, exactly the same way a "normal" (i.e., sighted) person would talk about his or hers.

Paul Allen does in fact consider himself normal. In his early seventies now, he radiates a sense of contentment based at least in part on the interesting, accomplished life he has led. The severity of his disability has as its counterpoint the resilience factors that have *enabled* him.

One of those factors is his feistiness, his stand-up nature. He might have been stuck in the closed, unsatisfactory world of the blind school, but he did not accept it. He lashed out there; he was a troublemaker. Once he got out, he was not going back, no matter what. That's the same irrepressible, gutsy character trait we saw in Claudia Thomas. Another factor is his courage, or boldness. On his first mountain climbing venture with Clarence Coffin, the Navy admiral who had befriended him, he refused to let himself be carried across the crevice. He insisted on getting across himself.

Those two characteristics—call them spirit and fearlessness—are what psychologists term "personality traits," the unique, intrinsic elements of character we all embody in one form or another, the psychological DNA that underlies who we are.

We might call natural curiosity, or "openness to experience," another trait characteristic. We all know people who are curious by nature, who have a drive that makes them want to explore the world around them. We know others who are shy, distant, more fearful and closed in, people who instinctively avoid rather than embrace new things. Mangok Bol, the Lost Boy refugee, has that innate exploratory drive. Paul Allen has that same drive. But without the ability to see, he turned to other senses: hearing and feeling. As a psychotherapist, he was hyperaware of his patients audially. He could hear their body language, the way they sat and moved in their chair, the sounds of their breathing. His sense of touch told him how they had arranged figures in his sandbox test (a common diagnostic technique) or rearranged them on his desk. As a massage therapist, he could feel the tension, the pain in his clients.

Allen acquired much of his knowledge through hearing and touch the way sighted people gain much of theirs through seeing. But it is the way he used this knowledge that is perhaps more interesting for our purposes. As a psychotherapist, he needed to employ a deep understanding of his patients' emotional lives. As a massage therapist, he needed an equivalent sensitivity to their physiological symptoms.

The common denominator here is empathy. Paul Allen's experience seems to be telling us that the ability to enter compassionately into another person's inner life can itself be a powerful element in the dynamic of resilience. It focuses a person outward. It gives meaning to that focus. Empathy is not usually emphasized in discussions of resilience. We believe it should be.

# 14

# Bobby Satcher

On March 7, 1965, civil rights protestors were savagely beaten by police for no more than trying to walk across the Edmund Pettus Bridge in Selma, Alabama.

More than forty-four years later, on November 19, 2009, astronaut Dr. Robert Satcher, who happened to be born in 1965, performed a different kind of walk, venturing outside the space shuttle *Atlantis* to install an antenna on the International Space Station. It was to be the first of two spacewalks for Bobby on that eleven-day mission, the second occurring four days later to perform further maintenance on the ISS. In total, the fourteenth African-American astronaut, and first ever orthopedic surgeon as well as oncologist in space, spent over twelve hours outside the craft, far longer than it would have taken those protestors to cross the Edmund Pettus Bridge had their walk not been so brutally interrupted.

"I want to be a role model for African-American youth," Bobby says today. "I speak to young people all the time, and I focus my remarks on the broader issue of whatever they dream, they can achieve. And when they see somebody like them just standing up and being there, well, let's just say that a picture's worth a thousand words. That's eighty percent of what needed to occur, the message coming across that if I can do it, so can you. Young people need someone to show them what they bring to the table, show them the possible and then help them achieve it. I wouldn't be where I am today without the mentors I had."

And where he finds himself, as an African-American orthopedic surgical oncologist and former mission specialist astronaut, is utterly unprecedented. The odds of achieving the level of success he has in these dual pursuits would be somewhat akin to winning Powerball and being struck by lightning.

"It's all a matter of perception," Ben Harvey, educator and cofounder of Authentic Education told the HuffPost for an article entitled "8 Habits of People Who Have Achieved Success Against the Odds" in July of 2017. "An unsuccessful person may think of starting a business but then encounters obstacles and thinks, 'What if I fail?' Whereas the successful person sees solutions: 'How can I learn more?' or 'How will I succeed?'"

The latter fits Bobby to a T. When he was growing up, it was common for kids to say they wanted to be an astronaut. This was the generation, after all, that had been raised on John Glenn becoming the first man ever to orbit the earth in February of 1962, piloting Friendship 7. The generation that watched the burgeoning Gemini and Apollo programs that followed Glenn's fellow Mercury Seven test pilots, which author Tom Wolfe so brilliantly captured in *The Right Stuff*.

Of course, in those days it might as well have been called the *white* stuff. It would be more than twenty years after Friendship 7 that Guion Bluford became the first African-American to travel into space aboard the space shuttle *Challenger* in August of 1983. That hadn't been the plan. In fact, the Kennedy administration had lobbied heavily for NASA to select an African-American astronaut and, toward that end, had actually selected Air Force pilot Ed Dwight to become the first African-American trainee with an eye toward becoming the first in space as well. A different kind of pioneer than John Glenn, but a pioneer all the same.

"Those plans all got waylaid when Kennedy was assassinated. And we've still got a long way to go in terms of getting African-Americans to participate in the space program. Representation is still low. Of all the astronauts in space, only seven percent, or about half the percentage African-Americans make up in terms of population, have been black. That needs to change. It's a work in progress. But the number of African-American physicians has gone down too, and that's something that requires even more diligence, continuous diligence. The institutionalized barriers for blacks are still there. Contrary to popular belief, they haven't been dismantled. When you see someone break through in areas where there hasn't been representation before, people relax and think we're okay. But the fact remains that it's still a lot harder for a black person to be successful. There are still a lot of barriers at all different levels."

Many of which Bobby faced too as an African-American striving to succeed in not one but two pursuits that are utterly dominated by whites.

"The belief that they will succeed no matter what can be seen especially in those that have had struggles in their path to success," psychologist Elizabeth Neal told the HuffPost for that same July 2017 article. "Confident individuals communicate with certainty that a challenge can and will be met effectively."

After receiving his doctorate in chemical engineering from the Massachusetts Institute of Technology (MIT), Bobby went on to graduate from Harvard Medical School in 1994, becoming a renowned orthopedic surgeon ultimately specializing in musculoskeletal oncology, limbs mostly, at the renowned MD Anderson Cancer Center in

Houston. On second glance, though, you realize that the road that led him into space was paved with books and dominated by education.

"I wouldn't be where I am without education," he said as part of NASA's Preflight Interview series in 2009. "I think it's something that we as a generation, I would say my generation, I think we kind of undervalue. Fortunately, there's more of a focus being brought on that now. And I'm grateful I was indoctrinated that way because it really does open up possibilities for you to the point where literally the sky's the limit. You can do anything you want once you have your education, and education is definitely the gift that keeps on giving. It drives you to continue to try to make yourself better, which, of course, opens up more and more possibilities for you."

What about the journey from MD into space?

"It was probably during residency and the inklings were there throughout the years," he told NASA for that same Preflight Interview series, "but I didn't really think it was a realistic possibility, and I think part of the thing that convinced me that it was a realistic possibility was seeing other people who I related to that were astronauts. I had the privilege of meeting Ron McNair; he came to MIT a few times when I was there as a student, and I knew about his story. He actually was from South Carolina also and got his PhD at MIT and then came to NASA and became an astronaut. During residency I actually met several physicians who were astronauts—Scott Parazynski, a couple other people—and just got the opportunity to really get to know them, and it was kind of that process and them sort of saying, 'Hey, this is something that you should seriously consider.' That was really the thing that kind of got me to the point of going on and finally deciding to apply for it. It had never been done before, and I really took to the idea of being the first at something."

As a surgeon, he had explored the inside of the human body but had a deep desire to take that drive toward exploration to the absolute limits. There was risk involved, of course, specifically putting aside the career he had so painstakingly built to chase a dream the odds were very much against him ever achieving. In 2016, for example, NASA received over eighteen thousand applications for the 2017 astronaut class, it's most ever. Out of that number, though, only between eight and fourteen will be selected. (In that year it was thirteen.) That means an applicant has only a 0.04 to 0.08 percent chance of being accepted into the program, and that comes with no guarantee that he or she will ever see the earth from space.

"I had people asking me why I was doing this, putting everything I'd built on hold, risking all the time I had invested in my academic career. There was a lot of advice coming from that side of my life, that I had amassed all these credentials, only to shift to an entirely different pathway. They thought I was risking my career."

He was also risking far more than that, as all astronauts do, especially in the wake of the *Challenger* tragedy that changed the way Americans viewed space travel, no longer taking it for granted. For every precaution and system redundancy NASA builds into space flight, something can, and almost always does, go wrong.

"There's risks in everything, though. Doctors are being exposed to COVID every day, sometimes all day. On the medical side, I did a lot of my training, my residency, during the height of the HIV crisis, and there was a lot of risk associated with that. There was so much fear associated with the disease on the front lines because nobody knew how to treat it. We were all terrified of a needle stick, being exposed. In all cases you do everything you can to minimize the risk, but the risk is still there. It's a matter of finding the confidence to work toward that something that's hard to do, bigger than yourself."

He went on to complete his astronaut training in February of 2006. And, it turned out, his medical training had prepared him for what he was going to face in the rigorous process that would ultimately lead to him spending 259 hours in space. Talk about overcoming the odds.

"The best way for me to frame astronaut candidate training is in terms of my medical training, because I think it was kind of analogous in certain ways to that. The last couple years of medical school, where you're rotating through the hospitals doing different clerkships in different areas like internal medicine, pediatrics, surgery, where you sort of learn the brass tacks, the nuts and bolts of those areas and learn how to function in a very general way before choosing a specialty. Mission training is similar in that you're either a mission specialist or a pilot or commander and you have specific tasks that you're going to have to do and your training is geared towards those tasks."

Education, education, education, in other words, something he preaches whenever he speaks at schools. Upon touching down fatefully on the moon in July of 1969, Neil Armstrong famously said, "That's one small step for a man, one giant leap for mankind." Well, in Bobby's mind, education can be a comparable springboard. Call it one small step at a time to make a giant leap toward your dreams.

"Both my parents came from large families, eight siblings in each. And every single one of them, all sixteen, went to college. My great-great-grandfather was a sharecropper, but all of his kids went to college too. Back then, because of Jim Crow laws, racial separation had been institutionalized. Higher education was prohibited except in schools that accepted black students—black-run schools, in other words. My great-great-grandfather relied on selling his produce to earn a living but received a lot of disapproval from his clients for sending his kids to college. Because he was black, they figured he didn't know how to do math and offered him less than his produce was worth. Once when he showed them up, he had to flee for his life. Walked all the way from Anniston to Birmingham, Alabama, sixty miles, before making his way to Cleveland. That reinforced his belief in education even more."

Bobby doesn't see his dual passions of space and medicine as mutually exclusive at all. In fact, he sees the former as a perfect complement for the latter.

"It's difficult to predict what the benefits of space travel and space-based research will be to those of us on the ground. There are things in our lives today, things that have transformed society, that are simply the result of exploration."

Among other things, Bobby cites MRI and CT scan imaging machines that owe their existence directly to space exploration. And the next step, as NASA boldly embarks on the newest phase of the space program by returning to the moon and journeying, eventually, to Mars, will produce even greater results as far as medicine is concerned.

"We're going to need technology that can take care of people for extended periods in space, three years or more for a Mars voyage. We're going to have to invent new ways to treat illness, perform surgery in space or a low-gravity environment like on Mars. Need is going to drive that sort of development, and it's going to lead to discoveries we never expected in the form of technologies we may have dreamed of but never would have otherwise realized. The needs of exploration drive what happens in the lab, and that eventually transfers back to Earth."

Bobby talks about advances in telemedicine, something we've started to see more and more of during the COVID-19 crisis, along with even more dramatic progress in robotic surgery, something very close to his heart as an orthopedic surgeon.

"Those advances and others have their roots in exploration because space forced us to bring technologies together, and develop new ones, that had never been done before. Going to Mars will require the next steps in telesurgery, in which a surgeon remotely guides the robot, or maybe even a robot capable of performing surgery on its own."

To Bobby's point, the list of medical innovations resulting directly from NASA and the space program is long and impressive, all due to the fact that people like him were willing to take the necessary risks because of the rewards to be reaped on the other side. Just to name a few:

- Digital imaging breast biopsy system, developed from Hubble Space Telescope technology
- Tiny transmitters to monitor the fetus inside the womb
- Laser angioplasty using fiber-optic catheters

- Forceps with fiber optics that let doctors measure the pressure applied to a baby's head during delivery
- Cool suits to lower body temperature in treatment of various conditions
- Voice-controlled wheelchairs
- Light-emitting diodes (LED) for help in brain cancer surgery
- Foam used to insulate space shuttle external tanks for better, less expensive molds for artificial arms and legs
- Programmable pacemakers
- Tools for cataract surgery

As far as robotic surgery goes, he mentions an operation that was recently performed on a patient in France by a doctor stationed in New York City. The future, to some extent, is now, an incalculable number of lives on earth having been saved by new technologies developed for space explorations.

Take a robotic arm developed by Canadian scientists and called, appropriately enough, Canadarm and its more recent offspring, Canadarm2.

"Taking Canadian expertise in automation, robotics, and imaging into the next era of innovation," reported the Canadian Space Agency in February of 2018, "pioneering scientists, engineers, and entrepreneurs have been developing cutting-edge spinoff technologies for industry, medicine, and other applications based on Canadarm, Canadarm2 and Dextre. Examples of these spinoffs include Neuroarm, the world's first robot capable of performing surgery inside magnetic resonance machines, and the Image-Guided Autonomous Robot (IGAR), a new digital surgical solution expected to increase access to life-saving surgical techniques to fight breast cancer."

The development of lifesaving technologies like that further affirms Bobby's unprecedented pursuits as both astronaut and orthopedic surgeon, pursuits he achieved only by overcoming stereo-types along with the odds. And he doesn't believe we're done yet, not by a long shot.

"I grew up looking at the Apollo missions; it's what made me want to become an astronaut. My class came in and we were supposed to go to the moon and Mars. We never got that far because our mission was to help complete the International Space Station. But we have the potential to do so much more than that. The space program needs to continue; I mean it has to. COVID has made everyone aware of their mortality and the fact that there are a limited amount of resources on our planet. Earth is a finite thing. Looking at space, at other planets, is eventually going to be a survival issue for us. We're going to need to go to other planets. We may need to put people on other planets."

Dealing with cancer, and now COVID-19 as well, on a daily basis has made Bobby realize all too well the nature of human fragility.

"The questions we're interested in are how the skeleton responds to external forces and how cancer spreads to the skeleton."

Perhaps space exploration might yield the next medical break-through, and not a moment too soon for his patients. And, as an African-American surgeon and astronaut, he is all too aware of the light the coronavirus has shined on the black community when it comes to treatment.

"The whole country can see it now, thanks to all the coverage of the dramatic disparity in access to care that has resulted in a far higher mortality rate for African-Americans. That's typical of the troubled relationship between African-Americans and the medical community."

In Washington, DC, for example, 45 percent of the population is black, but that community accounts for three-quarters of the deaths. In Louisiana, the ratio is 33 percent to 65 percent; in Wisconsin, it's 7 percent versus 39 percent.

"COVID has exposed all that, and now we have the opportunity to talk about it because of the national attention it's received. Something to build on moving forward."

Speaking of moving forward, Bobby is a big fan of science fiction and the vision the genre offers for our technological future. His favorites are the original *Star Wars* movies, the first three that ultimately became the middle trilogy.

"If I had to choose a technology to take from those films, my first choice would be the ability to go into hyperspace and travel large distances in short periods. As an orthopedic surgeon, though, I also always come back to the robotic hand Luke Skywalker gets at the end of *The Empire Strikes Back*. I look at those artificial tendons, the gears and gadgets. That was very convincing. We're not there yet in medicine, but we will be someday."

As for that someday, Bobby is happy to report a new enthusiasm for space on the part of the young people he frequently speaks to, almost like a second coming of wanting to grow up to be an astronaut.

"The recent commercialization of space, thanks to SpaceX and Boeing, has released this pent-up enthusiasm. These kids are aware the United States hasn't been flying spacecraft in their lifetime, but they want to be the ones to change that. Young people are still looking up toward the stars. The only way they will certainly fail is if they don't try."

~ ~ ~

## Reflections

Bobby Satcher, MD, PhD, NASA astronaut, has few, if any, peers as a role model for African-American youngsters. He focuses on their dreams; he tells them they can achieve whatever they dream of being. "And when they see somebody like them just standing up and being there, well, let's just say that a picture's worth a thousand words."

Satcher talks about the role models he himself has had, including Ron McNair, an African-American astronaut, also an MIT PhD, who died in the *Challenger* disaster.

Gus White, the Harvard orthopedic surgeon who is one of this book's authors, was also a role model and mentor for him. When

Satcher was finishing up his doctorate in chemical engineering at MIT and his MD at Harvard, he went to see White in his office. He wanted to know what his chances might be for an orthopedic residency. Orthopedic slots were notoriously hard to get.

"What are your grades?" White asked. Satcher's grades were all As and honors. "Orthopedic residency?" White said. "You're a national treasure!"

There were then very few black astronauts. McNair was the second to walk in space. There were also very few African-American surgeons; Gus White was the first black service chief at Harvard. It was a long shot that Satcher would have ever met an African-American NASA pilot or an African-American chief surgeon. A lucky chance. But as Louis Pasteur famously said, "Chance favors the prepared mind," and Satcher's mind was prepared. "You can do anything you want once you have your education," he says. "It drives you to continue to try to make yourself better, which, of course, opens up more and more possibilities for you."

Education—that is, the drive to explore and to absorb knowledge—is the theme of this interview. It's not too much to say it's been the theme of Bobby Satcher's life. His sidestep from medicine into space exploration is a case in point. The body's musculoskeletal structure and cancer's assault on bones are fields that can and do immerse surgeons and medical scientists for their entire careers. It's uncommon to see specialists in these areas suddenly switching to something completely different. Satcher did that. A new field of knowledge beckoned, and he jumped at the opportunity to explore its intricacies and secrets. Of course, Satcher's wide embrace of knowledge was evident earlier; he had completed his doctoral work in chemical engineering along with his medical studies.

Satcher exemplifies the drive to know. Underlying his extraordinary accomplishments is the need to encompass and cognize the world around us, to establish and expand our knowledge base. This is, without a doubt, a pillar component of human nature, a prerequisite for cognitive functioning. That same drive is a striking part, for example, of Paul Allen's life. We'll see it too in Herman Williams's interview later on. It is displayed most starkly perhaps in the story of how Mangok Bol transformed himself from a pastoral herd boy in one of Africa's most remote regions into a college graduate in what amounts to a different universe.

A senior American resettlement officer who worked with Bol and many hundreds of other refugees put it this way. "Education," she said, "is mental health." The connection with resilience is self-evident. Like empathy, like faith, like purpose, the drive to know draws attention outward, away from an inner self that may have been stricken by traumatic injury. Almost by definition, trauma cuts people off from who they were before. So often recovery means building a new self and a different life, "resurrecting" yourself, as Jim Pantelas saw it. For that, the drive to know new things and to reorder old things is the prerequisite.

"Education" in Bobby Satcher's terms, "opens up…possibilities."

# 15

# Matt Paknis

*The purpose of this book is to shed light on myths and realities of male trauma. It's to help trauma survivors who have difficulty disclosing their bad experiences with anyone, with loved ones, to learn how to share the truth to heal from, to stop, to prevent abuse, and to live well. My intention in sharing my story is to allow people a hopeful glimpse into how, with the right support, drive, and competencies, someone can turn gut wrenching circumstances and incredible pain into success, advocacy and resiliency.*

So opens *A Lineman's Dream*, the soon-to-be published instructional autobiography of Matt Paknis. The tentative title is an ironic choice indeed, given that the experiences it centers upon seem lifted from a nightmare.

"My parents met at the same high school. She was a cheerleader and he was a football player. So, everyone assumed I had this ideal childhood. They didn't know my father had physically abused me since I was a toddler, or for as long as I can remember."

"Without warning," Matt recounts in the book about an incident when he was nine years old and had just gotten home from school for lunch to find his dying mom being wheeled out of the house on a gurney, "my father let his fears and frustrations out on the back of my head with several slaps. This forced my face to slam into the sandwich my grandmother prepared and further damaged my already broken nose. I burst into tears. My grandmother and grandfather said, 'Oh, please, don't.' I heard my grandfather suck his tongue and shake his head, as if to say, 'Oh no!' Blood spread everywhere and I returned to school; red faced, bloodied, and hungry."

Far from ideal, right?

Not long after this incident, and as the physical abuse by his father continued, Matt was targeted, then groomed, and ultimately sexually abused by a neighbor.

"My perpetrator was a creepy neighbor who hung around too much," he writes, the pain and torment lifting off the page and striking the reader like a gut punch. "He was not involved in any youth organization. He was not a coach. He was not in my peer group. He was just a creep. He invited himself into my private area. He befriended my parents. He massaged my back after I fell out of a tree fort one day. He came back and asked me if I wanted more massages. I stated my mom always rubbed my back when I was sick or hurt. He told me not to tell my mom, or anyone else, that he was massaging my back. I did as I was told and kept it quiet. The massages led to him violating me. As he did this, I froze, like when my father was hitting me. Deep in my soul I felt smothered and weak, something I'd learn as an adult is a typical trauma response. This led to comprehensive childhood sexual abuse and molestation, on a regular basis, over the next three to four years except when we went away. I craved the attention and connection, but did not comprehend the abuse.

"Groomers know exactly what they need and where to find it," Matt adds. "They're predators. They see an easy target in a boy whose mom was in and out of the hospital and whose father wasn't really around even when he was, a public angel and private devil. I was traumatized and became extremely independent at a very young age, to my detriment. I was trained to not share my problems or to ask for help. Predators can see that. They lock in on it."

"Twenty-eight to thirty-three percent of women and twelve to eighteen percent of men were victims of childhood or adolescent sexual abuse," Melissa and Joshua Hall wrote for the American Counseling Association website in an article entitled "The Long-Term Effects of Childhood Sexual Abuse: Counseling Implications," proceeding to elaborate on those long-term effects. "Survivors often experience guilt, shame, and self-blame. It has been shown that survivors frequently take personal responsibility for the abuse. When the sexual abuse is done by an esteemed *and* trusted adult it may be hard for the children to view the perpetrator in a negative light, thus leaving them incapable of seeing what happened as not their fault. Survivors often blame themselves and internalize negative messages about themselves. Survivors tend to display more self-destructive behaviors and experience more suicidal ideation than those who have not been abused."

Among the other long-term effects the Halls reflect upon are depression, body issues, eating disorders, stress, anxiety, sexual inadequacy, and difficulty in establishing interpersonal relationships. Matt Paknis was too young to understand, and to integrate, his overwhelming traumatic experiences into his life or to channel his rage and anger with productive outlets. His anger manifested in obsessive thoughts and judgments, internal compulsions, and responses and rituals, including compulsive hair pulling, or trichotillomania, resulting in several large bald spots.

And on top of all that, Matt was dealing with the ever-declining health of his mother.

"My mother had three young children when she was diagnosed with stage IV melanoma at the age of thirty-six, a death sentence with a short survival prognosis, yet she never complained about her great pains," he writes in *A Lineman's Dream*. "Never griped after surgeries to remove her diseased lymph system or the related hemorrhaging. Her surgeries required over two thousand stitches. She never showed pity for losing her youthful legs and body at thirty-six to edema and scars. She never broke down during the eight-year valiant battle she waged, yet lost, against this insidious foe."

Sometimes life really does pile on. But you wouldn't know that from looking at Matt Paknis today. His bulk, powerful frame, and full head of hair make him look not so far removed from the football player who enjoyed brief stints with the New England Patriots and New York Giants after completing an All-Ivy career at Brown University. And speaking of football, Matt found significant respite on the field, where he excelled under legendary coach Ted Monica at New Jersey's Madison High School.

"Coach Monica was a disciple of Vince Lombardi, and they had a lot in common. Coach Lombardi's philosophies were influenced by his time coaching at West Point. Coach Monica received a Purple Heart in the Korean War. They knew each other, and Coach Monica helped the Packers on NFL Draft Day for years. Both were builders of men. They had the same kind of frame; bulldogs, kind of like human fireplugs. Coach Monica had this presence about him that automatically raised the level of energy in the room as soon as he walked in. He brought a Marine attitude to the field—*Semper Fidelis*, the motto of the Marine Corps which means always loyal, always faithful. You always knew he had your back, even though you knew he would test you, bringing out the most from your potential. I sensed that he went out of his way to look out for me. I never told him what I'd experienced, but I felt he knew I could handle and respond to adversity and challenge while looking out for my teammates. He died recently, and I was one of the eulogists at his service, so I've been thinking about this a lot lately."

For Matt, starring for Coach Monica at Madison High represented a milestone in his life, if not a turning point that sent him on to a Division I football career in college and flirtation with the NFL.

"I went from all that stress just a year or so before to being a three-year starter on three consecutive undefeated New Jersey state championship teams, the only sophomore starter that first season. And I was selected as co-captain my senior year when we finished the season top ranked in New Jersey. Being a part of this team pulled me through several acute childhood experiences [ACES], as sadly my mom finally succumbed to melanoma during my senior high school football season. Being part of that structure, that community, made me feel whole. We had no hazing, no bullying. Just being around the atmosphere Coach Monica created for his players, it was like an incubator, a family, a band of brothers."

Which was something that had been stolen from Matt's youth, what almost all kids take for granted. What they called everyday life, Matt saw as a kind of awakening. By eighth grade, he had freed himself of the systematic physical and sexual abuse he'd suffered for so long as a boy, an empowering milestone for him. He'd played youth football briefly when he was nine, but part of that experience triggered the fears that had dominated his young life.

"There were parts of football I loved in fourth grade. I loved the drills and the contact and the challenge. I loved to scrimmage. My size, strength, and agility made me equal to players two to three years older than me. I dominated practice but hated the coaches yelling and swearing at me and the team. That made me shake. It made my stomach hurt. I wondered what was wrong with me. I didn't realize I was afraid of them like I was afraid of my father. I guess I was responding to them like I responded to my father. I thought they'd attack me if they weren't pleased, so I tried to be perfect to please them and to keep them from hitting me, like I tried to do to keep my father from beating me. It was too much stress for me, a traumatized nine-year-old boy. Despite loving the game and the players, I couldn't take the anxiety and fear."

And then Coach Monica entered his life. Like all great coaches and leaders, he was very tough, but he showed his players they were valued and loved with his actions and efforts. He forged a fighting force with trust and interdependence. The support and encouragement spread throughout the school and community. It was a perfect salve for Matt's young, traumatized soul.

"Coach Monica was very demanding, sure, but he was also very progressive, and everyone on the team knew he cared. We were drinking Gatorade before any other high school, and he researched the latest lifting and stretching and running techniques. He cared about what we put into our bodies and how we developed our bodies. Our offensive and defensive schemes where chosen and adapted to best fit our talent. But more than anything he taught me how to trust again. Coaches sometimes never know the impact they have on a player's life."

And, thanks in large part to that impact, the man Matt Paknis is today emerged. But he had some other help along the way, particularly from a therapist he started seeing when he was twelve years old, giving him an adult to whom he could finally open up to.

"He helped me look at my life—the distortions, the fears I had about people, places, the world in general—differently. He helped me identify those distortions so I was able to make healthier choices in the moment as opposed to some of the bad decisions I'd been making. He created an environment in which I finally felt safe. He helped me become aware. One of the healthiest things he did one day was he told me, 'You know, Matt, I've asked your father several times if he'd be willing to meet with the three of us. Each time, he's said no.' This helped me realize he wasn't willing to improve our relationship, so I decided, emotionally, as an eighth grader, to distance myself from him. This was tough, but very healthy for me. Also, I noticed one time the therapist asked to see my father, alone. I sat in the waiting room and I could tell he was lecturing my father. I couldn't hear the specifics, but I could tell he was upset. I had never heard or seen anyone stand up to my father like this, standing up for my mom and me; he was like my advocate.

"What a blessing. It wasn't just about what he said; it was the fact that what he did better than anything was treat me with respect. He listened to me at a time when I was dealing with a lot of issues with OCD, obsessive compulsive disorder. I was truant, among other things. And he helped me clear up all the trauma so I could concentrate, enabled my basic functioning. All these very scary things were happening to me, and I could finally wrap my head around them. I tried to listen, tried to trust him, which was a rarity for me. The thing that helped me the most was the release of telling him all the stuff that was happening in my life, including the physical and sexual abuse. It felt so good to let it all out, all those things I'd been keeping in, that I couldn't share with my mom because she was so sick. Talking to him was very empowering. Up until then, I couldn't even put into words what was going on in my head. I was always trying to put up a strong front, until the therapist helped me realize there was nothing wrong with me, that being physically and sexually abused wasn't my fault."

What about those myths of male trauma, though, that Matt is so adept at conceptualizing?

"There's the vampire myth that when this happens to someone, they end up repeating the cycle. But the majority of people who are abused as kids, suffered these really horrible experiences, don't do that. Another myth that persisted for years, and continues to some extent, is that the abuser is some creepy person who lives in a dark house. But they're normally drawn from the likes of family, neighbors, teachers, coaches, priests, and Boy Scout leaders. I was a Scout when I was a kid and we had this Scout leader who every summer would pick one kid to take on a motorcycle ride. We all thought it was weird, but it was worse than that, because he was abusing the kids he picked out. It's not about sex or pleasure, and it's not about love either. It's about the need to be able to dominate and attempt to destroy another person, just like all bullying and abuse is.

"Another thing is that when this is happening within an organization, people know. That's the one common factor across the board—officials in the organization know. I don't care what anyone says after the fact; they knew. That's how the abuse is able to continue, how the abuser is able to remain a perpetrator. And enablers are like accomplices, just as guilty as the perpetrator himself. That's the one thing all bullies—verbal, financial, emotional, spiritual, physical, and sexual—have in common. No parent or teacher or adult ever came to them on the schoolyard or somewhere else and said enough is enough. Nobody straightened them out. Their behaviors never warranted severe consequences. They behave the way they do because they gained something from it as a kid and want it to continue as an adult."

Like Penn State's Jerry Sandusky, a man with whom Matt Paknis became acquainted when he was running the scout team offense against Sandusky's defense while serving as a graduate assistant offensive line coach there in 1987 and 1988. Matt sensed something was very wrong with the coaching staff's dynamics but assumed it was just overinflated egos and power. Clearly, Sandusky's abuse was not beyond Matt's comprehension, but it was difficult to accept given the setting and the program's reputation. He recalls initially spotting Sandusky poking and prodding middle school and high school kids enrolled in Penn State's summer football camps.

"He was always grabbing the kids and giving them knuckle rubs in the head. I watched and it made me very uncomfortable. We'd always been taught to only touch players and kids if you were teaching technique, while other players and coaches were watching."

"I took Sandusky aside and, in private, asked, 'Why are you doing that, Coach?' at one point during camp.

"'I just love the kids!' he said to me, and he said it with a smile.

"He was creepy. To this day, my greatest regret is not being more self-aware and self-trusting and questioning. I was twenty-four or twenty-five and working for the reigning national champions and caught up in the 'We at PSU do it the right way!' mirage. I never saw him abuse a child, but those Second Mile kids were always around.

"One day in the gym at Penn State, I was lifting with the players and stopped to talk with Sandusky, who was riding a stationary bike. He projected a bizarre urine-like aroma I associated with the scumbag neighbor who'd feigned interest in and molested me when I was a kid. In that moment, I shook and felt a guttural response but tried to ignore it and went back to lifting. My high school football experiences, in part, helped me transcend several acute childhood traumas, including sexual abuse, and I wanted to use coaching as a venue to help young men in a similar way, so I had erroneously assumed all coaches were good and decent and hardworking, like my coaches. But I felt this great dissonance over what I smelled on Sandusky, a man generally regarded as a defensive savant. He was thought to be a humble and decent person for founding and running the Second Mile, that nonprofit agency for disadvantaged boys he used as a beard to gain access to and groom his young targets, to violate and molest boys."

"As I read about the Sandusky scandal, in 2011, I became more enraged," *A Lineman's Dream* picks up. "I could not sleep. My heart pounded and mind raced. I broke out in a sweat. Tears welled in my eyes. I stayed up the night reading the grand jury's report and every Sandusky and Penn State related article on the internet. To amend my blindness, I needed to expose Penn State football and people who disguise abuse who are perceived public angels, like my father and Paterno and Sandusky and my scoutmaster. They are private devils. I wanted to help people better understand the massive fraud enacted to cover up the truth of sexual predators and the strategies their organizations use to hide, fool, intercede, perpetuate, and confuse to carry out their ruse."

Had Matt known or seen more in 1987 and 1988 or had been encouraged to question what we now know are red flags indicating abuse, he wonders about and agonizes over the pain he could have prevented. The sham of "Happy Valley" and the gaping wounds it left on so many could have been curtailed much earlier.

Meanwhile, he's built a dedicated and successful career helping organizations thrive with healthy leadership and team principles. He's an entrepreneur and much sought-after corporate consultant and speaker and conducts leadership seminars as well, in which his own management and coaching experiences and lessons are prominently incorporated. And, in a fitting tribute to Coach Monica, he serves as a mentor to the Brown University football team. Matt's also a father of three himself now, the kids all in their twenties.

"Now I'm the parent. I do my best to foster the kind of connection and loving relationship with my kids my own parents weren't able to have with me. I was worried when I first had kids, very cognizant of not repeating anything I'd experienced. I raised them the opposite of how I was raised, which was hard because I didn't have a role model to go by. Some people are more natural parents than others. You don't get a report card. You don't get graded. It doesn't come with an owner's manual. You love and protect your kids and do your best to be a role model for them and to do the best you can."

*Positive beats negative. Light beats darkness. Good (honest, selfless, self-critical behavior) beats evil (lying, selfish, narcissistic behavior). Hope, healing, and support works and is available. It's not your fault! You are not alone! Healing is possible! It's never too late!*

—The opening of *A Lineman's Dream*

~ ~ ~

## Reflections

Many of our interviewees speak of the love and support of parents as a crucial element in the strength they bring to withstanding and recovering from trauma. But what happens when the normal parent/child relationship is turned upside down, when a parent not only doesn't demonstrate love but abuses a child physically? How does a child process the psychological injury of that betrayal of trust? Matt Paknis experienced exactly that with a violent father and a mother too ill to stand up for him. To add to the misery his father was inflicting on him, an older neighbor was at the same vulnerable time in his childhood sexually molesting him.

The father's physical abuse and the neighbor's sexual predation had certain common features. Both were situations where adults brutalized a young person as an outlet for their own needs. About sexual abuse, Paknis says, "It's not about sex or pleasure… It's about the need to dominate another person." The same can be said for child beating. The child is a vulnerable and available target for the parent's anger, frustration, and unhappiness and the resulting uncontrolled urge to act out violently.

As a child, Paknis was unable to understand what was happening to him, and in common with most other abused children he turned the pain and shame of the experiences inward. The result for Paknis was not different from the consequences common in abused children— emotional and physical disorders of various kinds, the desire to run away, his truancy.

For many abused children, the psychic injuries can persist well into adulthood and disrupt the ability to achieve a contented, satisfying life. But Paknis managed to confront the damage he suffered, recover from it, and go on to create a robust, accomplished life for himself. The steps to his recovery illustrate the way support from others and an individual's own capabilities often crystallize in resilience.

First was twelve-year-old Paknis's fortunate encounter with a therapist who helped him understand that the abuse he was suffering was not his fault—that is, the therapist helped him turn away from self-blame, guilt, and shame. Most important, the therapist was a willing listener. He gave Paknis the release of sharing "all the stuff that was happening" in his life with a sympathetic audience instead of bottling up his thoughts and feelings in secrecy.

Sharing, i.e., communication, is of the essence in focusing outward, beyond the internal pain of the trauma. We've seen time and again in these interviews how having some sort of outward focus—short-term goals, enduring purpose, education, vocation—is so significant in mitigating and overcoming adversity. In Matt Paknis's story, the release from secrecy to sharing was empowering for a child who had up till then only been the victim of other people's power.

We've also seen in our stories the importance of having mentors who intervene at critical moments in a person's life. This might happen in a quick interaction or in a long term, more intimate relationship. For Matt Paknis, as badly damaged as he was, a long-term mentor was called for. He found that person in Coach Ted Monica.

For a child, family love provides far more than a diffuse feeling of comfort.

Supportive, loving parents engender security, confidence, trust, discipline, and independence. Parents are the primary role models for positive interpersonal relationships. All these things get conditioned into a well-structured psyche that is prepared to that degree to face challenges and bear up under adversity. In Matt Paknis's childhood, he experienced none of this.

What he found in Coach Monica was more a parent than a mentor. Monica provided first of all a safe place. On the Madison High team there was no bullying or hazing. Monica was a disciplinarian but also protective of his players. He stood up to bullies. He gave Paknis a safe haven, which we know is so important to those recovering from deep, long-term psychic injury. He built confidence, and he did it in a way that was encouraging but measured, which introduced the realism that Paknis needed. He taught trust and discipline. He gave Paknis the resources a more normal childhood would have given him. Monica was, Paknis says, "like an incubator," an apt metaphor since under his tutelage Paknis was, in a sense, reborn.

Paknis brought to this process an attitude of receptivity, an openness that was not destroyed by what he had gone through. A large, powerfully built man, he also brought his physicality and love of football. That gave him a ready field for the expression of his will to recovery. Finally, it was sharing his experiences with his therapist that had initially relieved his anxiety and fear. We've seen the significance of sharing stories in the lives of Jim Pantelas and Claudia Thomas, strengthening not just for the listeners, but for the tellers. In Matt Paknis's career as a leadership seminar figure and corporate consultant, we can see that process highlighted even more dramatically.

The DVD cover of *41*, the movie based on Nick O'Neill's life.

# 16

# Dave Kane and Joanne O'Neill

*Nick O'Neill was one of those kids you figured God must have smiled on. Funny, handsome, talented, Nick had it all. With a boy like that, caring and wise beyond his years, there's no telling how Nick O'Neill would have left his mark on this world.*

—Channing Gray, from the March 2, 2003, edition of
the *Providence Sunday Journal*

The day before he became the youngest victim in Rhode Island's Station Nightclub fire that claimed a hundred lives, eighteen-year-old Nick O'Neill was in the passenger seat of his father's car heading to his girlfriend Gabby's house.

"Nicky's band was going to open for Great White on Friday night, and I asked him how much money he was making," recalls long-time Rhode Island radio talk show host and performer Dave Kane. "He gave me this spiel about the owner giving him tickets to sell, which made no sense to me since most of his friends couldn't even attend the show because they weren't eighteen yet. I was trying to give him a show business lesson and asked Nicky why he was selling God's talent so short.

"'The show must go on, Dad,' he told me. And those were the last words he ever said to me."

"He was sleeping when I left for work," Nicky's mother, Joanne O'Neill, remembers. "When I got out of work at seven on Thursday night, he was already at the Station Nightclub. He'd met [Great White lead singer] Jack Russell, and Jack invited him to come by early to shoot pool and talk music. That's what he was doing when I called him. 'You're going to have a lot of stories to tell,' I said to him. 'I love you.' 'I love you too,' he said. And then I hung up."

The relationship between an aging rocker and the young firebrand wasn't all that surprising, given that Jack Russell to a large degree *was* Nicky back when he was eighteen. A lanky, striking talent with flowing blond locks that left him mistaken for a Hanson brother at times who didn't just command a stage, he owned it. Nicky's whole life in front of him while Russell's reunion tour was being staged in venues that were a far cry from Great White's heyday.

Nicky was never far from Dave and Joanne's minds through the night. He'd gone to the show with Jon Brennan, "JB," who played lead guitar in the band Shryne, for which Nicky sang lead, performing with a presence and charisma far beyond his years. At eighteen, he was already a star; the world just didn't know it yet.

Dave and Joanne settled in to watch the eleven o'clock news, tuning in just as the broadcast was airing a bulletin about a fire that had broken out at the Station Nightclub. A film crew was en route, but no footage was available yet, and rumors were rampant with a flood of police and fire calls blasting over the emergency band, calls being put out for backup fire and rescue crews from communities neighboring West Warwick, Rhode Island, where the Station was located in what had once been a P. Brillo's restaurant with max capacity listed at sixty people.

Over four hundred were crammed into the old, rickety one-story wood-frame structure the night of the fire. The Station actually dated back to 1946 and had been subject to numerous renovations over the years, the kind of building held together in patchwork fashion by duct tape. It didn't hold sound in very well and, responding to a bevy of complaints from neighbors, owners Michael and Jeffrey Derderian had installed black foam soundproofing up the walls and along the ceiling. The fire-retardant variety was pricier, so the brothers opted for a cheaper brand. And they allegedly had no idea Great White would be incorporating pyrotechnic special effects for that evening's show, via cannons that would shoot fireworks into the air as Jack Russell launched into his opening number just past eleven o'clock.

Five minutes later the building was an inferno, already collapsing to the ground. The columns of fire had ignited the soundproofing foam stripped across the ceiling, the fire spreading almost instantly down the walls. A television cameraman from the station for which Jeffrey Derderian served as a reporter captured the second-by-second spread of the flames, on hand for a story on nightclub safety in ironic counterpoint.

"I called Nick about four or five times," Dave, who wasn't yet married to Joanne at the time, recalls. "He didn't pick up, but we weren't aware of how bad it was at that point, so I thought maybe he'd lost his phone or been injured and couldn't answer. We went to Rhode Island Hospital where most of the injured had been taken and started hearing these crazy stories. I thought people were conflating things, embellishing. I got furious. How could it possibly be as bad as they were describing?"

"They had no record of Nick being there and suggested we try Kent County Hospital instead," Joanne picks up.

There they found a semblance of hope. A nurse upstairs where most of the victims were being treated checked the records and said she thought Nick was downstairs in the actual ER and went down to check. For those brief moments, Joanne and Dave breathed a bit easier and allowed themselves to hope. Then the nurse returned, looking grim and glum with the news that she had mistaken Nick for another young man named O'Neill who'd been brought in. False alarm.

"We tried to get to the site, but the roads were all blocked off," says Dave.

By that time, the Station was already long gone. The fire had engulfed the entire building in mere moments, the nightclub going up in flames like the tinderbox it was. The number of casualties in the four-hundred-plus-person crowd mounted by the minute, along with the death toll that continued to rise as the scope of the disaster became clear. Nicky had been directly in front of the stage, not the star of this particular show but as close to the action as he could get.

"They sent us to the Holiday Inn at the Crossings," David continues. "It's a favorite spot for celebrations and events, but it was clear from the clergy and grief counselors who were already there that this was no reunion. We explained why we were there, and they asked for the name of Nicky's dentist."

"I finally got his friend John Brennan, JB, on the line," Joanne follows. "He said Nick was right next to him when he made his way out, but they must have lost track of each other. He said Nick must have gotten out."

She and Dave didn't let themselves hope this time; they'd already experienced seeing it dashed. They knew.

Parents always know.

Nicky was gone.

But he wasn't, and that's the real story here.

"The morning of the fire," recalls renowned Rhode Island psychic medium Cindy Gilman, "I fell into what's called psychic shock. It happens when something terrible is about to happen, and the last time I felt anything like this was 9/11. I couldn't sleep, I couldn't eat, I cancelled all my appointments with clients for the day. Then the next morning, the morning after the fire, a young blond man appeared to me. I say young man, but I wasn't sure at that point whether it was a boy or a girl until I heard him speak.

"'Call my father,' he said to me and then he was gone.

"I had no idea, of course, who he was, who his father was, or what had happened to him. He appeared to me later and made the same plea, then a third time taking a different form that made me realize it was the Station fire. I pulled out my address book and opened it randomly: to the Ks where there was only one name listed: Dave Kane.

"Dave answered, and I asked him if there was anything I could do.

"'How did you know?' he asked me.

"'Know what?'

"'I lost my son last night in the fire.'

"And then he hung up."

"I called Cindy back a few days later," Dave recalls, "and she told me the whole story. I'd had her on my radio show enough times to know she was telling the truth, but I still wasn't ready to believe it."

"Nicky just wanted his parents to know he was okay," Cindy Gilman explains, "that he'd made it to the other side."

This was Saturday or Sunday, two or three days after the fire that had started at 11:08 on Thursday night, and Nicky's body still hadn't been identified among the victims.

"We began getting phone calls from a strange number we'd never seen before," Dave relates. "But there was never anyone there when I picked up. So I called the phone company, AT&T, directly to find out who it was. They kept checking and finally told me it was a nonworking number registered to no one."

Then yet another glimmer of hope.

"The phone rang Monday afternoon," Dave remembers, "and Nicky's number lit up in the caller ID. But when I answered, no one was there. I kept shouting 'Nick, Nick!' but there was nothing. We thought maybe, *maybe*, he somehow survived and wandered off. Lost his memory or something."

Monday night they got a call from the police department in North Providence where Dave's legal residence was, informing him that Nick's body had finally been identified. The next morning, the funeral home called to tell him they were holding some personal items that belonged to the boy, and Dave drove there immediately from the Pawtucket, Rhode Island, apartment he shared with Joanne to retrieve them.

"Nick's cell phone was in a Ziploc bag, totally waterlogged. It didn't work. It couldn't work. It was impossible to turn on."

Joanne and Dave are not alone in believing they've experienced the impossible.

"The popular race car driver Dale Earnhardt Jr. believes his deceased father Dale Earnhardt Sr. saved his life by physically pulling him out of a burning car," Christine Duminiak wrote for the Open to Hope website in April of 2012.

"From the movement I made to unbuckle my belt, to laying on the stretcher, I have no idea what happened," Earnhardt told Mike Wallace of *60 Minutes* in 2004. "How I got out… I don't have an explanation for it other than when I got into the infield care center, I had my PR man by the collar, screaming at him to find the guy that pulled me out of the car. He was like, 'Nobody helped you get out.' And I was like, 'That's strange, because I swear somebody had me underneath my arms and was carrying me out of the car.' I mean, I swear to God."

"And that was your dad?" Wallace asked him.

"Yeah, I don't know. You tell me. It…freaks me out today just talking about it. It just gives me chills."

Count Earnhardt among the 45 percent of Americans who believe in ghosts, according to a HuffPost/YouGov poll as reported in *USA Today* in October of 2017. According to that article, a Pew poll in 2009 said 65 percent of Americans similarly believe in the supernatural. Meanwhile, 49 percent believe that they've had "a religious or mystical experience." That same poll noted that "about 29% of Americans told Pew in 2009 they have felt in touch with a dead person."

Joanne and Dave buried their son Nicky before a standing room only crowd at a Lincoln, Rhode Island, church, more than a thousand mourners squeezed inside or milling about in the frigid night. Through much of the service the music of Nicky's band Shryne played, all of which he had written.

*Sometimes things just fall apart*
*Aging slowly in your heart*
*Sometimes we end up all alone*
*Oh my darling, please take me back home.*
*As the seasons pass, my youth betrays me*
*And as I look back, it's you that's fading*
*Oh, don't you forget this*
*Once you find your heart*
*You'll find your forgotten bliss*

It was the biggest crowd Shryne had ever played for.

Normally, that would be the end of the story. Normally, the overwhelming, unimaginable grief would have passed, at least become easier to bear, through the course of time, though the hole left by losing a child can never be filled. Life may go on, just never the same.

But Nicky wasn't finished yet.

Dave, Joanne, and others who knew Nicky well, not so well, and in one case not at all, began getting signs that were impossible to ignore. Lights flickering, meaningful songs playing whenever they turned on the radio, sightings over and over again of Nicky's favorite number 41 until neither Dave or Joanne could leave the house without spotting it on a license plate, seeing it printed on a restaurant receipt, or pulling over randomly to ask directions at a place that turned out to have a "41" street address.

"We started wondering if forty-one was just a number that popped up more often than others," Nicky's oldest brother, Christian, recalls. "What else could it be?"

Many of those songs and flickering lights happened when the clock struck 41 after the hour. But why 41?

"There are forty days of Lent," Dave says, "Easter is the forty-first day. There were forty days and nights of rain in the Great Flood that stopped the day after, the forty-first."

"It didn't all hit me at first," Joanne picks up. "You distract a kid so the doctor can give him a shot. I was distracted so the signs weren't hitting me. I needed time to process them."

"I'd say look at that," Dave agrees. "But in the beginning I took all this as a nice coincidence. But then it started to really pile up and at some point the pile got so high, I knew I couldn't be imagining all of this. Sure, I'd heard that people get signs like that, but I was getting billboards."

"Consider this," Dave elaborates further in *41 Signs of Hope*, a book he wrote documenting all the experiences for others who are similarly grieving. "Nicky lived to the age of eighteen years and twenty-three days. Those two numbers add up to forty-one. The Station nightclub was located at latitude 41.41. The number of the fire call box at the Station site was 4414, and the company that made the soundproofing foam that got much of the blame for the fire's quick spread was founded in 1941."

The book, it turns out, contains 41 chapters. Just a coincidence, its publisher New River Press insists.

And it didn't stop there, not even close. Her son Chris bought Joanne an antique music box for Mother's Day, one that needed to be manually wound in order to work. He gave it to her that morning and, at precisely 9:41, it began to play.

Even though it hadn't been wound up.

Since that fateful night in February of 2003, Dave has been contacted by hundreds of parents faced with the loss of loved ones, mostly children as well. Some just want a shoulder to cry on. Others are looking for reassurance, while still more want to know what they *should* be looking for. The calls and emails persist to this day, Dave cast in the role of ad hoc grief counselor, offering a unique message of hope.

"Mostly, they're looking for affirmation that they're not crazy when they get a sign from a loved one who's passed. Validation that what they think they may be experiencing is real instead of a product of their imagination. I had coffee with a woman once who thought she was getting signs from her daughter. She had a bunch of them but was still not putting a lot of credence in the signs. She called one of those nine hundred numbers to speak to a psychic and, not surprisingly, got nothing. Then she had an actual session with a medium who hit everything on the head, but she still wasn't convinced. So while we're talking, she burst into tears. I thought I might have said something that hurt or offended her, but she said that wasn't it at all, that the medium told her she'd know it was all real when she saw the crown and the hands. Still sobbing, she pointed to the Claddagh ring I was wearing, which has a crown and hands in the center."

That was the message of a play Nicky wrote two years before the fire called *They Walk Among Us*. Almost eerily, it centered around teenagers who die before their time and return as guardian angels, lending a helping hand for those who need them the most. He never got to play the lead role of Cyrus that he'd written for himself, which ultimately went to his brother David, a professional actor. His older brother Chris staged the play on several occasions and ultimately, with the help of filmmaker Christian de Rezendes, turned it into a movie filmed on stage over several performances. Chris and Christian also helmed a documentary entitled, appropriately enough, *41*, which stunningly chronicled Nicky's story both before and after the Station fire. This time he was indeed the star.

The film went on to receive considerable acclaim at any number of film festivals and landed a distributor. But it was a different award that Nicky's family is most proud of, specifically the Best Screenplay Award at Michigan's Black Point Film Festival that went to Nick

O'Neill for *They Walk Among Us*. Nobody mentioned it was awarded posthumously.

But not everyone agrees with the family's view of the world, like Paige Whitley.

"To conclude," she wrote for the Ohio State University online magazine in March of 2018, "people want to believe in mediumship because there is confirmation on the afterlife, they get to find out if their loved ones that have died are doing well and watching over them, and since it's gaining popularity on social media it seems more acceptable. People go to mediums in a vulnerable state and choose to believe it because they are tricked into giving information to a medium and fall into the hole of it all seeming 100% real. Mediumship is very hard to measure, and mediumship is very hard to disprove; therefore, people will support it. There isn't a placebo effect or anything like that but even if it's all fabricated, it gives people a little bit of happiness and mediums will thrive off of that."

"Psychics are out to fool you," Susan Gerbic adds in the *Skeptical Inquirer*, also in March of 2018. "Yep, and they are good at it too. Don't think you are going to out-think them or show them up; you are in their territory…. And the psychic is so nice! How could they be lying? In the end, it is not the responsibility of the skeptics to prove that the psychic can't talk to the dead. The psychic is making the outrageous claim, so the burden of proof is on them to prove that they are communicating. If someone tells you that they can fly without any device or aid, you are going to say 'Show me' not 'Let me prove you can't fly.' So why is it any different with psychics? We need to start pushing the burden to prove the ability to communicate with the dead. If it were true, it would change the world overnight."

In which case Dave Kane believes the world's already been changed.

"Here's what I say to people. Look, if I invite you to my house for a dinner party and I tell you the buffet is in the dining room, if you don't go in the dining room, it's not my fault you didn't eat. I tell you what I know to be true and you decide for yourself. This is how we got through, how Nicky helped us get through."

And to help other similarly aggrieved families, Dave is writing a second book that will be comprised of the stories of others who communicated with their loved ones after those loved ones passed. He's hoping that getting the tales down on paper will help them as much as it helped him.

"When people come to see me, I usually have only their first names and an arrival time," Robert Brown, one of the world's most renowned psychics, wrote in the foreword to *41 Signs of Hope*. "From the start of the appointment, I tell everyone that I don't know what information, if any, will come through. Any reputable medium will not guarantee that the person you are seeking to contact will make a connection, and I tell people to run a mile from any medium who says that he or she can guarantee it. If mediums can categorically attest to being able to just get anyone they wish, then surely they are also saying that they have a hold over your loved ones. They do not. A medium merely has an ability."

That's what Brown told Dave and Joanne at the outset of their session after they'd taken the train to see him in New York, a few months after the fire. A recording of that session feels like a conversation between Nicky and his parents, with Brown acting as a kind of interpreter, the medium nailing the boy's mannerisms, vernacular, and even speech patterns to a T. As amazing as that sounds, the final moments of the session were really the only thing the still grieving couple needed to hear.

"He just said something," Brown related to Dave and Joanne. "I don't know what it means, but he wants me to repeat it exactly as he said it. 'The show must go on. The show must go on.' Does that mean anything to you?"

~ ~ ~

## Reflections

We had a difficult time deciding whether to include this interview in *Overcoming*. Of our three authors, one of us thought that belief in the paranormal was fairly common to the human experience and was a legitimate subject for both ourselves and our readers to look at. One of us believed that Dave Kane and Joanne O'Neill's belief about their son's post-mortal communications was delusional and that delusion was not a psychological phenomenon we needed to include in a book on resilience. Our third partner looked at the subject in a more noncommittal and less confrontational way. We were unable to resolve our differences. Readers, we know, will bring their own views to the subject.

In the end we decided to include this story. As one researcher put it, "There are multiple and sometimes unexpected pathways to resilience." This interview draws attention to the complexity of human psychology, not least in the constellation of resources that bear on coping with tragedy.

One aspect of the resilience dynamic that is almost never mentioned in popular books but that is receiving increasing attention from clinical psychologists is repression, technically "repressive coping." We've encountered this before, in our interview with Josh Perry, the Down syndrome actor who simply did not acknowledge his limitations. In Josh's case, we saw that his refusal to dwell on or even consider the impediments of his condition enabled him to achieve goals that might otherwise have seemed improbable.

Repressive coping refers to the ability to turn away from the negative emotions that characterize common responses to trauma. It can take the form of unrealistic optimism, emotional dissociation, denial—or even, as in the Dave Kane and Joanne O'Neill case, a conviction that events in this world are impacted by forces outside the reality we experience through our senses and intellect. All of these can be characterized as defense mechanisms, psychological strategies, often subconscious, meant to manage stress and protect the self against the disturbing and harmful emotions that so often follow an experience of tragedy. We know, too, that the extreme difficulty of accepting the loss of a child and the simultaneous need for comfort are normal reactions to this level of shock.

At the same time, though, surveys indicate that a large percentage of people believe that supernatural events like miracles are real. As we cited, 45 percent of Americans believe that ghosts exist, while 41 percent think that extrasensory perception (telepathy, for example) may be possible, and 29 percent believe in astrology. And it's not just everyday people. A number of serious scientists, including leading figures, accept the reality of paranormal experience. Alan Turing, for example, the brilliant British mathematician who broke the German Enigma code in World War II, believed that clairvoyance was real. Theoretical physicist Freeman Dyson wrote that "the hypothesis that paranormal [events] are real but lie outside the limits of science is supported by a great mass of evidence." Even William James, the great philosopher and psychologist of the nineteenth and early twentieth century whose *Varieties of Religious Experience* is still a classic, believed that when it came to "ghosts and all…though the evidence be flimsy in spots, it may nevertheless collectively carry heavy weight."

In considering Dave Kane and Joanne O'Neill's experience, while two of our authors think along very different lines, the third may have an insight both can accept. Belief, he says, lies beyond science. It ranges along a spectrum, at one end of which lies the paranormal, at the other end religious faith. At the very least, we all agree that the Kane/ O'Neill account points to the complex and sometimes mysterious nature of the mind's struggle for post-traumatic equilibrium.

Oretha Tarr (center) with Betsy and Andy McNeil.

# 17

# Oretha Tarr

*Imagine living in a world of war for your entire life. It is in your heart and soul. It is part of who you are. For just a moment, put yourself there. Only then will you begin to understand the horror of what I went through during the Liberian Civil War.*

—Oretha Tarr, from an essay in *Journeys*

Oretha Tarr was nine years old when she saw her childhood home in Liberia for the last time in 1996. It was the third war Oretha had witnessed in her young life, following violent outbreaks in 1990 and 1992. But, from a historical perspective, those three outbreaks are combined into what is known as the First Liberian Civil War that would ultimately claim two hundred thousand lives (10 percent of the nation's population) and send a million more fleeing to refugee camps, a virtually unprecedented displacement of a populace. And

1996 featured a staggering escalation in murder and mayhem that lasted for 134 straight days, in which Oretha was swept up and swept away.

"I remember running, being told the whole time to keep up. We were running for our survival. I saw people killed along the way. A woman's daughter was killed and she dragged the girl's body with her for miles and miles. We were crawling in the grass to avoid bullets. I remember people screaming, kids sobbing, parents crying out their kids' names after they'd been separated amid all the gunshots. So we came across this church and thought it would be a safe place to hide for the night. Only inside there were dead bodies, dead bodies piled everywhere. The rebels had massacred everyone who'd been inside the church. It smelled so bad, but we had no other place to go. We had to stay. I remember you couldn't drink the water because cholera was spreading. You had to pour a little bit of bleach into the cup; it was the only way we could drink it."

Her mother had stayed behind with Oretha's siblings and stepfather, leaving Oretha with her grandmother and other family members in a displaced persons camp not far from the border with the Ivory Coast. She spent just over two years in that camp until her biological father located her in 1998 and took Oretha to live with him and her stepmother. She was able to visit her mother at least sporadically until 2000 when civil war loomed anew, forcing her new family to flee once more, across the Ivory Coast to a refugee camp in Ghana, where they lived in a ramshackle home with a single bedroom that was shared by all family members. They had no car, no running water, no electricity. And she hasn't seen her mother since, in over twenty years now.

Fortunately, her aunt (the sister of Oretha's biological father) had a daughter who was living in New Jersey and was willing to sponsor her family in Ghana as part of a refugee program in May of 2003 that has since been discontinued.

"It wasn't just us," Oretha recalls. "There were almost thirty of us living under the same roof."

Prior to the start of school in September, a friend of the family agreed to take her in. She was fifteen at the time and big for her age. Her lack of formal education in a West African region where schooling comes with a significant fee led to her being placed in the eighth grade at Carteret Middle School, where her size, accent, and race made her a target for bullies and ridicule. In reality, her knowledge level made her a better fit for several grades lower, but Oretha was deemed too old to enter elementary school.

"In Ghana, at least my biological dad was with me. I came to America without my parents or siblings. It was so scary, and the kids teased me a lot. The way I dressed, talked. English is the first language of Liberia, but there are sixteen different dialects. So my English didn't sound the same as theirs, and I couldn't understand a lot of what they were saying, so they teased me more. They called me 'grandma,' because I was so old. I didn't know how to ride the buses and didn't have the money for them. So I walked to school, forty-five minutes there and forty-five minutes back every day."

Oretha found solace in her relationships with her teachers, particularly one she remembers as Ms. James.

"She was very nice to me. When I told her I was sleeping in an unheated beauty salon that was next to the family's house, or in the doghouse in the backyard with the dogs, she gave me warm blankets. When I told her I got to school early to eat breakfast in the cafeteria because that and the school lunch were the only meals I ate, she brought me food so I wouldn't go hungry. The woman I was living with in New Jersey used to ask me, 'Did you get three meals a day in Africa?'"

Oretha thinks about Ms. James a lot, always fondly. Wondering how much harder things would have been if it wasn't for her becoming the first adult outside of her own family to truly take an interest in Oretha. Another woman she calls "Ms. Maggie" took her to the local church regularly and made sure she had food to eat when she was hungry and struggling.

"People like that came to my aid. They saved me."

But the woman in whose house Oretha was living in New Jersey was the polar opposite of that.

"She took advantage of me. Seized my paperwork and wouldn't give it back to me, which made me her prisoner. She threatened to report me to the authorities, tell them I didn't have any documentation, which was a lie. She threatened that they were going to send me home. I went to school the next day and never came back."

Liberia, 1996: *It all changed in an instant when I saw my friend Prince, the son of our chief, running through the town screaming. His screams were louder than anything I had ever heard before. He was screaming, "Run, leave your houses now! Take all you can and leave! The rebels will be attacking the city tonight!" At that moment my life changed forever.*

Oretha had an uncle, her mother's brother, living in Rhode Island, and that became her next stop in June 2006. She was almost nineteen now and enrolled as a sophomore at the inner-city Providence, Rhode Island, high school E-Cubed Academy, where at least she didn't have to pay. That's where she met a teacher named Betsy McNeil.

"We had an elective class where students could choose to sign up for something that interested them," Betsy recalls. "Oretha knew she needed to work on her speech and diction, so she signed up for an advisory I was doing called Oral Presentation. She was a very nice girl, special in her own way and not afraid to tell her story. She wanted to become an accountant and help her family back home. Her dream was to bring her mother to America. I found her to be a wonderful, hardworking, caring person who just wanted to do right for her family. Everything was always about her family."

Betsy and Oretha struck up a friendship to the point where Oretha began opening up about the hardship she was suffering at the hands of the uncle in whose house she was living. He was cruel and lashed out at Oretha at the slightest provocation, like coming home late or not doing the chores he assigned her or forgetting to return the cordless phone to its cradle. She was little more than an indentured servant to him. But she found solace at E-Cubed Academy.

Until winter came.

Oretha had left New Jersey with only the clothes on her back, no sweaters or a winter jacket in the humble wardrobe she'd accumulated in the meantime, something Betsy McNeil recalls all too well.

"So I went to Marshalls and bought her a winter coat for her birthday in November. I left the receipt in the bag so she could exchange the coat if she didn't like it. When I gave her the bag, she looked at the coat, looked at the receipt, and started to cry.

"'What you paid for my coat,' she said, 'would put all my brothers through school back home for a year.'

"That was Oretha," Betsy continues. "Always thinking about her family, like I said."

And Betsy McNeil was always thinking about her.

"It makes me feel good to make someone else feel good, to make a difference in their life. There've been times in our life where my family hasn't had a lot of money, so I know what it feels like. I'd rather do something than get something. It's a wonderful thing to make someone else happy."

Betsy recalls a time when the great African-American author Maya Angelou came to the Providence Performing Arts Center to do a reading. The theater distributed some free tickets to all the high schools in the city, and Betsy made sure to snare one for Oretha.

"She decided she wanted to meet Maya Angelou afterward. She tried to get backstage but someone stopped her, so she tried again and this time made it through and got to Maya Angelou's dressing room. Another security guard tried to move her away, but Maya said she could come in and meet her. So Oretha introduced herself and they actually chatted for a while. That's Oretha," Betsy adds with a smile. "Very resourceful."

Oretha had brought a copy of Angelou's book *I Know Why the Caged Bird Sings* for the esteemed author to sign but had left it by her seat when she made her way backstage.

"She gave me an address to send the book so she could sign it, but I never did. I wish I had."

She started attending the nearby Ebenezer Baptist Church and found great solace in the church family she found there. But it was another family that made an even bigger difference in Oretha's life. Donna and Tom Sherman, who hailed from the seaside suburb of Narragansett, Rhode Island, read a story about Oretha and Betsy's friendship in the *Providence Journal*, featuring a picture with Oretha wearing that coat from Marshalls.

"The Shermans saw that article and contacted me. They said they wanted to help me, and they helped me apply for US citizenship because I'd have to be a citizen to bring my mother over."

"It was around Christmastime," Donna Sherman recalls. "We were with family, and I was thinking how fortunate we were. I'd left the newspaper opened to that article on the counter and when I looked at it again, I knew I had to do something. So instead of buying Dunkin' Donuts gift cards for anyone and everyone, my husband Tom and I decided to send Oretha a check at the school for a hundred and forty dollars. Out of the blue I got a call from her and Betsy McNeil just to say thank you. Oretha even invited us to her high school graduation. I went with my sister, but I realized I didn't really know what she looked like except for that one small picture in the newspaper, and I couldn't figure out which girl she was. But she found *me*. I asked her how she knew it was me, and she said she just did. She had so much pride she was graduating high school. She hugged me and just cried and cried."

The relationship grew, Donna being the person Oretha knew she could call when things became difficult at home with her abusive uncle, abuse in Liberian culture classified instead as punishment or discipline. One Christmas, when she had nowhere else to go, the

Shermans invited her into their home for the holiday. A longtime tradition in the Sherman household was for Tom to read "The Night Before Christmas" to their children on Christmas Eve, a ritual that stopped when the kids grew up and moved away. On that night, though, Tom read the poem to Oretha. She'd never had a Christmas stocking before, and the next morning, among the other gifts she'd found stuffed inside was a keychain flashlight.

Months later, after attending Fourth of July fireworks, it was pitch black outside. The tiny flashlight was all that kept Oretha and a friend from getting hopelessly lost.

At the bottom of her stocking that Christmas morning, she also found $200 stuffed into the toe. That was on top of a comparable amount Donna's friend Maria had given the young woman as a gift after Donna had told her Oretha's story in Rhode Island Hospital, where Maria was in the final stages of the serious illness that would ultimately claim her life.

"When Maria died, Oretha came to the funeral. I don't even know how she learned about it or how many buses it took for her to get to the church."

It was actually a deacon at the Ebenezer Baptist Church she'd grown close to who gave her a ride. Oretha was attending Rhode Island College at the time, and Donna encouraged her to make the most of her education by getting a degree. What Oretha dreamed of as well was becoming an American citizen. At the time, there was a $680 fee associated with the paperwork. The Shermans gave Oretha $500 of it and made her promise to save it for when that time came, which it did on September 15, 2016.

"I had been dealing with my own health-related issues but came out of them just fine," Donna recalls. "And that made me realize how lucky I was, made me ask myself why I did okay when so many others in life don't do okay. I have a wonderful family. We're so fortunate and sometimes you take that for granted. So I wanted to do something for someone else, to make a difference. I wish everyone thought that way because the world would be a much better place if they did. We're all in this together.

"And Oretha has brought so much into my life. You can't give people money if you don't have enough to share, but giving your time is just as important, maybe even more so."

Oretha had moved to Indiana prior to becoming an American citizen, where she still lives not far from Notre Dame University, and began seeing a man to whom she'd ultimately become engaged and have two sons with. When her fiancé's father had a stroke, Oretha became his caregiver and has since carved out a career as a home health-care aide, specializing in people with disabilities, while amassing enough credits to graduate from college in the near future. Her goal is to continue her schooling to become an occupational therapist.

"It hurts so much for me to see what my fellow immigrants are going through today," Oretha notes, swallowing hard. "People who are mean and don't want us here haven't been through what we have, haven't experienced what we have. I thank God I came here when I did because if I tried now the immigration people probably wouldn't let me. I'm so lucky."

A strange way to describe life from someone who fled her home to avoid execution squads at the age of nine and has since become her own light shining through the darkness that had once threatened to swallow her. Oretha and Donna Sherman speak on holidays, birthdays, and plenty of other times during the year as well.

"Donna Sherman once asked me, 'Do you ever have bad days?'

"I said, 'No, they're always good.'

"Because that's the way I look at life. Even bad days have a light behind them. You have to be positive. Persevere, always hope, because there's always tomorrow and tomorrow might be brighter. I pray and trust in God. I am in this country, even though my biological parents aren't with me. I don't have to walk forty-five minutes back and forth to school. I don't have to go sleep in a doghouse or hair salon. I have electricity and running water. I don't have to sleep in the bushes to hide from soldiers."

> Liberia, 1996: *My family and I started to run. Although we did not know where we were going, we just followed the crowd that we met along the way. Life in the entire country was disrupted. There was no more work or school. We went into survival mode. We were running for our lives. We were beyond desperate for peace. I watched people die from stray bullets. Some of my relatives were killed. My paternal grandfather was killed by the rebels for no reason. They took him to the beach and, along with fifteen other men, slashed his throat in front of our entire family.*

That's another excerpt from the essay Oretha wrote in 2007 that was included in *Journeys*, an anthology comprised of art, poetry, essays, and short stories created by the students of E-Cubed Academy that was published in 2012.

Prior to her move to Indiana, Oretha also managed to complete three semesters at Rhode Island College and landed a job in the Admissions Department, specializing in immigrant applicants. So it should come as no surprise that Oretha's Facebook feed is dominated by optimistic posts and memes centered around hope and positivity, like one that reads DON'T GIVE UP! GREAT THINGS TAKE TIME. To make some of those things take less time, though, Oretha helps others like her in Mishawaka, Indiana, and the surrounding community with the process of becoming American citizens.

"Some of them have no legal documentation and they're afraid of being deported. I'm so grateful to God for what I have, but also to the Shermans, and I want to do for others what the Shermans did for me. If you go through a lawyer, you have to pay. So I started a kind of immigration clinic to teach people like me how to go through the process online, just like I did when the Shermans showed me. Some of the people I help don't speak English at all. Notre Dame graduate students come in and help me with the translating, and there are lawyers who live around the college who help too, and they never charge us anything. These immigrants need to integrate into the community. They need to know where to go to find the help they need. If I can't help them, I find someone who can."

Such ad hoc immigration clinics have become crucial way stations to help recent immigrants settle in, and Oretha wants to help the newly arrived avoid the pitfalls that plagued her when she settled in New Jersey. But her number one goal is to bring her mother to America to live with her. Betsy McNeil recalls Oretha insisting she introduce her to her mother over the phone.

"We couldn't really understand each other so Oretha had to translate. Her mother just wanted to thank me for all I had done, which I didn't think was much. Her mom had to light a candle in the middle of our conversation so she could see, because it had gotten dark and she had no electricity."

"I have children of my own now," Oretha says, "which makes me miss her all the more. It's taken a long time, forever, but we're getting very close and soon now she will be coming. I can't wait. It will make my life complete."

*I know I am blessed because I am living in a country that is so peaceful. I don't have to wake up every day worrying that I will be killed. I am safe and warm.*

—Oretha Tarr, from an essay in *Journeys*

~ ~ ~

## Reflections

Resilience means literally "to leap back." We use it to indicate the ability to recover quickly from injury or adversity. The violence Oretha Tarr experienced as a child didn't call for resilience; it called for a way not to recover but to survive. Together with relatives, she ran from the carnage for all she was worth. That was the survival instinct kicking in, pure and simple. The brain's fight-or-flight mechanism was screaming "flee."

Once Oretha was safe physically, other kinds of traumas set in. She was subject to squalid, crowded living conditions in Ghana. When she came to the US as a refugee, she was bullied in school and beaten and abused psychologically by an uncle. Oretha was not emotionally robust, unsurprising given a childhood lived amidst bloodshed and associated horrors. What she needed was solace, solace and a safe haven. She needed a way to heal. Psychiatrists tell us that finding a safe place and emotional connection are often the first steps in recovery from childhood trauma.

Oretha found solace in her relationship first with some of her teachers who were moved by her situation and befriended her, then by a family that read about her in a local newspaper and came to her with warmth and help. She found a safe haven in her church family. These were therapeutic. Oretha's faith, though, was on a different level.

Through everything, Oretha's belief in God was unshaken. Faith can work in various ways. For Oretha, it seems to have given her an underlying sense of optimism, a way of looking beyond her immediate troubles to something better.

Faith is a way of getting beyond oneself, which is itself an essential element in resilience. Having a goal, an objective, works similarly; it focuses the victim of adversity outward, away from one's own suffering and toward something motivating and meaningful. From the time of her arrival in the US, Oretha had an overriding goal—to bring her mother to live with her. At the time of our interview she had not been able to do that. In the current climate (this interview took place in March 2020), the chances that she might succeed in the near future were not good. But the goal persists, bringing with it an indispensable sense of purpose.

In her American circumstances, with all its troubles, Oretha felt that those teachers and families that reached out to her with comfort and assistance saved her life. Those relationships triggered in her the desire to help others as she herself had been helped; they mobilized her native sense of empathy, which came into play when she began her work life, helping immigrants. Social scientists have found that empathy, the exercise of compassion for others, is another primary element of resilience. Oretha's journey—from survival, to healing, to purpose—traces the landmarks of recovery from even profound trauma.

An example of Echo's art.

# 18

# Echo

"I create the background first," Echo says of the abstract art that has become a kind of lifeline for him, "starting with a few colors that I like and want to work with, a mix of lighter and darker. I just go with it. I don't think about a painting until I'm more than halfway in."

The same, you might say, is true about his life.

"I was born a girl physically, but I've identified as a boy for as long as I can remember. When a bunch of us used to role-play as kids, I always played male characters. Sonic the Hedgehog was my favorite."

Echo's eye-catching art is clean and expressive, full of stunning images often enclosing partially hidden, or obscured, faces. What the drawings lack in definition, they more than make up for in perfectly balanced color schemes and memes that command the eye. Many are on display on his Facebook page under "Echo McSparkles," mixed in among messages and comments typical of a twenty-four-year-old.

"Something hits me and I start drawing. In a lot of paintings, I do incorporate one of the characters from my book."

*When I opened the door to his office the man greeted me with a smile. "70589. Just the guy I wanted to see." I shut the door behind me, slightly startled by his cheery attitude. He should be furious with me. I turned around and all of the pride I had felt going down the stairway flushed out of me when I met Vincent's cold, ruthless, yellow eyes.*

The hero's character is never named, his entire dehumanized identity reduced to a number. It's a theme that reflects Echo's struggles with his own identity growing up. And, in a form typical of Echo's pointedly themed art, when he draws him, the book's narrator has horns. Does that make him the devil or, more likely, a character struggling with the duality of his own nature? You'll see that reflected in the fact that all the pictures of 70589 currently displayed on Echo's Facebook page picture him in dual images, almost like a perspective framed by a funhouse Hall of Mirrors.

*There was a long silence where neither of us spoke, and I took the time to look Vincent over. He seemed different that day. His clothes seemed less tidy, the dark circles under his eyes more noticeable, and in several places on his head it appeared as though his blonde, usually well-kept hair had developed a will of its own. Wisps of it stuck out defiantly from the rest, making it look almost as though he had just rolled out of bed. I looked into his eyes. Something seemed different about them, but I couldn't figure out what it was.*

Echo's art is as smooth and rhythmical as his prose, though more open to interpretation. Part of that is due to the nature of the medium itself. But another part owes itself to the fact that, like many artists, Echo has spent his life as a keen observer of the world around him. An outsider viewing the tight klatches of humanity, among which he didn't feel he particularly fit.

*I screamed and pleaded for help, but my cries were useless. There was no one around to save me. I tried to immerse myself somewhere else, in a warm bed or an embrace from someone I care about. Someone who would lean in close to my ear, their head on my shoulder, and whisper "It'll be alright. I've got you. There's nothing to be afraid of." But those things don't exist anymore, they were from a world untouched by this darkness, this hopeless nightmare world, where escape was futile and freedom was fleeting.*

"I actually classify myself as gender fluid. I identify as a he or a him. I feel like a he most of the time, but other times I feel like a she, and sometimes I don't feel like either. I've always dressed as a male, always got boyish haircuts.

"I had a pretty bad time in middle school. I was on Adderall for my ADHD, which makes you feel like a kind of zombie, so I wasn't very social. I'd sit and write or draw all day. I didn't have a lot of friends, and I was dating someone who was abusive. He was mostly mentally abusive, but once he tried to strangle me. I was with him for about a year. Art was a great release for me. I think I may have picked it up from my older sister Kimberly, who painted a lot and drew a lot. I so looked up to her. She was a great inspiration to me."

Note Echo's use of the past tense. Because in 2011, Kimberly was walking to her nearby high school. Like so many teens, she was listening to music through her earphones and didn't hear the school bus coming when she entered a crosswalk. She was struck and killed. Echo was called out of his eighth-grade class and summoned to the office, where a neighbor was waiting to take him home. The neighbor wouldn't tell him what had happened, but Echo knew it couldn't be good.

"Kimberly was an amazing person. She even wrote a book that almost nobody knows about. That made me want to write mine. She was the person I wanted to be more like, and her death made me even more introverted for a very long time. I had to go into therapy, but I didn't open up to the therapist beyond showing her my sketchbook. I watched her expression wrinkle as she flipped through the pages. 'These are very dark,' she told me."

Echo doggedly searched all the meager titles his school library had on mental illness and realized he had all the symptoms of post-traumatic stress disorder. His art became the key to his recovery, diving into his sketchbook or a full-blown painting. Sometimes he'll stare at a blank canvas for the longest time, fearful he'll never be able to paint anything. Then, inevitably, something strikes him and he begins, not exactly sure where he's going but certain that he'll get there.

"I did photography for a while too. But when you're taking pictures you're limited by the lens. When I'm sketching or painting, I'm not limited by anything."

Echo resists labels, not identifying himself as gay or transgender necessarily, though he remains almost exclusively attracted to girls.

According to a February 2019 article posted by the Trevor Project, "Overall, 1.8% of youth identified as transgender. The almost 2% prevalence rate is more than double the previously available estimate of 0.7%. The prior estimate was based on the patterns of transgender identity among adults. However, it was noted that the 0.7% estimation would be inaccurate if younger cohorts identify as transgender at a sharply higher rate than 18–24-year-olds. This data reveals that younger youth are indeed identifying as transgender at an increased rate."

And, as it did for Echo, that poses any number of challenges.

"Transgender youth reported significantly increased rates of depression, suicidality, and victimization compared to their cisgender peers," that same article on the Trevor Project site continued. "Notably, in the past year, one in three transgender youth reported attempting suicide, almost one-third reported being a victim of sexual violence, and more than half reported a two-week period of depression."

Staggering statistics from any perspective, truly mind-boggling. A 2016 study by the Williams Institute at the UCLA School of Law found an estimated 1.4 million adults identified themselves as transgender. But since "younger adults are more likely than older adults to identify as transgender," it's a safe bet that number has risen considerably since that particular study was completed. Many current estimates put the number at closer to two million, though three million is considered by some experts to be more accurate. And that doesn't necessarily include the number of transgender individuals keeping the truth of how they identify a secret.

It would be a misnomer to call Echo the typical transgender boy, or girl, because there isn't one, any more than there is a typical straight boy or girl. The common denominators of social alienation, depression, and the struggle for acceptance remain the truest of transgender tragedies. Echo has experienced them all and continues to deal with them to varying degrees, his attempts growing more successful as he has learned to accept himself.

"My book is set in an underground facility. 70589 has been taken off death row and sold to this secret facility where his memory is wiped. And the whole book is about him trying to remember who he is as he tries to get out of that place. In taking away his name, they're trying to take away his humanity. He's trying to redeem himself, overcome his mental illness."

In counterpoint to 70589, the evil, irredeemable Vincent represents the depths of human depravity, seeing our unnamed narrator as no more than an object, a technological play toy to be experimented on and subjected to torture.

*His eyes were like black coals, and when I looked into them I saw nothing but an empty black void, reminding me of the water I had just almost drowned in.*

And, speaking of mental illness, Echo had his own bout with that, at least in some respect, back in high school.

"I didn't have any friends, and I was moving back and forth between my dad's house and my mom's house. I was getting what I'd call softly bullied because I'd be sitting alone at a table in the lunch room and I'd hear people giggling and saying stuff just loud enough for me to hear. There was some psychosis I was experiencing at the time too that led to panic attacks. I'd start crying and my parents would yell at me to stop. I kept all that bottled up for too long. I probably should have gotten help at the time but I didn't, and it stunted me as a human being before I finally admitted myself to a hospital."

Echo was older then, twenty-one. Like many LGBTQ youth, he'd been unable to do that in high school but now ended up in a program run by the Triangle Group, an outpatient program that revolves around a combination of counseling and group therapy. He was also prescribed meds. Instead of too little too late, call it just enough just in time.

That said, art remains the best therapy for Echo.

"I'm in a different place altogether when I'm creating. When I'm writing, a whole world opens up to me; I can do whatever I want. When I'm drawing, I start by just putting the paint on the canvas. I don't know where the painting is going to take me or how I'm going to get there. It's more free form. I've painted over things dozens of times until I find something that I really like and then I go from there."

Echo's book reads like a literary blend of famed young adult author Robert Cormier's *The Bumblebee Flies Away* and Stephen King's most recent opus, *The Institute*. In those tales, too, the characters are battling their surroundings, prisoners of their own psyches more than the walls that enclose them. Interestingly, though, Echo's underground facility is shoddy and run-down, far from sleek, shiny, and futuristic. It seems to be crumbling, wasting away, an apt metaphor for the moral decadence that defines it. In that sense, 70589's literal rise runs parallel to the facility's steady deterioration, a descent akin to Edgar Allan Poe's "The Fall of the House of Usher." To put it another way, there's hope for 70589 and there's even more of it for Echo, although it hasn't been easy.

But is 70589 his alter ego?

"A little bit, yeah. We have a lot in common. My paintings are self-representative, but I paint him instead of me. He's a projection of me, and I'm pretty much feeling what he's feeling."

Echo hasn't written very much lately, in large part because the opportunity and access haven't consistently been available.

"A friend of mine and I were homeless for the month of October. I didn't have any money or any other place to go. It was scary. We really thought we were going to die. Then I said, no, we're going to go camping, it's going to be great. So I sold my gaming gear to buy a nice tent and we lived in a campground. Both of us finally got jobs and were able to get this run-down, shabby apartment until they moved up to Maine and I came back to Rhode Island."

"They" refers to Maroby, who is bisexual and identifies as they/them, which is the case for many in the LGBTQ community who resist the labels cast by gendered pronouns. Echo and Maroby started out as friends, but it's developed into more of a serious relationship, and Echo will be joining Maroby up in Maine within the next six months or so. Maroby's family has secured a camper on their property for Echo to call home.

Echo's own parents divorced after the death of his older sister Kimberly. His mother now lives in Florida, and they video chat occasionally. Echo gets along relatively well with his father these days, but he doesn't talk to him all that much, having left home originally years back under less than ideal circumstances.

In the meantime, he's been working at East Side Mart, a convenience store in Providence, Rhode Island, owned by the family of a young woman named Courtney with whom Echo has been friends since kindergarten. The Smiths not only gave him a job but also a place to live at their home. A roof now, instead of a tent, over his head.

"Courtney was always there for me as a kid, and she still is."

Courtney's father, Paul Smith, the owner of East Side Mart, puts it this way:

"I've known Echo on and off for many years, mostly when he and my daughter went to high school together. He's a hard worker, I can tell you that. When he moved in with us, I asked him to help out around the house to earn his keep, and he's really chipped in there. At the store, I haven't had a single complaint from a customer. He's attentive and is capable of handling a shift all by himself. He likes learning new stuff and is really attune to the whole retail experience. I think he'll still be searching for himself for a few more years and that he'll be able to work his art more and on a bigger level."

"He's a strong, positive individual," Courtney, who calls Echo her best friend, says. "And he's resilient. Whenever the world tries to knock him down, he won't give in or give up. He always finds a way to get by. When he ended up homeless, it was really cold, but he made the best of it, just like he did in high school. I talked to my father about him moving in with us, and he said as long as I didn't mind sharing my room, my space, with him. And he's been a really good influence on me. He's inspired me to try painting, encouraging me and teaching me to just go with the flow."

Echo's life mantra, you might say.

"Moving in with the Smiths helped me out a lot," he says. "I look at all the past trauma I've experienced and want to come out of it a better person, looking toward a brighter future. Something less dark. I work on myself a lot."

Most recently, he moved in with an ex of his. They're still friends and so far, so good, making the arrangement a transition before Echo's move to Maine, where he'll have that trailer parked in the driveway to resume his writing as well as continue his painting. Toward that end, the top post on Echo's Facebook page currently features a painting labeled "a work in progress," just like him.

"Everybody is a work in progress in some way. We're all striving to find our better self. I don't know mine, but hopefully I'll be someone more accomplished. I'd like to sell more of my art, be more professional. Art's what I do to get me through the day. It keeps me alive in a way. But I want to feel more whole and complete."

Interestingly enough, he's already helped others with their art.

"Say an artist says to me all they're painting is mountains and they want to know how do they not paint mountains. I tell them to go with whatever your hands want. Paint a galaxy—the sky's literally the limit. I've actually worked on some paintings with other artists, and

I found that kind of group painting—picking up where somebody else leaves off—to be a great process. You get to find your own style because you're working off somebody else's lead. It forces you to create something different than you're used to."

Echo doesn't see himself at this point going into anything like art therapy as a profession, but he is interested in helping the LGBTQ youth following in his wake find the right path. The right path for them, that is.

"I would say to them get out of your chair and go talk to somebody. Try to make at least a small group of friends. Even if it's really hard, get out there and socialize. Never assume people are going to come to you. You have to get out there. I did that with a small rave crowd when I discovered the club scene. You meet people, make new friends. Keep looking until you find that group that makes you feel better about yourself."

Echo knows he's far from alone in a growing community of transgender youth and young adults, a lot of whom are experiencing many of the same hardships, challenges, setbacks, and angst he's come to know all too well.

"I would say to them to be yourself and don't be afraid to reach out to people and make friends. Don't be afraid to reach for help."

~ ~ ~

## Reflections

The question often is not, "What strengths do we bring to bear in overcoming trauma?" Rather, it's "What strengths help us to *endure* trauma?"

Looking at Echo's life, the latter seems most relevant. Establishing a stable identity is a universal process as we develop and as confusion resolves into a mature sense of who we are. When gender dysphoria is an issue, confusion is often magnified and prolonged. Sexual identity is such a central element in our makeup that conflict in that sense of ourselves can spill over into other emotional problems or exacerbate them. Echo was given the amphetamine mix Adderall to treat his ADHD. Looking through books on mental illness, he found that PTSD symptoms matched much of the torment he was feeling. He experienced panic attacks. He felt isolated, alienated, so distressed that he checked himself into a hospital. He was a young person under siege.

We know the awful statistics on suicide rates among transgendered young people. When the kinds of mental problems Echo describes mount, they sometimes simply become unbearable to the person suffering them. But Echo, as troubled as he has been, has never succumbed to that extreme. A leading psychiatrist at Harvard's McLean Hospital explains that extremely ill, potentially suicidal patients often have something in their lives that keeps them moored to life. And as long as the desire to live has something to hang on to, the psychiatrist has time to try to treat the illness and help the patient stabilize and ameliorate his or her life. For Echo, that lifeline has been art. Art therapy has a respected place in the repertoire of psychotherapies, starting with the distinguished psychiatrist Carl Rogers and his thinking about interpersonal, patient-centered therapy. "Art allows us," says Natalie Rogers, Carl's daughter who has developed this aspect of her father's approach, "to go into our pain, rage, and grief. Using art is sometimes much more effective than words to deal with some of these very difficult emotions."

Typically, so-called expressive art therapy takes place in a patient-therapist context. But for Echo, art has little or nothing to do with the standard doctor-patient therapies he's experienced. Art, he says, "keeps me alive in a way." But art for him is self-therapy. It's an avenue generated by his intrinsic talents and desires. Art functions for him as a way of observing himself and his problems, especially the identity issues that have been so disruptive in his life. He paints faces, partially hidden or fractured. His writing, with its nameless heroes struggling to remember themselves or escape the places of their imprisonment, are transparent projections. "My paintings," he says, are "self-representative." The nameless hero in his writing? "He's trying to overcome his mental illness."

We understand from this interview something about how far Echo's problems reach. We know from others we've encountered in this book how necessary it is to recognize a problem before healing can take hold, which is such an obvious element in Echo's striving to, as he puts it, "feel more whole and complete." Our ability to look in some kind of objective way at who we are is an essential part of our desire to understand our lives, what they mean and where they might be going. That's normal, we believe, in the human experience. Can we also say that it's not just understanding ourselves that's at issue but how it is that we change and transform ourselves, how we shape our identities differently from one phase of life to the next to be better reflections of who we are, or who we hope to become.

Photo blurred for safety and security reasons.

# 19

# Steve

"Just to make clear," Steve says, "I'm not the kind of SEAL who went out and killed a bunch of bad guys. Yes, I deployed and was gone from home for more than two-thirds of my career, but I was born one decade too early and missed the really good combat every Frogman wants."

That career spanned twenty-eight years, covering parts of three decades, during which the world changed right before Steve's eyes. And while he may have missed "the really good combat," he ultimately trained several of the SEALs who participated in the May 2011 raid to capture or kill Osama bin Laden. Indeed, Steve saw the SEALs, and their Frogmen precursors, from a variety of perspectives, starting with joining the Navy at the age of seventeen fresh out of high school.

"Becoming a SEAL for me started literally on the first day of boot camp in 1983. We had a physical training instructor wearing this blue-and-gold shirt that read SEAL INSTRUCTOR. He reminded me of my dad. After I smoked the initial tests, he pulled me aside.

"'What are you gonna do in my Navy, son?' he asked me.

"'I'm supposed to go into aviation, serve on an aircraft carrier.'

"'Are you interested in becoming a Frogman?'

"That was the first time I ever heard the word, but the instructor proceeded to tell me all about the SEALs and showed me a short movie, *The Men with Green Faces*. I was hooked from the get-go. Every Wednesday during basic training, before the day started, I'd do screening tests for BUD/S [SEAL basic training] just to get more physical training in. My company commander blew his lid.

"'They're all fucking crazy,' he told me.

"'Okay,' I said, 'I want to lose my mind.'

"I went through BUD/S and I checked into my first Team when I was nineteen years old. The very first morning at quarters I met a salty Frogman master chief named Ed Schmidt. He was from a completely different era. When he was a nineteen-year-old 'FNG,' it was World War II and he was swimming across the beaches of Normandy, Sicily, and Africa. He was originally NCDU, Naval Combat Demolition Unit, and was trained at Fort Pierce, Florida. He had a swagger to him, an extreme air of confidence. You could see the experience in his eyes and the lines on his face. He had broken service, missed Korea, but came back in right at the beginning of the Vietnam conflict. He was an early member of SEAL Team Two and made several deployments to the Mekong Delta. I wanted to be just like this guy."

Steve ended up serving twenty-six of his twenty-eight years of service in Naval Special Warfare as a SEAL under the United States Special Operations Command. And he spent the bulk of that service, the fourteen years spanning 1987 to 2001, with the Naval Special Warfare Development Group (a.k.a. "DEVGRU"), the crème de la crème of special operations warfare. True to the legacy of Ed Schmidt and Rudy Boesch, he became a master chief, and command master chief, after his deployment days were over.

"DEVGRU [which is also known within the Joint Special Operations Command, JSOC, as Task Force Blue] is the place ninety-nine percent of Team guys aspire to go. It's a selection course for the most extreme operations anyone can ever imagine. Six months of the most intense selection and assessment training a guy can receive. Sure, BUD/S was tough, but this was a different sort of tough.

"I saw combat in Panama. Conducted operations in Bosnia, Somalia, and Iraq. But they weren't the kind that everyone envisions or sees on TV and the movies, not mine anyway. I've got buddies who saw that kind. I've lost friends and Teammates in combat. In the Teams and special operations, it's all about timing and luck. I've got a friend who's the luckiest bastard in the world. He's seen way more combat than any one operator should get to see. He was in Grenada, Lebanon, Panama, Bosnia, Afghanistan, and Iraq. He's a contractor with the CIA doing what you think a guy like that should do. I've still got friends there at DEVGRU and other Teams. Just about all of them are older, senior guys. A couple were on the bin Laden raid. Some were on other raids and hostage rescues. They all worked for me at some point, and I knew them all in some other capacity. They were junior to me and went through BUD/S after me.... Like I said, I was born a decade late and my timing was off."

Especially after 9/11.

In August of 2001, Steve left DEVGRU and was assigned to the newly established training detachment on the East Coast. On September 11, he was at Camp Lejeune, North Carolina, helping train a couple of platoons in urban combat in preparation for what was envisioned as a quiet six-month deployment overseas when the Twin Towers were struck.

"We knew what our place was—we were the trainers—but we weren't happy about it. We were a bunch of pissed-off dudes who only wanted to deploy into the new combat zone of Afghanistan but were now supposed to train the guys who were going to do that instead. Not a good time to be in the 'trainer' position when your Teammates and country are at war."

Never mind that Steve was the one responsible for training his SEALs to do what they did and come home safe and alive. Never mind that the prowess and skills they repeatedly exhibited, sometimes doing two or three missions in a single day or night, had come, at least in part, from his teachings. What frustrates him is that during his tenure, the Teams spent the bulk of their time training for missions and deployments that never came. Steve isn't a "let the other guy do it" type; he wants to get it done himself, get his own hands dirty.

"We were grinding through the 1990s. You'd train so hard because you were training for missions that rarely happened. But we were training for the hypothetical, instead of training like guys are today for the known. They know they're going to Iraq, Syria, or Afghanistan in three or six months. It wasn't like that for us.

"That said, leaving DEVGRU was the toughest thing in my career because I loved being there so much. So many people, when Sunday evening rolls around, say, 'Damn, I've got to get to work tomorrow.' Well, I looked forward to Monday mornings. I hated days off. I just wanted to get back at it, and I relished overseas deployments. I was married to my first wife back then, and she refused to wash my work clothes that one-third of the time I was home. I think she hated the fact that I loved what I was doing more than I loved her. She didn't understand, she didn't get it, and that's why we ended up divorced. My first wife despised the Navy, despised the Teams. I had no business getting married when I was twenty-five, and the divorce rate was around ninety percent at the time because we were gone two hundred days a year. I loved parachute training, did over twelve hundred jumps. I loved combat diving. It didn't matter what day of the week it was. The funny thing is I've never enjoyed recreational scuba diving at all. Like my first platoon chief, Roger Gant, said, 'Son, the mailman doesn't take a walk on Sunday.' You will not find me putting on a mask and fins to look at rocks and fish. I can remember some guys sticking a cartoon of me on a wall. I'm strapped with gear with a gun in my hand, pictured with my wife and two kids who are all crying because I didn't want to go home.

"'You love being here more than you like being with your wife and kids,' one of my Teammates said to me by way of explanation.

"'Doesn't everybody?' was my response."

Behind Steve's love for virtually all things associated with being a SEAL, there was one thing he didn't—specifically, blast exposure. Simply stated, that's the term associated with being in the proximity of explosions related to demolitions of any type, rocket or artillery fire, and being exposed to the percussion that is now known to wreak havoc with the central nervous system. Something Steve came to know all too well.

"The cumulative effect of blast exposure is causing cognitive changes in military personnel. That cumulative effect can be seen in gait alteration and vascular response in certain individuals with repeated sub-concussive blast exposure. This hazardous exposure is especially worse on the range safety officer [RSO]. On average an RSO within a SEAL Team training command can be exposed to blast overpressure, BOP, that far exceeds safety parameters. The limit is supposed to be seven to ten supervised rocket firings. Excessive BOP/blast exposure is thought to contribute to traumatic brain injury [TBI] and has a history of causing memory loss and sleep disorders. I have personally done ten times the recommended number in one day just with shoulder-fired rockets when I was assigned to the training cadre at DEVGRU. We were stretched thin, and I was the only RSO available to supervise the safe firing of the shoulder-fired rockets."

Steve also suffered a serious training injury in 1992, after he'd been part of the assault team for five years. It happened when the team was conducting a CQC (close-quarter combat) training event.

"I was to be one of two primary entry men following an explosive breach on an exterior balcony door at our live-fire training facility. We were to rappel halfway down to a balcony, me and the other operator, and hold cover [security with weapons drawn] for the breacher who would place the charge and then rappel over the side of the balcony, under cover of that balcony, and detonate the charge. We would then finish the descent onto the balcony immediately following the detonation and make initial entry, clearing the way for the rest of the team to rappel down and enter. I was in a set point position and situating myself in order to hold adequate cover from my side for the breacher. My number two was in the process of doing the same when my device failed and I smoked into the balcony below, about a fifteen-foot fall, hitting the back of my head on the railing and breaking my back. Luckily, I was wearing body armor which contained my torso and kept me from rupturing any internal organs. I was unconscious for the better part of an hour and didn't come to until I was in the emergency room of the local hospital, hooked to an EKG with an IV inserted. Traumatic brain injury wasn't a very big thing at that point in time, and me being knocked unconscious wasn't as big a deal at the time as breaking my back."

Steve's back healed enough for him to return to work, at least in the training cadre, and he resumed full active duty a year after the accident, throwing himself back into the process full tilt.

"That was 1992, and I didn't address my TBI until 2019. The resulting post-traumatic stress disorder [PTSD] hit me gradually over time. Hypervigilance, explosive anger and mood swings, not being able to sleep or stay asleep, thoughts of suicide—the list goes on. I thought it would all go away after I retired and settled into civilian life, because I was deeply disturbed and troubled by all of this shit going on in my head. I was very wrong; it never went away. I didn't want to appear weak or as a pussy. I was a tough guy, a SEAL, and I wasn't supposed to feel this way. I was stronger and better than that. What I didn't know was that I had a problem deep in my brain caused by blast exposure and training accidents over the course of my career, and I had no control over these reactions and feelings. When I retired in 2009, part of my exit physical screening was to explore whether I had experienced a TBI due to vehicle-borne improvised explosive devices [VBIEDs] or IEDs. That's all they wanted to know.

So, naturally, since I hadn't ever been hit by one of those, I said no and that was that. That was as much as they wanted to know.

"When I first came into the Teams, I read a book by a Vietnam-era SEAL who talked about what he went through when he got home after all the trauma he suffered, how he lost his marriage. My platoon chief was a Vietnam vet, so I asked him about it."

The chief proved less than sympathetic about the issue.

"What a piece of shit," Steve recalls him saying. "You don't listen to shit like that. You don't talk about it. Don't be a pussy. If you got that kind of shit in your head, get the fuck out."

In other words, back then in the 1980s, and for years afterward, the treatment for PTSD too often was denial. It was a phrase not to be spoken, and SEALs, both past and present, who'd suffered from it weren't acknowledged.

The list of Steve's deployments with the Teams spanned nearly fifteen years and took him to South and Central America on the trails, respectively, of Pablo Escobar and Manuel Noriega. He was deployed for a stretch in the Balkans and was deployed, on call, for the Summer Olympic Games in 1992, 1996, and 2000, just in case, as they say. When you're a SEAL, there's a lot of "just in case."

After leaving DEVGRU just before 9/11 as one of the three assault team chiefs himself, he went on to serve as part of Operation Enduring Freedom and Operation Iraqi Freedom. He was a command master chief at two Naval Special Warfare commands before his retirement in 2009. Well, kind of retirement, anyway. Steve went to serve for eight years as the deputy range program manager for Naval Special Warfare Command in Coronado and also worked for the then newly established NSW SERE program, a survival school created for the SEALs and SWCCs (Special Warfare Combatant-Craft Crewmen), another integral component of Naval Special Warfare.

Simply stated, Steve's résumé is so impressive that it strains credulity. It was during the tail end of this phase of his career, though, that an incident in 2008 near the SEAL base in Coronado (near San Diego,

California) crystallized the one part of his career you won't find on that résumé. Steve had just returned from his last deployment. He and his second wife were getting an ice cream when a car with music blasting pulled into the parking lot. Steve asked the driver to turn it down, dial it back a notch.

When the driver refused, things started to get heated.

"I was in Condition Red. Never heard my wife warning me off."

Finally, Steve slapped the guy's windshield to get his attention and avoid doing something much worse.

"It shattered, like someone had taken a baseball bat to it."

A local cop arrived and peacefully defused the situation after gleaning that Steve was on the Teams and then learned he'd just gotten back from overseas.

"A hairpin trigger like that is a big part of PTSD. I didn't know. I never tied everything together."

The lingering effects of his traumatic brain injury, blast exposure, and any number of rough-and-tumble parachute landings had produced a cumulative result, piling on, and it was only getting worse. Then in 2019, Steve was out in New Mexico visiting his father when his PTSD struck full bore, triggered by a near traffic accident when his father narrowly avoided T-boning a truck in an intersection while they were doing fifty miles per hour.

"I was deeply shaken. I'd almost been in a helicopter accident on a deployment and I had a flashback to that moment. My dad and I were on our way to meet a member of his circle of friends for coffee. This gentleman had been flying a B-52 as part of Operation Rolling Thunder in Vietnam. The plane got its tail blown off, but he managed to eject and spent a hundred and eleven days as a prisoner of war in the Hanoi Hilton. Then he went back into the service, got his master's in psychology, and became a counselor for the Veterans Administration specializing in PTSD. My father had to go use the bathroom after telling the story of our near accident, and his friend got this serious look on his face.

"'You look visibly shaken by this,' he said to me. 'Are you okay?'

"'No, I don't think so,' I told him."

As sometimes happens with post-traumatic stress disorder, the near car accident had released all the pent-up feelings Steve had been holding in for years. He'd already left the Navy for good and moved with his second wife from Coronado to upstate New York to start the next phase of their lives. But Steve knew he was going to lose the marriage, and potentially much more, if he didn't seek help at long last.

"I called my wife that day and described to her what happened. 'Are you okay?' she asked me. 'I don't think so,' I told her too."

His first wife had never really gotten him, but his second wife did. She was a retired Navy chief herself, having served as administrative chief at SEAL Team Four. She also had worked at the Pentagon for the Joint Chiefs of Staff. Steve couldn't bear the thought of losing her too, especially after moving their post-military lives to the Finger Lakes Region of New York where their property sits on one of those lakes, which is great, except for the lack of waves on which he can surf as he'd grown used to off the San Diego coast. Steve knew he had to get help, to save himself as well as his marriage.

Thanks to the intervention of his father's POW friend, Steve contacted a commanding officer he knew at Special Warfare Command Headquarters and explained what was happening.

"All the crazy shit going on in my head. It wasn't always like flashbacks or anything like that, but I couldn't do anything about it, had no control. My wife told me how she was always walking on eggshells with me, that she never knew how I was going to react, or overreact, to something. I had no idea. I'd just learned to live with it. I didn't know how to ask for help."

He ended up being put in touch with a fellow retired SEAL from the Wounded Warrior Project, who told him about Home Base, an innovative, intensive two-week program designed to treat warriors suffering from a myriad of psychological issues, including PTSD.

"Home Base saved my life. It was like a kind of twelve-step program, how denial gives way to recognition. The more you acknowledge what's happening to you, the more you talk about it, the easier it gets to deal with. I've got this, and this is what I'm doing to get treatment for it. It's hard to do, hard to talk about. But once you start, you get a greater understanding of what you're going through. You come to terms with it.

"Initially, I spent a week as an intake patient, getting tests and speaking with the medical professionals and staff. Less than a month later, I spent another two weeks as an outpatient with a whole group of veterans going through the same stuff I was. I saw a variety of therapists at Home Base who put their finger right on what was happening to me, both mentally and physically. I'm a hundred percent better than I was fifteen years ago. Those weeks there were equivalent to a whole year of therapy."

Those weeks had indeed saved Steve's marriage and, very likely he believes, his life. And part of the reason he agreed to be included in these pages was to get the word out to others in the military community who find themselves in a similar place and either don't know where to turn for help or are ashamed to try.

"Home Base asked me to record a video interview for their annual Veterans Day telethon. I'd never done anything like that before, just like I've never done anything like this before. But anything that helps somebody in need, count me in. I'd say to Home Base, 'You guys saved my life. Just tell me what I can do for you.'

"The first thing I'd ask someone who needs help is, what happened? What brought you to this point? I'd want to know if they were a danger to themselves, and I'd strongly recommend they go to Home Base—I've already referred two SEAL friends there. One thing I've found is that sometimes guys telegraph their feelings on social media as an early warning sign, so if I'm worried about somebody, I'll check out what they've been up to on Facebook or Instagram. We need to get past this 'don't be a pussy' mentality. I tell the guys I talk to, 'I'll go with you. There's a place we can go. I'm going to get you to someone who can help you.' The problem is a lot of Team guys are afraid to step into the deep end of the pool. But you've got to take that jump for the sake of the rest of your life. I don't care what anyone says—you can't fix it yourself. But everybody can find something to save them.

"I'm a lifer. I loved doing everything I did as a SEAL. That's why I reenlisted, that's why I stayed in as long as I did. I'd found a group of people I wanted to be around. It was the comradery, the brotherhood, being part of something much bigger than you. And it was all worth it."

There were other Ed Schmidt, Roger Gant, and Rudy Boesch types in his life, mentors who were also role models, and now Steve wants to be that for the next generation of SEALs. He believes he is in control of the PTSD that for so long controlled him without him knowing. He wants those younger SEALs to know where to find and seek help if they need it, not to wait thirty-plus years to ask for help the way he did. To not be afraid to admit something's wrong and let it consume them as it consumed him. He was mentored by some of the best and went on to mentor more of the best himself. Toward that same end, he looks forward to helping the warriors to whom he's passed the baton, now with a firm grasp at long last of the condition that had tried to squeeze the life out of him for so many years. Steve's taking that part of things slow to make sure he's ready, his own treatment barely a year in. Maybe even do some volunteer work at Home Base.

"You have to be accountable for your own actions. I learned that the hard way with my personal life. Everybody has regrets about how they handled certain things, and I wasn't taking accountability for other things. Now I've taken unconditional ownership of everything I do. I'll ask young people who I'm working with, what is your passion, what is your *why*? I was lucky enough to find mine when I was seventeen years old, and it's important for everyone to find theirs. It's all about understanding yourself, mastering yourself. I'm still doing that, still a work in progress."

~ ~ ~

## Reflections

Abraham Maslow, the founder of humanistic psychology, posited that in the hierarchy of human needs, the highest is the need, or desire, for what he called "self-actualization," the instinctive drive to fulfill one's unique potential. Maslow regarded this as a universal in humanity's psychological makeup. We are all motivated, he says "to become more and more what we are, to become everything that we are capable of becoming."

This drive often realizes itself when we find a vocation, a calling that enables us to express our unique gifts and talents. Steve found his calling at the age of seventeen in a Navy boot camp when his instructor told him about SEALs. There was something about the extreme physical training, the competitiveness, the risk and danger of the endeavor. "I was hooked from the get-go," he says. What hooked him was that SEAL training took physical, mental, and combat preparation to the peak of what was possible. This was for Steve self-actualization in its fullest sense. It expressed who he was.

Two things distinguish SEALs and U.S. Army Special Forces. First is the level of training, which pushes "operators" to the limits of their capabilities. Second is the all-encompassing nature of the calling. Callings provide a pathway to self-fulfillment, but they do not commonly encompass the entirety of a person's life. A devoted doctor can maintain a rich family or civic or religious life outside his or her calling. A scientist or artist or furniture maker can do the same. A SEAL or Green Beret is more like a monk. For the most part, their world is determined and bounded by what they do.

"I hated days off," Steve says. "I just wanted to get back at it." One of his fellow SEALs said, "You love being here more than you like being with your wife and kids." His response: "Doesn't everybody?" SEALs are away two-thirds of the year. The divorce rate, at one point, was 90 percent.

The commitment of these warriors to their profession is intensified by the mortal nature of it. Theirs is a calling that demands an everyday willingness to put one's life at severe risk; this calling is, literally, worth your life. That intensifies every aspect of it: the physical and skills training, the interpersonal relationships, and the mindset. There's a "holism" about being a SEAL that puts them in a distinctive and largely separate world.

All this comes through loud and clear in Steve's telling. The question his interview poses is: What happens when the mindset that envelopes this world is challenged? That's what happened to Steve when the years of blast exposure, a bad head injury, and other training accidents left him with TBI, traumatic brain injury.

Without understanding the cause, over time Steve's behavior changed. Hypervigilance, explosive anger, sleeplessness, suicidal thoughts—he exhibited all the earmarks of PTSD. In the SEAL mindset, though, anything other than mental toughness was not permitted. Acknowledging problems like these would be considered weakness. "Don't listen to shit like that," as his old chief put it. "Don't talk about it; don't be a pussy." When trauma upsets the sense of self, what happens? One common answer is denial. For a SEAL, whose vocation defines so much of his life, denial is multiplied by an order of magnitude.

For Steve, that denial, or repression, persisted for ten years after his retirement. Then a close-call accident brought all of the pent-up emotional turmoil to the surface, which triggered deep fears about his fragility and about everything in his life he stood to lose. That broke through the SEAL mindset, and he found an intensive treatment program that helped him acknowledge what had happened to him and bring it out in the open where he could, with the help of therapy, start dealing with it.

This is not an unusual story. It's about the difficulty of recognizing the effects of trauma and the necessity of acceptance as a prerequisite to healing. What *is* unusual about it is that the all-encompassing nature of the SEAL identity makes acknowledging mental or emotional problems so extremely difficult. The great revelation here for Steve was that accepting his vulnerability and seeking treatment did not stigmatize him; it did not affect his SEAL identity. What it did do was help him understand what he was going through and allow him to come to terms with it.

Steve had mentors who taught him what it meant to be a SEAL, who helped forge his identity. They helped him grasp how becoming a SEAL gave him the ability to fulfill his need to become, in Maslow's terms, everything he was capable of becoming. The best mentorship opens possibilities; it expands the sense of who you are. Coping with the trauma of PTSD expanded Steve's sense of who he was, of what a SEAL was. It rearranged the borders of his mental landscape. Accepting that larger version of himself saved his marriage. It may well have saved his life. His message to younger SEALs, his own mentorship, is that SEALs are not invulnerable, that vulnerability is nothing to be ashamed of, that it needs to be incorporated in their definitions of themselves, because it is a reality. And because doing so may well save their lives too.

Roca at work.

# 20

# Roca

"I used to do a lot of long-distance running," says Molly Baldwin. "When I had a lot going on, it always put me in a different place, a different space, a different perspective."

Something she still needs, given her calling as the head of Roca, the organization she founded that's devoted to offering hope in the form of second chances to America's most high-risk youth, culled literally from the streets often in the form of gang members. (Roca is Spanish for "rock," in recognition of the fact that Roca initially helped underserved Hispanic youth.)

"The 1,300 young people we serve are at the core of urban violence and are living in some of the most traumatic situations imaginable," an October 2019 white paper entitled *Roca's Intervention Model* laid out. "They are individuals with complex needs, often being both victims and perpetrators of violence. They are 16-to-24-year-olds whose brains will not be fully developed until they are 25, with trauma delaying this further. They are kids, emotionally stunted by the horrors they experience and witness."

The top of the first page of the white paper features the tagline LESS JAIL, MORE FUTURE.

"It's a long-distance run for the young people we work with," Molly explains, "a marathon. Young people who've been hurt and who've hurt other people, who are caught in a cycle of violence they can't break. We try to get them onto a different road, create a safe enough environment so things can work differently."

Thousands have now traveled that road since Molly founded Roca in 1988 as anything but an ordinary social services agency poised to serve high-risk kids to fulfill a mission statement that has remained consistent for over thirty years, at least in spirit.

"There's no finish line, because there's always going to be someone else to help. There's that and the conditions of the country—and the world—in the moment. There's a lot that's broken, and our program is designed to serve high-risk young people who are not yet ready, willing, or able to change."

"Roca's mission," according to the organization's 2019 annual report, "is to be a relentless force in disrupting incarceration and poverty by engaging the young adults, police, and systems at the center of urban violence in relationships to address trauma, find hope and drive change."

The penning of this chapter coincides with an unprecedented movement toward racial justice across America, with protests taking place daily from coast to coast. Umbrellaed under the moniker of "Black Lives Matter," the social strife owes its existence to the unnecessary and brutal deaths of George Floyd and others that have ripped the scab off our country's ever-strained racial relations. In that sense, Roca was bandaging the wound long before pretty much anyone else was paying attention. The organization wasn't just ahead of the curve; it developed the road map for what the protests that have drawn hundreds of thousands to the streets in the midst of a pandemic are demanding. Right now, that map is limited to five sites and eight programs across Massachusetts and a comparable two-year-old program in Molly's native Baltimore. It's not too much of a stretch, though, to see Molly Baldwin's vision expanded in cities all across the country.

Roca's time, you might say, has truly come.

"Trauma does not have to define you," proclaims the cover page of that same 2019 annual report, a credo for Roca's youth workers who define themselves by persistence in treating underserved youth often lost in a cycle of despair, crime, endless probation, and recidivism. And the results speak for themselves, as delineated in the report:

> *97% of Roca young men who completed the first two years were not re-incarcerated. 70% of Roca young men who were placed in a job held their job for six months or longer. Only 33% of Roca young men served from 2012–2019 recidivated within three years. That's a big drop from the over 50% national average. And, perhaps most impressive of all, of the more than 85% of young men who come to Roca with a violent record, four out of five stop engaging in violent crime.*

"The young men in the program all have a history of high-level felony charges, all of them," says Molly. "That's what gets you in the door. And our approach with them is all about building relationships and creating a space where people who've been hurt, and hurt other people, can slow down and learn some other skills so they'll feel, think, and act differently.

"Over time, we've really learned about how the brain figures into all this. People who've been traumatized and feel threatened all the time live in a constant fight-or-flight mode. Living in the bottom part of their brain and reacting in ways that make perfect sense at the time but are ultimately self-destructive. Our goal at Roca is to teach young people how to rebuild those neural pathways and address trauma so those in our program can actually change the behaviors that brought them to us in the first place, the end goal being that they can feel, think, and do differently. Make the right choices instead of the wrong ones. It's all about creating an environment safe enough for them to see the world differently."

Toward that end, Molly says, "Roca has developed an evidence-based and data-driven intervention model." She works on the prevailing theory that those who enter the Roca system are processing information in an entirely different way, responding to that constant stress they're under where a simple stare or bump in a crowd can lead to the flaring of tempers and, all too often, the drawing of guns.

"They cannot in that moment access the thinking part of their brain. When I started out in this, I was pretty much a classic youth worker—in your face and all that stuff. But I took a step back and started looking at what we were doing, the biology of what we were doing, and asking if it was doing any good, if there was a better way. We ended up changing the way we went about things, a different approach to affecting how the young men we were working with think, feel, and do. That's why this is a long-distance run, not a sprint."

Roca worked with Mass General Hospital to develop a tailored cognitive behavioral theory (CBT) approach to emotional regulation taught and mentored by frontline workers. It's a simplified, interactive plan that is highly flexible for Roca's young people, responsive to where they are emotionally and physically—whether they are at Roca headquarters, on the street, at lunch or in a car; whether they have three or thirty minutes for CBT engagement. Every interaction is planned, intentional, and tracked in this interactive plan that has since become the cornerstone of the organization's efforts and outreach in dealing with the trauma that's at the root of the issues being experienced by virtually everyone who comes through its doors.

"Trauma," that 2019 annual report tells us, "is fear that never turns off. It sends our brain to survival mode, as if the brain is responding to a threat, just like the brain functioned when the traumatic incident initially occurred. In survival mode, the pathways to The Thinking Brain are effectively blocked—the brain focuses on survival ("fight, flight, freeze"), lets the Limbic System and the Brain Stem take over, and is not open to learning or change. For people who experienced trauma, threats as severe as shootings and as mild as constructive criticism from a boss trigger the survival response regularly, and they struggle to make balanced decisions until they feel safety."

Sounds great in theory, as many cerebral analyses do, the difference with Roca being how they put it into practice with young men like Chris Mullins. Before the now twenty-eight-year-old Chris became a Roca youth worker, he fit the profile of that traumatized young man to a T. At twenty-two, he'd managed to avoid prison but was on probation on a drug charge for possession with intent to distribute, and it seemed inevitable that before too long he'd be looking at the world through a razor-wire-topped fence.

"I'd never heard of Roca," Chris tells us. "Then this random guy came to my house looking for me. I figured he had to be some type of law enforcement so I kept avoiding him. One day, I opened the door and there he was. He told me he was there to help, that the state of Massachusetts had a program for guys like me and my name had popped up, like winning a raffle. It turned out to be more like winning the lottery. Henry came to my house a few times before we actually went to the Roca building, and I got into the program that teaches guys how to work: get up early, follow the rules, go to your job, then move on from the program when you're ready to handle a job on your own."

That Transitional Employment Program is another cornerstone of Roca's modus operandi, putting high-risk youth on Roca work crews that fill municipal contracts in landscaping and construction, among other labors. And "Henry," Chris's youth worker also known by Hea Tha, is a Cambodian refugee with a background that was dominated by trauma of its own right, though a different brand than that experienced by the typical young man in the Roca program.

"I ended up in a work camp after Pol Pot and Khmer Rouge came to power," Henry recalls in perfect, though accented, English. "My family was separated and taken away except for two sisters who were too young. I had to sneak out of the work camp to take care of them, make sure they ate. They stayed home but they still had to work. We were all between five and ten years old, and we were all put to work as slaves. You know how to read, they kill you. You know how to write, they kill you. You speak up, they kill you. You don't get your work done, they kill you. It was genocide. I never overcame that. I still have nightmares. Becoming a youth worker at Roca drove the negative energy out of my mind. I know that I'm able to help other people, know that I'm a value to other people, and I'm stronger because of that."

Henry spent time in seven or eight refugee camps spread across Thailand, Malaysia, and Singapore. He ultimately immigrated to America with much of his family but found himself in and out of trouble constantly, much like the typical Roca youth he would later make a life out of helping. Unlike Chris, he was unable to avoid prison and ended up behind bars for drug trafficking.

"When I got out, a man kept showing up at my house. The first day I came home, he was in my driveway. I thought he was undercover and told him to leave. But he came back the next day and said he wanted to help me. I asked him why.

"'Because you saved my son's life,' he told me.

"Before I went into prison, I'd dropped his son off at the hospital after a fight. That's all I did, and this man offered me a job because of it when I needed a job the most. It turned out he was the CEO of a major company, and he offered me a job delivering packages at night. He believed in me, trusted me. I was an ex-con, so he couldn't have me on the books and had to pay me under the table. That allowed me to pay off all my debts, but I wasn't happy. I spent a lot of time alone driving at night, and my mind was processing what might be in those boxes I was delivering, that it could be valuable, and I was afraid the temptation might lead me to relapse and then I wouldn't be helping this man at all. So I quit, and he blessed me and told me to make the most of my second chance."

And Henry did, though his road to becoming a Roca youth worker with a substantial caseload was hardly typical, if there even is such a thing.

"I went to Roca to protect my brother because the members of the gang he was a part of didn't want him there. I didn't realize then that I was the one who needed protection from all this kind of stuff. My brother taught me how much Roca had done for him. They were there for him, convinced him he could be a good person. My brother ended up working for Roca, and then I did too. And now I have purpose. I don't have much, but I have a lot. I tell people the best thing that ever happened to me was getting arrested. Because if I didn't get arrested I'd probably be dead or in jail for a really long time for something much worse.

"I love working at Roca because I have my purpose. My work can make a difference in someone else's life. In the seven years I've been there, I've only taken two weeks off, and I work seventy- to eighty-hour weeks. I can't feel good about myself going on vacation when my kids need me. And I made a vow to myself to give back, volunteer at least half the time. So I get paid for forty hours, when I work eighty."

That kind of dedication explains why Roca gets the results that it does, in stark contrast to other, normally state-supported social services agencies.

"They're real consistent and always push me down the right path," says Derrick, a current participant in the program from Chelsea, Massachusetts. "It's nice knowing someone out there cares. A lot of us grew up in a fucked-up lifestyle and no one cared about us. Roca shows that they actually do."

"I use CBT [cognitive behavioral theory] every day because it helps me with self-control," adds Luis of Springfield, Massachusetts. "I used to be the kid that would get mad about everything. But the other day, someone said something about a gang I was in, and back in the day I would have fought him. But now I know it's not worth it."

Ron Mitchell, who heads Roca's Springfield-based program, smiles at hearing that.

"Roca is all about giving kids the opportunity to have a second chance. You can't give up hope on a person, even when they have a setback or relapse into their old behaviors. That's what makes Roca different. We don't give up on kids. We want them to know they have options, that they don't have to be a product of their environment. It's not just shoot or be shot, end up in jail or end up dead. They have more in them than they think. They have more choices beyond what they know. And we're going to be there to applaud their successes and catch them when they fall. We want to prove to them that we'll still be there to help them get back on the horse."

Mitchell, who's fifty-three now, knows of what he speaks. He had his own share of brushes with the law as a younger man and teen and served some time in prison that helped solidify his commitment not only to his own future but also that of others. And he knows that Roca's unique cognitive behavioral theory approach works.

"Here's an example: Roca had this young man. He was in a park when some rivals showed up. In his mind, he resorted right away to the fight instinct. Called a friend and asked the friend to bring him his gun. Then he thought about all the kids around him in the park and the costs of using that gun. So he backed up and called his friend again, told him not to bring his gun. He told us how he'd used CBT. He believed in it. It's small things sometimes, like the way someone like him responds just to a look. They call that 'smoke,' and young men like him, when they use CBT, they realize the person wasn't even looking at them."

In other words, Ron explains, Roca's program is all about not just changing the way young men think but also how they process information.

"Change is possible," Molly Baldwin explains. "You can't undo the past, so you deal with it. Show these kids that life is worth living. Learn what's going on with them; how the think, feel, do cycle can put them in a place of joy and hopefulness. Get them to slow down enough by forging the kind of positive relationships that create a safe place, something a lot of them have never known. You want to show them an alternative so they think, 'I could be like that.'"

Molly talks about the Roca "Circles," modeled after those of a peacekeeping variety enacted by Native Americans centuries ago. Police officers and community leaders participate, along with the likes of Derrick and Luis, and Chris Mullins before them.

"It shows everyone involved that we're so much more alike than we are different as human beings."

"Roca is the only organization that I know that doesn't give up on you," says Captain David Batchelor of the Chelsea, Massachusetts, police. "Their model is different because with most programs, you violate a rule and you're out. Roca allows you to fail and brings you back for programming."

But why did Molly choose this as her life's path?

"It was a calling. I grew up in a privileged family, and I knew when I was a kid the world wasn't everything people were telling me it was and they didn't get it. I'd get incredibly sad because I couldn't figure out why I was seeing things they weren't. I knew people had a choice, that they could change."

She doesn't consider herself or Roca to be miracle workers. Even though some of Roca's work can be called miraculous, there are also dark moments that bring home the harsh realities of the world the group inhabits with a vengeance.

"I remember a particularly snowy winter we had in 2015. On one of our work crews, a young person ordered another member of the crew's execution. They were rival gang members. I never thought in our experience something like that could happen. Kenny getting killed was the hardest period of my leadership."

Indeed, Roca is all about breaking the cycle of violence and danger, but some cycles can't be broken.

"Roca offers another way to respond in contrast to the mindset you have coming in," Chris Mullins explains. "Young men entering the program react the same way. For me, if I felt disrespected, it would have to be handled. Maybe not violently and maybe just telling them to go fuck themselves. Show you're not a punk and you're not going to take shit from anyone. Look, a lot of bad things have happened to them, and CBT doesn't eliminate everything they bring in with them, but it pulls you away from your old habits. CBT shows you that you don't have to fight, numb yourself, or bury things. It literally reprograms your brain to deal with things."

Chris isn't the only Roca youth worker who knows the program as a participant, but he offers a unique perspective as to why he stayed around on the other side to form the kind of transformational relationships between high-risk youth and their youth workers that have come to define the organization.

"It's a debt I've got to pay. What someone did for me, I've got to do for someone else. When you think about what you got from that and now you're helping others who are in the same position you were—that means something."

Chris leaves out mention of his own struggles while in the program. He suffered years of relapse, almost died, and fought off the desire to take his own life. Setback after setback neither soured Roca on him nor led people like Henry to give up. Far from it.

"They have to relapse in order to grow," says Ron Mitchell. "It's part of the process. They didn't want us in their lives, but we kept showing up and we keep showing up until they realize we're there to help them."

And now Chris is on the other side, doing that very same thing.

"A lot of people don't become part of what helped them. The ones who do become poster children for giving back."

Leorah Weiss-Newall, a Baltimore-based youth worker who goes by "Leo," gets that. She came to Roca from another social services organization, which has given her a unique understanding of why Roca succeeds where others fail.

"I think someone who's dedicated, someone who's open, someone who's not afraid to keep showing up and coming back," she says, in describing the more-or-less typical Roca youth worker. "Someone not afraid of some minimal harassment. Being a woman, I have a different perspective than the guys do, and I have to connect on a different level. And that's okay because I'm different from the other lady social workers these kids have had in their life. There's a lot I don't know about their experiences, but I'm there to learn. And they figure out pretty quick that I'm on their side.

"A lot of guys I've come into contact with, it's just a matter of having someone in their life who's persistent and someone they can develop a therapeutic rapport with. That allows us to be successful. They know we're going to keep showing up. Guys who keep ducking out on me know I'm not going to give up on them. I'm going to be around, and they can always reach out to me and they know that."

And why did Leo choose this career path?

"My family adopted my sister who's special needs. That made me understand how fortunate I was, all the crazy shit she went through before she moved in with us. And that made me want to help people who weren't as fortunate as I was."

People like Raequan, a participant in the fledgling Baltimore-based program.

"Now I stop and think in that split second. I am now able to think about possible outcomes of my situation before I choose wrong. Everyone should give Roca a try because it will help save you in the long run and could save your life."

Or Antoine.

"I'm working this now. I've failed like ten times, but I'm gonna get it right. Roca helps me practice, and helps me help myself."

J. T. Timpson, one of those who oversees the organization's Baltimore program and a lifelong resident of the city, knows of what Raequan and Antoine speak.

"Our commitment to change the lives of young people is real," says the burly former high school star athlete. "A lot of programs have already failed these kids and given up on them. The first thing we bring to the table is the credibility behind what we say we're going to deliver. The reality is being a part of Roca is a decision they don't have to make. We make the decision for them. We're going to build relationships with these young people. We're going to get to know their families and friends, and we're going to service the family and individuals around that young person too. I tell them that my job is to love them whether they like me or not. I don't care. No matter what, I'm going to be back knocking on their door tomorrow. I'm going to be in their driveway. I'm going to be outside their house. We don't give up on them, and we don't let them give up on themselves."

J. T., now forty-three, escaped the streets thanks to being a stellar athlete. He was "protected" from that life, shielded from it. He didn't realize his own level of trauma until he went to work for Roca, finding that he had resorted to the very thinking from which he thought he'd been insulated and found himself practicing the principles of CBT. He and Molly Baldwin had enjoyed a long relationship before things were up and running in Baltimore, adding to Roca's work across Massachusetts and establishing a model for the rest of the country.

"Our commitment to changing the lives of young people is real," J. T. says. "I've worked for a lot of different organizations. Roca brings something different to the table. Since I've been on the board, all the things I'd hoped for have come true and much more. The commitment level to the community, commitment to change, commitment to helping young people understand that change is possible are all real."

J. T. and Ron Mitchell, who both know this world at the street level, stress that Roca doesn't and can't succeed in a vacuum. Another of the program's unique strengths, J. T. explains, is enlisting community partners in a coordinated effort.

"Our best friends in Baltimore are the police. We can't do anything without the police. They know what we're doing is in their best interests; they get that. The whole city does. They want things to change, to get better. That's what we're about, and they're committed to helping us."

Roca is fortunate for having built strong alliances and relationships with foundations and municipalities, as well as corporate leaders who provide funding for the good of the community and humanity in general. In Baltimore, top corporate leaders believe activism is integral to their corporate identity and crucial to attracting young, talented employees. Companies devoted to reducing crime and helping disadvantaged youth offer their employees a greater sense of purpose and quality of life in their communities.

But Leo highlights another challenge that comes with the job: negotiating the treacherous waters of the system itself.

"The frustration is so great on so many different levels. You see these kids getting disrespected as they try to work their way through all these bureaucracies. They're told they didn't fill out a form right, so their probation officer is going to violate them. They show up for a meeting on Tuesday and get told it was changed to yesterday and they get violated. It's worse than violence. People deserve to be treated like people."

The racial inequities Leo and other youth workers have to deal with are systematic to a society in desperate need of change. According to the NAACP, African-Americans are incarcerated at more than five times the rate of whites. And they receive sentences averaging around 20 percent higher than whites. Racial profiling hasn't gone away, recent events being all the proof we need of that.

And the emotion stemming from that reality is magnified by a deeply felt history of subjugation and denigration—slavery, Jim Crow, segregation, and prejudice. The public murder of George Floyd wasn't just horrifying; it triggered an already primed psychological bombshell. It's no wonder the alienation runs so deep and why it's so difficult to wean these kids into a mindset where they think it's possible to make it.

Every decent person who saw Floyd murdered was enraged by it and wanted to somehow express their anger and revulsion. That's what all the protests were about, all the calls to "do the right thing," not only to reform police departments but to expose the depths of racism in the society so it can be addressed more effectively than it has been. We're seeing the results of that on the streets (this is being written in June 2020). But many of the young people Roca deals with can't see a way to make a positive impact. Instead they're driven deeper into their antagonism and self-destructive behavior.

"Look at the country," says Molly Baldwin. "The racism and bias make for adversity that's very difficult, sometimes impossible, to overcome. And you have to understand that these kids are severely traumatized by it by the time we get them."

Molly herself doesn't seek or make a big deal out of accolades, like winning the Boston Bar Foundation Public Service Award in 2016. That's not her style. For her, the job is its own reward.

"I've been at this a long time, but I understand it differently now than when I was younger. It's such an extraordinary privilege to walk down the road with people you're trying to help be better."

~ ~ ~

## Reflections

Molly Baldwin and Roca are about healing long-term traumatic injury. They work almost exclusively with young people whose lives have been embroiled with gangs, criminality, and violence, young people who have been convicted of crimes and imprisoned or are on a one-way road to court and jail. Almost always, Roca's clients have grown up in harsh, dysfunctional, often violent circumstances, none more desperate than Cambodian refugee Hea Tha experienced under the Khmer Rouge regime of mass murder and enslavement followed by life in a series of refugee camps.

We've seen similar kinds of profound trauma in other interviewees. Oretha Tarr and Mangok Bol were both victims of years of catastrophic violence and deprivation. Mangok and Oretha both came through those experiences intact, for reasons we have tried to define. But for Roca's clients, the damage they suffered has become embedded, chronic. It's resulted in sociopathic behavior and mindsets that veer instinctively toward violence. "Young people who've been hurt and who've hurt other people, who are caught in a cycle of violence they can't break," in Molly Baldwin's words. These are young people who have been defined by trauma. But Baldwin and her street workers tell them, "Trauma does *not* have to define you."

Baldwin founded Roca in 1988. Through much of its existence it was much more like a standard community center in the impoverished, immigrant-heavy locality, Chelsea, Massachusetts. Somali refugees, Bosnians, South and Central Americans, Cambodians, Afghans, and others were resettled there in recent times, following earlier immigrant communities of Irish, Italians, Poles, and Jews. In that environment, Roca helped and supported everyone who might have appeared on its doorstep, with counseling, health and nutrition programs, job development, cultural activities, athletics—all the usual endeavors of dedicated settlement houses and community centers.

Perhaps inevitably, Roca became progressively more engaged with gang work and youth/police interaction. That was, in fact, Molly Baldwin's initial motive even before she started Roca. She engaged herself with young gangbangers and wannabees, knocking on doors, meeting them on the streets, keeping on them relentlessly, cajoling, counseling, telling them to get back to school and do their homework, putting herself on the line to help them in every way she could think of.

That relentless persistence and availability is *the* defining characteristic of Roca's caseworkers. It is also the essential first step in the behavior-changing approach known as CBT (cognitive behavioral theory) that now informs Roca's work with young people in trouble.

The insight that Baldwin and Roca eventually came to was that thinking is inseparable from emotions. The neuroscience behind this was developed by Antonio Damasio, the director of the Brain and Creativity Institute at the University of Southern California. Damasio has shown how the brain's decision-making mechanisms are interconnected through neural networks with its centers for emotional reaction. "Feelings come first," he argues in his seminal book *Descartes' Error*. "They constitute a frame of reference... Their influence is immense."

"People who've been traumatized and feel threatened all the time," Baldwin explains, "live in a constant fight-or-flight mode... Our goal is to rebuild those neural pathways."

The necessary first step in the process is to establish a connection. That's what is behind Roca's relentlessness. A connection makes the case that despite everything—the violence, the incarceration, the antagonism—someone does, in fact, care. There is a caring presence knocking on the door, immediate and available. Once that is established, a safe haven of sorts opens up where anger and defensiveness aren't automatically triggered. That's the beginning of changing the emotional pattern that allows a different sort of thinking. Caseworkers, many of whom as young people were themselves entrenched in street crime, provide models for a new level of thought. Roca programs then provide training in work habits and skills for those who are ready. These are steps in a pathway of cognitive reworking.

Ultimately, the changes in thinking can lead to a sense of purpose, which so often is the great driver of resilience and recovery. The startlingly effective insight here is that thought is nested within a structure of emotion and that to affect deeply conditioned patterns of behavior, it is necessary to first wean the emotional system from fear and anger to affiliation and empathy, which equally inhabit the mind's deep structures.

Herman (left) pictured with his wife Jeannie and Dr. Gus White.

# 21

# Herman Williams

*Herman J. Williams was on the verge of living his ultimate dream of becoming an orthopedic surgeon to elite athletes—when his life took a shocking detour.*

*"Herman!" screamed his fiancée Jeannie, as he lay lifeless on a gymnasium floor.*

*How could a healthy 31-year-old collapse during an afternoon basketball game with his fellow medical residents?*

*"No pulse!" they shouted. "He's not breathing."*

—From *Clear: Living the Life You Didn't Dream Of*
by Herman Williams

The rest, as they say, is history. Herman survived, but his dream didn't.

"I had entered the gym that April day in 1991 on the verge of living my dream. Now I was being wheeled out on a gurney, unconscious, and totally unaware that in one fateful heartbeat, or technically, lack thereof, death had killed my dream. Doctors determined that I had Right Ventricular Dysplasia, a rare heart disease that causes fat to replace muscle. This condition triggers vulnerability to dangerous arrhythmias; antiarrhythmic medication was the only treatment at the time."

But a more experimental treatment had just become available in the form of a small pacemaker with the capability of a defibrillator that could be implanted in the patient's chest.

"Every time your heart races into an irregular rhythm or stops altogether," Herman explained in *Clear*, "the device will shock you to restore a normal heartbeat. The shock will save your life."

Instead, it only added to his trauma; it was so painful when a shock was delivered, terrifying him whenever it went off. Eventually, Herman began suffering from post-traumatic stress disorder, or PTSD. Initially, he grew so terrified of being jolted in public that he didn't want to leave the house.

"Then I began having 'Phantom Shocks.' Waking up in a cold sweat, believing that I'd been defibrillated, even though the device showed no shock had been given."

In a perfect world, the device would have allowed him to resume his chosen career path of becoming an orthopedic surgeon specializing in the treatment of professional athletes. And that is the exact path he was on, after a chance meeting with the team doctor for the Los Angeles Rams.

"He made that dream seem attainable when I rotated through Dr. Clarence Shields' practice as a medical student. Since I actually worked with an African American man who was the team doctor for the Rams, he inspired me to dream big and apply for a fellowship in sports medicine at the Kerlan-Jobe clinic where he worked. Dreams fall into two separate categories in my mind: Those one in a billion dreams like, I want to be president someday, and those one in a million dreams like mine which was to become the team doctor to the Los Angeles Lakers someday. I will never forget my father telling me that as a black man you can do anything you want, except to be president, because we'll never have a black president in this country."

He chuckles at that.

"I grew up with limitations on my dream because I was black. But all that seemed about to change. It was a pipe dream at first, but I was putting the pieces into place to make it a reality. I met one of the current team doctors, he was my mentor, I got into one of the most difficult orthopedic residencies and I knew the sports medicine program that took care of the team. It was like, 'I'm coming, baby!' Then the cardiac arrest. When you lose your dream, the first thing is to make sure that it's gone. Losing my profession, losing my skill, was unbearable. I had to try to come back. The problem was, first, all the medications I was on messed with my vision. I was in surgery one day when the attending physician asked me to close the wound. But my vision was too blurry to manage it. I had to tell him I couldn't see. Then there was the internal defibrillator that was like a time bomb ticking in my chest that could go off at any time, including when I was operating. I had to leave surgery at that point. I had no choice."

It didn't go well at first.

"That ripped open a black hole inside me that was sucking me into a deep, dark depression," he writes in *Clear*. "It forced me to reflect on the meaning of life and death. Who am I? Why am I here? If I could not execute the first life mission that I had chosen, what would I do now? My dilemma reminded me of a famous quote by Langston Hughes: 'Hold fast to dreams, for if dreams die, life is a broken-winged bird that cannot fly.' My wings were definitely clipped.

"When something devastating like that happens to you, you need time to absorb what it means and mourn what you've lost. Then you need to train your focus forward, find a new dream to replace the one you've lost. I started putting together a plan B. I began to look around, at the skills I had and how I could best utilize them. Well, I had an MD, I understood health care. So I went back to school.

That meant I wouldn't have to worry about getting a job now that I couldn't be a practicing doctor anymore. It would also allow me to pace myself while I recuperated physically. I had already gotten a master's in public health from Harvard University, but it was five years later, and the public health landscape had changed completely. The most logical choice would be to bridge my medical training with business, so I got my master's in business administration at the University of Washington. The medical school there gave me a job in the admissions office to help recruit minority students while I went to school to help finance my education. The dean of the medical school, Benjamin Belknap, did everything he could to help me with making connections and support. And it wasn't just him; people came from all over the place to help me."

After that, Herman began charting a new path for himself as he embarked on an exciting, but totally disparate, career track than the one he'd spent much of his life dreaming about. What, though, does the former practicing physician prescribe for someone facing a comparable predicament? What's his recommendation for treatment?

"Surround yourself with people who care about you and will be honest with you. Establish a new dream, a new network. I hadn't gotten as far as I did to just give up. I believe there's something bigger than you out there. There's got to be a bigger plan for me to accomplish, I'd tell myself. And when you believe there's something out there bigger than you, that's going to help you improve your situation. You have to find joy in adversity."

Herman pauses before expounding on that unique philosophy.

"The key is to believe that suffering and adversity are part of the process of getting to something greater than you are. It assumes that you can't get to certain places without experiencing some degree of adversity. For an African-American male to set a goal to be the head of anything in this country is still associated with overcoming adversity. You're a trail blazer. You have to start on your journey knowing the steps you need to take to get to your destination. And you need to find joy in that journey, not just in getting to where you want to go."

Herman ended up with a great career in hospital operations, always as a prominent physician administrator in positions such as Chief Medical Officer or Chief Clinical Officer. After business school, he started as a healthcare manager for Pacific Northwest Healthcare Consulting from 1994 to 1997. That was followed by an eighteen-year stint with several large hospital companies overseeing various large hospital networks, until he was severed after a merger wiped out the entire upper echelon of his company. It was like déjà vu all over again, as Yogi Berra might say. Another dream lost, albeit after a much longer tenure. So what did Herman do?

"You set out on one path and all of a sudden you find yourself on a different one. I wanted to be team doctor for the Lakers, and I ended up someplace entirely different but just as good, maybe better. You look back at where you came from, and it's even better than what you thought you wanted. You have to be open to the fact that maybe there's something better for you out there, that the dream you lost was just a side road to prepare you for something else."

In Herman's case, that road came with any number of guides who led him where he needed to go, specifically Kent Wallace, then vice president for medical affairs at Vanguard Health Systems based in Nashville, Tennessee. He created a position for Herman because he believed in him.

"Herman's job was to run physician leadership groups across America to influence people to let them know that our hospital CEOs want to hear and resolve problems that physicians were having," Wallace reflects on Herman's tenure with his company. "This involved nearly five hundred physicians at more than twenty-five hospitals. The problem was that physicians felt CEOs did not listen to their irritants, nor did the CEOs implement solutions. Herman created a national environment to do that. Herman can move across all lines of individuals in the hospital. It's like he's taken his gentle bedside manner as a physician into conference rooms, where he can heal administrative and management conflicts as a conciliator or facilitator. And that's what makes him so successful at what he does."

"It wasn't my original dream, but it's become my legacy, something I can put my name on."

What Herman wasn't counting on was how close he kept coming to having his name prematurely etched on a gravestone. Incredibly enough, in addition to having to learn to live with his internal defibrillator going off whenever his heart rate elevated, often at the least opportune times, twice more his heart stopped, and he had to be resuscitated by passersby who just happened to be trained in CPR. He often thinks of the irony that not enough bystanders step forward when people have cardiac arrests and go down in public, though not in his case.

"Every time I needed a bystander, there was someone there, someone who was willing to take responsibility for doing something. Had they not, I wouldn't have survived."

And if that wasn't enough to add to the myriad of health issues he's suffered for thirty years, he also had to deal with suffering a stroke.

"Something was gravely wrong when I awoke the next morning at 6:15 on February 18, 2013," Herman writes in *Clear*. "I jumped out of bed—and almost fell over. I couldn't stand. I knew immediately, thanks to my medical training, that I was having a stroke. I tried to shout, 'Jeannie!' But an unintelligible sound came from my mouth. She turned on a lamp and ran around our king-sized bed. As I stood on wobbly legs, she appeared to be coming toward me in slow motion. Immediately recognizing the classic signs of a stroke, including slurred speech, she sat me on a vanity bench in the bathroom and called 911. When we arrived at the hospital, the only treatment that I was a candidate for was the blood thinner Heparin, delivered via IV. This would hopefully dissolve the clot and give my body a chance to resolve this on its own. I couldn't speak at all and they simply admitted me into the Neuro-ICU, and all we could do was wait for the final outcomes. My life was in God's hands. While we waited, to my horror, an echocardiogram revealed a three-centimeter clot in the lower chamber of the right ventricle of my heart."

Fortunately, God's grasp was firm, as Herman found himself hurdling another of life's obstacles, finding the resilience to overcome yet another bout with adversity. He didn't throw in the towel and concede to a Universe that seemed to have it in for him. Instead he looked it in the eye and the Universe blinked, even though Herman lost the ability to speak for three long days and feared he'd uttered his last word for good. But even that failed to deter the relentless optimism that carries him through every day.

"That is the day that I declared I would devote the rest of my life to doing everything I could to improve the lives of others and to help them see the beauty of life. I began to clearly understand what the late author and poet Maya Angelou meant when she said, 'Life is not measured by the number of breaths we take, but by the moments that take our breath away.'"

Remember, his book *Clear* is subtitled *Living the Life You Didn't Dream Of*. Emphasis on *didn't*. So you might say, *should* say, Herman is preaching what he has practiced his entire professional life. With that in mind, he firmly believes that the last thirty years, since his heart stopped on that basketball court, prepared him for dealing with the COVID-19 crisis.

"I got put in a better place. It made me more nimble, readied me to deal with the pandemic both personally and professionally. What a blessing, as it turned out."

On the personal level, Herman has to be even more careful than most, virtually all, when it comes to catching the virus. But what is his advice for dealing with adversity in a world riddled and dominated by the coronavirus, COVID-19?

"First of all, your life isn't over; your life has changed. The main concept of resilience is adaptability, the ability to adapt to your new life. Gather the facts: What are the new risks, what is the new reality, and how does it affect you? When you have the answers, you're in a position to create a new model for success that is adaptable to this new situation. Look, things are just not going to be the same. COVID represents a paradigm shift. We will never go back to living the way we did before this started. The whole dynamic of people being around other people has changed for good. You may hate the idea of what's being forced upon you, but the fact is your ability to survive could depend on social distancing. The people who are going to succeed out of this are the people with the most innovative, compassionate ideas. Sometimes when you lose everything, it's a wake-up call."

For Herman, compassion is an indelible element to achieving success, as is empathy. "I heard about this very successful restaurant owner in New York City who's going to let health-care workers eat for free in his establishments for a year after the coronavirus crisis is over. That came out of nowhere."

That restauranteur is hardly alone. As the *New York Daily News* reported on March 26, 2020, "Generous eateries across the five boroughs are offering free food to school kids, health care workers, first responders and others in need, even as they're forced to eat huge losses with the ban on eat-in customers due to the coronavirus pandemic."

Compassion and empathy. And in Herman's mind, these are the kind of people, what he calls the "best and the brightest," who will find their way back to the top, or at the top, once this is all behind us.

"Making a difference in people's lives brings me peace. It makes me feel like I'm making this world a better place to live in. I don't expect anything out of it; I've already gotten so much out of life, so many wonderful experiences. I want others to benefit from the things I've benefitted from."

Toward that end, in *Clear* Herman offers what he calls the Four Themes of Surviving and Thriving:

- Believe in something bigger than yourself.

- Know that your higher power, or spiritual entity, has a greater plan for your life than you can conceive for yourself.
- Understand that suffering is a relative experience and that resilience always trumps pain.
- Appreciate and accept that the unwavering devotion of your loved ones can provide you with the power to prevail.

Of his own life, Herman adds this in *Clear*:

*"My current position as Executive Vice President and Chief Clinical Officer at RCCH Healthcare Partners allows me to help improve healthcare for people across America. That ability has steadily increased since my first hospital operations job when I was taking care of one hospital; I now oversee Quality and Clinical Operations for [eighteen] facilities. Having risen from that devastating moment when I realized I could not be an orthopedic surgeon—to the honor of serving in this position—exemplifies the power of helping people. I wouldn't be here without Kent Wallace's continuous orchestration of my ascent to RCCH Healthcare Partners. I would not have reached that point without Hugh Greeley's training. And without the influence of Richard Williams, Don Parks, and Gus White, I may not have reached the pinnacle of my medical training, where I was the day I died on April 28, 1991, as I celebrate [thirty] years of living a new dream and enjoying an awakening about how I lived to tell about it."*

His wife, Jeannie, has been there for him every step of the way. So has his son Cole, whom he calls "a shining light amid the darkness" for giving him a reason to keep fighting when he could have just given up. He writes:

*"I found immense, overwhelming joy in the simple things that I had been doing for years and years: hugging Cole; waking up beside Jeannie and loving that we had a whole new day ahead of us; greeting strangers in the elevator at work; savoring a sweet, creamy cup of steaming coffee; enjoying the warm sunshine on my face. I loved the*

*feeling of simply being alive. Breathing, walking, talking, encountering people at work, greeting complete strangers in public, marveling at the majesty of nature, relishing the taste of delicious food, being acutely aware of the joy of laughing or playing music."*

All because he lived the life he didn't dream of.

"My reason for living," Herman says, articulating the mission statement for his life, "is to make sure that everyone I encounter is better off in some way when they leave me."

~ ~ ~

## Reflections

The seventeenth-century philosopher Baruch Spinoza wrote about deep emotional distress, that the suffering it causes "ceases to be suffering as we form a clear and precise picture of it." One way of counteracting trauma, for example, is by finding meaning in it, thus forming Spinoza's clear and precise picture. If you can identify some purpose in the distress you are undergoing, you can not only protect yourself from being consumed by it, you can use that suffering to grow morally, spiritually, and in your effectiveness as a human being. Think of Nelson Mandela, imprisoned for twenty-seven years, part of the time at hard labor. Mandela was in despair for years, until he began to see, in his words, that "the suffering I am enduring is part of a larger plan." His suffering had led him to a different, far more effective vision of how to fight apartheid. That was its meaning. Herman Williams puts it a little differently. "The key is believing that suffering and adversity are part of the process of getting to something greater than you are." Suffering for Williams led to a far larger understanding of life's meaning and ultimate value.

What's so singular about Williams's experience is the many crises he has undergone: cardiac arrest, severe anxiety, loss of his career, loss of another career, more cardiac arrests, stroke. The repeated bouts with adversity Williams has suffered have focused him, in a way we haven't seen before, on the *problem* of suffering. Not *How do I overcome this adversity I am suffering*, but *What is the meaning of suffering in my life?*

His answer to that is that the journey itself has significance in making him see life in a larger, surer way. And since the journey has meaning, he considers the adversities he has suffered not as painful challenges but as steps along the way. You have to learn, he says, "to find joy in the journey, not just in getting where you want to go."

That's a remarkable insight, that we should embrace the adversities that afflict us because they constitute a further step toward the realization of our better selves. The guru of American leadership studies, Warren Bennis, emphasized essentially the same point. Leaders, Bennis maintained, are almost always forged by the hard adversities they face—Bennis calls them "crucibles." Leaders are transformed by these experiences. They emerge from crises with a clearer understanding of their own moral values. They find meaning and strength in themselves, and a heightened sense of resolve and purpose. Almost always, Bennis wrote, undergoing hardship enhances empathy, and true leaders, he says, "are richly endowed with empathy." Herman Williams would undoubtedly say that Bennis's remarks about leaders apply to all of us, as they most certainly do to the crucibles he himself has lived through.

We emerge from adversities, both Williams and Bennis say, with stronger, better selves. In previous interviews we've seen exactly this. We haven't encountered anyone who suffered through multiple crises as Williams has, but we have seen what happens when trauma destroyed the lives our interviewees had built for themselves. Like Williams, Claudia Thomas lost the ability to practice surgery. Jim Pantelas lost his business. Mangok Bol's path in life was destroyed before he had even embarked on it. But for each of them, adversity wasn't an end-of-the-road catastrophe; it was an opening to something else. "You get the opportunity to be resurrected," is the way Pantelas put it. You come through it, he might have said, a different person.

In each of those stories, our interviewees had re-created themselves. In fact, creating yourself in one way or another seems to be a constant theme when it comes to resilience. What this suggests is that we human beings have a drive toward self-realization, toward finding a purpose in our lives, that demands to be filled. If that drive dies, we can be overwhelmed by frustration, self-pity, and paralysis. But it doesn't die easily, as Herman Williams's story demonstrates so vividly. It persists for us to draw strength from even in the face of the severe traumas we are all likely to suffer at some point as we make our way through life.

# CONCLUSION

# How We Survive, Learn, and Overcome

We began writing this book just before the coronavirus pandemic arrived. Then, as we interviewed our participants and thought about their experiences, we found ourselves in the middle of it. Here we were, writing about the life crises people had endured and overcome, and suddenly all of us were facing an unprecedented crisis that was killing tens of thousands of people and testing everyone's powers of coping and resilience.

With everything else COVID-19 does, it focuses people's minds on the most important things in their lives. What is it that is most valuable to us that we have lost? How can we reshape the way we live and think in order, first, to sustain ourselves, and then to come out of it whole, maybe changed, but whole?

In essence, that's what all trauma does. Trauma focuses the mind on things lost, and then on what might nevertheless be found. Traumatic events, the kind we were hearing about from our interviewees, challenge us to muster the resources of our minds, bodies, and imaginations in order to heal and come out on the other side, changed maybe, but whole. COVID aside, we know we are all bound to suffer trauma in our lives: a bad injury, serious illness, deep emotional distress, natural disaster, the loss of people dear to us. Something powerful and threatening is going to afflict us—there's no getting out of it. Being human means being vulnerable to harm and loss. But being human also means that we have strengths we can call on in times of anguish and distress. If vulnerability is inherent in our human condition, so is resilience and the will to recovery.

The array of character traits and drives evident here present a mosaic of the elements that comprise resilience. Some we see in one or another of our interviewees, some in several. Others seem universal. Taken together, they convey a picture of our psychic immune system's response to severe stress. We approached these interviews thinking we would be able to explore elements of that immune system in order to name them and understand them better. Others have done that, or something like that, but we believed that with our varied backgrounds and perspectives, we might be able to throw a different light on this dimension of what it is that makes us human. Fighting through despair and hopelessness is part of the instinct for survival. Striving for meaning and purpose is as well.

Gregory Fricchione is a psychiatrist whose long experience with seriously ill and dying patients compelled him, he writes, "to journey into the world of human limit questions." In one after another of our stories, we too find ourselves in the realm of human limit questions. In desperate situations of loss, what are the essentials in our makeup that keep us alive and impel us toward healing? For Fricchione, the overarching healing element is attachment, empathy, and love, revealed not only in successful therapeutic treatment but in human evolution and neurobiology. In our own explorations we saw a taxonomy of strengths, a few of which seemed to be irreducible, bedrock elements of our common humanity.

Krystal Cantu, for example, the one-armed weightlifter, embodied an unadulterated need to strive, to confront, to overcome, to find a way even when there seemed to be no way. Hers wasn't just the fortitude to wordlessly endure, which some have and some do not, but a built-in, undeniable will to contend against whatever fate offers. Jim Pantelas knew about that when he said he had no choice. "You don't have an option," he said. "You get out of bed in the morning and go forward." In the killing fields of Nuba, Tom Catena would simply not give up because it was somehow ordained that he had to "do his job."

If contending, or striving, is a primal motive force, we need to then ask—what is the necessity it serves? Our interviewees provide the answer here. In almost every one of our stories, whether it is the teenage wrestler Don McNeil, the Lost Boy Mangok Bol, the female football coach Heather Marini, the trans young man Echo, or the Down Syndrome actor Josh Perry, the answer is: purpose. "Man's main concern," says Auschwitz survivor and psychiatrist Viktor Frankl, "is not to gain pleasure or to avoid pain, but rather to see a meaning in life." Meaning, or purpose, can be a specific goal that mobilizes our determination and abilities or a vocation that allows us to realize our unique gifts and talents. To live a purposeful life may be a path to what Abraham Maslow called self-actualization, but it's undeniable that everyone seeks in his or her own fashion to find meaning—in family, in friends, in helping others, in work, in faith. To have no meaning at all is an invitation to apathy, alienation, and self-destruction. The pursuit of meaning is an antidote to despair; having a purpose counters the immersion in loss that inevitably accompanies trauma.

Can we not say, then, that both striving and the search for meaning are primary components of the psyche, lighted up for us when we look closely at what makes us resilient.

These interviews strongly suggest that another foundation component is empathy. We see that time and again. How do sufferers overcome suffering? So often they do it by reaching out to help others. Matt Paknis, abused sexually and physically as a boy, puts

his experiences out front when he talks to others in leadership meetings. Jim Pantelas, the lung cancer survivor, finds telling his story to
a roomful of people is a pathway to healing, this for both himself and
others. Ann Hagan Webb, who established an organization to bring
victims of priest abuse together, tells us that, "Hearing someone else
tell their story, you think, 'Oh my goodness, I felt that too.'"

"It validates your experience," she says.

Research on empathy has a rich recent history, from the prima-
tologist Frans de Waal, who traces compassionate connection through
the evolution of our species, to the neuroscientist Donald Pfaff,
whose studies reveal the brain structures that move us toward emotional engagement with others. "How plausible," Pfaff writes in *The
Altruistic Brain*, "our built-in kindness actually is, how scientifically
reasonable it can be to rely on the idea that we are wired from infancy
to 'do the right thing.'"

These and related studies in biology, psychology, and sociology
focus on the significance of empathy for evolutionary success. But
we see here how empathy functions not just for the flourishing of the
species but as a central component in the recovery from trauma. Nor
is this a mystery. Reaching out, giving our attention and energy to
others in need, focuses us away from our own inner turmoil and can
renew or reinforce our desire for meaning and purpose. Two of our
authors (AW and DC) have found, for example, in their study of physicians that "empathetic care not only improves patient outcomes but
provides meaning and satisfaction that enhances the well-being of the
caregiver and counteracts physician burnout and dropout." We see the
same principle in the waves of public support for medical personnel,
delivery people, first responders, mail carriers, and garbage collectors
during the COVID virus lockdowns. Our reliance on others generates
not only gratitude but a reinforcing sense that our well-being is tied
to their well-being, a web of mutual healing in a time of great stress.

If empathy is a hard-wired element at the core of resilience, what
then about love? Empathy is fellow feeling, compassion, the openness

we have to entering the lives of others with sympathy and understanding. Love derives from the same psychological substratum, but magnified. Love is empathy concentrated and crystallized, the most intimate connection with another of which we are capable. "An even deeper mystery than the secrets we keep," the novelist Richard Russo writes, "is the mystery of the way our hearts incline toward this person and not that one, how one soul selects another for its company, how we recognize companion souls as we make our way through the world… We love whom we love." Love is rarely if ever mentioned in studies of resilience, yet getting a close-up look at love may help us better understand how it is that deep caring for others works to counter trauma. The story of Mike and Kathy Goldberger and their son Kevin illuminates this subject in an unexpected and deeply heartfelt way.

Can we not say, then, that empathy and love are base elements that the human psyche mobilizes in times of crisis—base elements actually of the psychological substructure at all times. The deep desire for meaning or purpose, we think, is another of the fundamental drives that define us, most especially when we are tested by trauma. Each of these drives, it seems to us, refers back to the idea of man and woman as strivers, contenders in an arena full of unpredictable dangers and sudden onslaughts, always prepared by their nature to fight, often to fail but also often to win—that is, to be resilient.

We see faith, too, as a common if not quite universal element in resilience. Many researchers have shown a correlation between faith and well-being. Southwick and Charney document some of the most important of these studies in their own discussion of the components of resilience. What we have seen is that our interviewees often mention faith as a great strength for them, whether or not we have asked them specifically about it. They talk about it in different terms. For some, a belief in God, or in something "larger than themselves," is a source of general comfort, an underlying optimism that things will eventually work out. For Claudia Thomas, it is a conviction that God watches over her personally, especially in times of greatest need. For

311

Tom Catena, belief empowers the conviction that we are all brothers and sisters, children of one God—which is for him a stimulus to empathy, care, and purpose.

"Faith" may be complex, but at least it's easy to name. Another fundamental component of resilience doesn't have an easy defining term, except perhaps as a counterpart to faith. "Reason" has traditionally been considered the opposite of faith. But reason connotes more than our rational capability; it is our desire for knowledge that can be processed by our reasoning minds. It is our native curiosity, the built-in drive we have to understand the world. Joseph Soloveitchik, the Jewish sage we've quoted earlier, refers to "cognitive man," meaning by that, man given to learning and utilizing knowledge. Bobby Satcher exemplifies that drive, calling it simply "education." Mangok Bol is a model of its importance. So are Paul Allen and Herman Williams. But every story of someone who has needed to construct a different life in order to recover from trauma illuminates this drive. Re-creating a life takes both mental flexibility and the openness to understand and encompass new things. Here we see again that though resilience has its own distinct profile, the underlying components are deeply embedded in normal psychology, which is why, perhaps, that resilience comes so readily into play when we are subjected to traumatic injury.

Education, then—the desire to learn—seems to us one of the factors that operates at the core of human resilience, along with "striving," "purpose," "empathy," "love," and "faith." We see other factors at work too: self-awareness, anger, determination, endurance, persistence, optimism. But the instinct to strive, to find meaning, to seek out others, to believe in something beyond ourselves, and to acquire knowledge seem to us to be the core.

These we see as the essential components of resilience. They speak to the way we heal, and they embody the very essence of what we've been calling our common humanity.

Of all our interviewees, Herman Williams stands out. He is the orthopedist in training who suffered a near fatal cardiac arrest while playing basketball, which turned out to be just the first of various severe traumas he was to experience as the years passed. He stands out because having to cope with these many events has led him to reflect on the meaning not of one event or another but of suffering itself. He tells us that we need to see the adversities we suffer for the new strengths they give us, for the new perspectives we achieve, for the deeper understanding of those things that are of most value in our lives. Adversities, if we look at them correctly, propel us toward realizing a better, fuller version of ourselves. We need to not just suffer them, Williams says, but to embrace them.

Not everyone might agree with that conclusion. We can all think of traumas that, though we might bounce back from them, leave severely negative imprints on our lives. But the takeaway message from Williams, and perhaps from all of our interviewees, is that whatever the depth of the trauma, it is still, after all, possible to affirm life. It's impossible to forget Mary and Jim Costello, whose daughter Jill fought and lost her battle with lung cancer.

"My daughter taught me what you need to celebrate, you always need to celebrate," Mary Costello said, "whether there's cancer in the picture or not."

Viktor Frankl, facing the end in the Auschwitz death camp, came to the same essential wisdom, though he put it in terms of meaning. "We may also find meaning in life," he wrote, "even when confronted with a hopeless situation, when facing a fate that cannot be changed."

Mary and Jim Costello would agree with that. So would Herman Williams. Maybe that's where any exploration of resilience should lead, to the recognition that life itself somehow asserts its claim to meaning and value. And that resilience is, at bottom, the affirmation, and often the celebration, of that simple fact.

If resilience speaks to the ultimate value of life, it also affirms our common humanity. We opened this book with that affirmation.

"When a surgeon makes an incision and looks inside the body, we are all the same. Underneath the surface we are all brothers and sisters." But our interviewees are telling us a larger truth: it's the reality of the spirit that most essentially makes us brothers and sisters. Anxiety and fear are the fellow travelers of pain and suffering. But so are courage and fortitude. And knowing that, we are better prepared to face the crises that appear suddenly and without reason in our lives—not just as individuals undergoing our own trials, but as we now know in a way we didn't a year ago, in the lives we share together as a people.

# ACKNOWLEDGMENTS

It's not common for a book to have three authors, so by way of background—Jon Land is a story writer, and each of the interviews in *Overcoming* is a kind of short story; David Chanoff is an independent scholar who has written about health care, refugee issues, and moral decision making; Dr. Augustus White is a world renowned surgeon and professor of medical education who initiated and has guided this book throughout. It's worth noting that three of our interviewees— Claudia Thomas, Bobby Satcher, and Herman Williams—were mentees of Dr. White's at Yale and Harvard.

*Overcoming* would have remained an unfulfilled aspiration were it not for the generosity of Mr. Donald L. Saunders. We are grateful to him for making this book possible and for his enthusiastic encouragement at its inception and his ongoing support. Others we need to thank include Dr. Stephen Southwick who, along with Dr. Dennis Charney, wrote *Resilience*, a storehouse of information on a subject that engaged us with its invitation to observe and reflect on this essential dimension of mankind's instinct for survival. An initial conference at Massachusetts General Hospital's Benson Henry Institute for Mind Body Medicine stimulated and furthered many of the ideas incorporated in *Overcoming*. Stephen Southwick and Dr. Gregory Fricchione were present at that meeting, along with Dr. Herbert Benson, the Institute's founder and emeritus director. We would like to thank each of them for their contribution to our initial thinking.

Others we would like to acknowledge include Dr. Jeannette Post, and Jim Post, co-founders of Voice of the Faithful, a worldwide organization of Catholic lay people engaged with issues of priestly abuse and Church accountability. Dr. Marni Chanoff, a psychiatrist with deep experience regarding emotional injury and recovery, was helpful in providing insight into how minds function under great stress. Yolanda Bauer, Dr. White's administrative assistant, was essential in keeping the three of us coordinated and moving forward with due speed and collegiality.

The following individuals and organizations have been helpful to us over the years in developing and furthering our ideas about resilience, humanitarian values, and the immense power of the human spirit. We thank them all for contributing to the background that has made our efforts in this book possible:

Dr. and Mrs. Todd Albert, Coach Tommy Amaker, The Late Dr. Mark Bernhardt & Mrs. Renee Bernhardt, Beth Israel Deaconess Medical Center (BIDMC), Department of Orthopaedic Surgery, Blue Cross Blue Shield of Massachusetts, Ms. Verona Brewton, Director, Minority Initiatives, ZimmerBiomet Inc., Bristol-Myers Squibb Foundation (John Damonti), Dr. J. Jacques Carter, Dr. Leigh Callahan, Dr. Kevin Churchwell and Gloria Respress-Churchwell, Dr. Phillip Clay, Ms. Claudette Hodges Crouse, Dr. Robert Crowell, Culturally Competent Care Education Program, Harvard Medical School, Dr. Anthony D'Amico, Rodger L. and Gloria F. Daniels Charitable Foundation (Richard J. Hindlian, Co-Trustee), Mr. Kevin and Mrs. Jennifer DaSilva, Dr. Claes Dohlman, Mr. Michael Douvadjian, Dr. Daryll Dykes, Mr. Vincent Fath, The Late Dr. John Feagin, Dr. Gary and Linda Friedlaender, Otis Gates, III, Dr. Mark Gebhardt, Chair, Orthopedic Department, BIDMC, Dr. Harris Gibson, J. Robert Gladden Orthopaedic Society, Mr. Fred Green, Dr. Thomas Green, Dr. Vartan Gregorian, Arthur and Barbara Higgins Charitable Foundation, Daniel E. Hogan Spine Fellowship Program, BIDMC, Mr. Elwood Howse, Mr. Jamie Hoyte, Dr. Serena Hu,

Dr. Joseph K. Hurd, Jr & Mrs. Jean Challenger Hurd, Mr. Thomas Jones, Mr. Charles Keene, Mr. Wendell Knox, Dr. Melvin Law, and Dr. David Levine.

The Macy Foundation, Massachusetts General Hospital, Department of Orthopaedic Surgery, McKesson Foundation, Chancellor Keith Motley, Movement is Life, The Late Reverend Willie Naulls and Dr. Anne Naulls, Dr. Michael Parks, Dr. Bendt Petersen, Dr. Preston Phillips, Dr. Alvin Poussaint, Dr. Roderick Randall, Attorney Macey Russell, Dr. Isaac Schiff, Dr. Thomas P. and Cynthia D. Sculco Foundation, Dr. Manish Sethi, Dr. Helen Shields, Dr. Randolph C Steer, Dr. and Mrs. Louis Sullivan/Sullivan Family Foundation, Inc., Dr. William and Julia Taylor, Dr. Samuel Thier, Dr. Michael Watkins, Dr. Yashika Watkins, The Augustus A. White, III, MD Family Trust, Dr. Richard Allen Williams & Minority Health Institute, Dr. Nelson Wivel, Dr. Willard Wong, and Zimmer Holdings Inc.

Finally, we acknowledge with gratitude and pleasure the constant encouragement and moral support we received from Anita and Atina White and Lissu Chanoff.

~ ~ ~

Following is a short list for readers who might wish to look at a few of the most important books and authors we've cited in *Overcoming*.

Southwick, Stephen M., and Dennis S. Charney. *Resilience.* Cambridge University Press, second edition, 2018.

Fricchione, Gregory. *Compassion and Healing In Medicine and Society.* Johns Hopkins University Press, 2011.

Pfaff, Donald. *The Altruistic Brain.* Oxford University Press, 2015.

Frankl, Viktor. *Man's Search for Meaning.* Simon & Schuster, 1984.

Soloveitchick, Joseph. *Halakhic Man.* The Jewish Publication Society, 1983.

Damasio, Antonio. *Descartes' Error*. Putnam, 1994.

White, Augustus, and David Chanoff. *Seeing Patients*. Harvard University Press, 2011 (paperback edition, 2019).